THE LIMITS OF REALISM

THE LIMITS OF REALISM

CHINESE FICTION IN THE REVOLUTIONARY PERIOD

MARSTON ANDERSON

University of California Press
Berkeley   Los Angeles   Oxford

University of California Press
Berkeley and Los Angeles, California

University of California Press, Ltd.
London, England

© 1990 by
The Regents of the University of California

Library of Congress Cataloging-in-Publication Data

Anderson, Marston.
   The limits of realism: Chinese fiction in the revolutionary
period / Marston Anderson.
      p.   cm.
   Bibliography: p.
   Includes index.
   ISBN 0-520-06436-4 (alk. paper)
   1. Chinese fiction—20th century—History and criticism.
2. Realism in literature.   I. Title.
PL2442.A53   1990
895.1'35109'12—dc20   89-31543
                                                  CIP

Printed in the United States of America
1   2   3   4   5   6   7   8   9

Contents

v

Acknowledgments

Research for this book was begun while I was studying at Fudan University in Shanghai from 1980 to 1982 on a grant from the Committee for Scholarly Exchange with the People's Republic of China. I am indebted to my sponsors and to the staffs of several Chinese libraries who made their collections available to me. These include the Shanghai and Beijing municipal libraries, as well as the libraries of Fudan University, Beijing University, and Sichuan University. While in China, I had the fortune to interview three of the authors whose works I discuss in chapter 4 of this book: Ai Wu, Sha Ting, and Wu Zuxiang. I am most thankful for their time and hospitality.

Parts of chapters 2 and 4 of this book appeared as the article "The Morality of Form: Lu Xun and the Modern Chinese Short Story" in a conference volume edited by Leo Ou-fan Lee, *Lu Xun and His Legacy* (Berkeley and Los Angeles: University of California Press, 1985). A somewhat altered version of the second half of chapter 2 appeared as "The Specular Self: Subjective and Mimetic Elements in the Fiction of Ye Shaojun" in the journal *Modern China* 15, no. 1 (January 1989).

A note on format is in order here: The *pinyin* romanization system has been used throughout. In a few cases, when citing from works that employ a system other than *pinyin*, I have changed the romanization in the quoted passage for the purpose of consistency. References cited in the footnotes are generally given in an abbreviated form; for full titles and publication information, please refer to the selected bibliography.

A great many teachers, colleagues, and friends will rightfully recognize their influence on some part of the argument of this book. Although mentioning them here seems a poor return for their generosity, I would like to thank in particular the following: Cyril Birch, Jeff Hanes, Theodore D. Huters, Leo Ou-fan Lee, D. A. Miller, Masao Miyoshi, Lung-kee Sun, and James Tate. Finally, I dedicate this book to my parents, Marbury and Sylvia Anderson, with deep gratitude for their support and love through years of what must have seemed an interminable process of education.

I

Introduction
Writing about Others

In 1928 Lu Xun 魯迅, by common consent the greatest of twentieth-century Chinese writers, satirized the literary polemics of his day in an essay entitled "The Tablet":

> The fearful thing about the Chinese literary scene is that everyone keeps introducing new terms without defining them.
>
> And everyone interprets these terms as he pleases. To write a good deal about yourself is expressionism. To write largely about others is realism. To write poems on a girl's leg is romanticism. To ban poems on a girl's leg is classicism.

Lu Xun then goes on to recount a joke about two shortsighted rustics who fall to arguing over the inscription on a votive tablet; they ask a passerby to mediate their quarrel, only to be told, "There's nothing there; the tablet hasn't been hung yet."[1]

Lu Xun wrote "The Tablet" at the height of the Revolutionary Literature debate of 1928, when he was under attack from a clique of left extremists who found his work and political stance insufficiently militant. Understandably, Lu Xun felt embattled, besieged by dogmatists who viewed literature exclusively through the lenses of theories that were themselves mutable and ill-defined. He saw the literary revolution in which he had played such a crucial role being turned into a mock-heroic battle of isms, a noisy polemical fracas about a literature that—in terms of creative output—had yet to materialize. Lu Xun was not alone in these concerns. At one time or other nearly every important author of the 1920s and 1930s decried the extent to which the discussion of literature in China had become saturated with theoretical abstractions. Shen Congwen 沈從文, for example, reviewing in

---

1. Lu Xun 魯迅, "Bian" 扁 (The tablet), *Yu si* 4, no. 17 (23 April 1928); reprinted in Lu Xun, *Lu Xun quanji*, 4:87.

1930 the achievements of the New Literature movement, was struck by the gap that had developed between the theoreticians' recommendations and the content of the literary works actually being published; he frankly recommended that authors ignore the latest "news from the literary scene" and attend instead to their writing and to life.[2] But such a detached attitude was easier to recommend than to achieve; as Lu Xun's exasperated tone in the passage quoted above suggests, the theoreticians had become too assertive to ignore.

The apparently inflated power accorded to theory in modern Chinese letters can only be understood in the context of the cultural emergency from which the new literature was born and in light of the particular kind of literary borrowing in which Chinese intellectuals were engaged. Lu Xun observed in another essay that "revolutionary literature as it flourishes in China is quite different from revolutionary literature elsewhere; it did not arise in the high tide of revolution but developed because of a setback in revolution."[3] One could emend this to suggest that modern Chinese literature developed from a series of setbacks, beginning with the failed 1898 reform movement and continuing through the Japanese invasion in the 1930s. In the intervening years Chinese reformers suffered one disappointment after another. The 1911 revolution, which rid the country of imperial rule, awakened hopes that a strong, modern nation could finally be forged in China, but the republican government established to replace the monarchy rapidly crumbled, its authority usurped by warlords. Then, in 1919, China suffered international humiliation when the Western nations at Versailles decided to cede the province of Shandong to Japan, a decision that provoked the student demonstrations on May 4, the date by which the larger cultural movement of the late 1910s and 1920s is now known.[4] Finally, in 1927, the coalition between the Nationalist and Communist parties, on which many had pinned their hopes for finally achieving a unified national rule, was violently severed when Jiang Jieshi 蔣介石 (Chiang Kai-shek) initiated a cam-

---

2. Shen Congwen 沈從文, "Xiandai Zhongguo wenxue de xiao ganxiang" 現代中國文學的小感想 (Modest impressions of modern Chinese literature), *Wenyi yuekan* 1, no. 5 (15 December 1930), pp. 159–62.

3. Lu Xun, "Shanghai wenyi zhi yi bie" 上海文藝之一瞥 (A glance at Shanghai literature), *Wenyi xinwen*, 20–21, 27 July and 3 August 1931; reprinted in Lu Xun, *Lu Xun quanji* 4:291–307, here p. 296.

4. For a full history of the May Fourth movement see Chow Tse-tsung, *The May Fourth Movement*.

paign of terror against the left wing of the alliance. The period that produced the new literature was thus a frankly traumatic one, during which repeated shocks and dislocations were visited on individuals and on the nation at large. Although in retrospect both faces of the Chinese revolution—political and literary—have taken on an aura of inevitability, it is worth remembering that the militancy of those days was bred in the frustration of repeated historical reversals.

Of course, modern Chinese literature did more than just mirror the chaotic condition of its age, for it had been burdened from birth with an enormous responsibility. Chinese intellectuals resolved to remake their literary culture only after their efforts at political reform had failed, and they did so with a specific purpose in mind. They reasoned that literature could reach a deeper level of cultural response than political manipulation had succeeded in doing; a new literature, by altering the very worldview of its readers, would, they hoped, pave the way for a complete transformation of Chinese society. Increasingly challenged by the West, they scanned Europe's diverse cultural weave for the strand that held the secret of its "wealth and power"; in their haste they eagerly seized on the isms by which Westerners categorized their own tradition. These offered a necessary grid through which to view the vast quantity of new ideas and new information that suddenly became available when the doors to the West were opened. May Fourth intellectuals did not have the luxury to slowly explore the philosophical and social ramifications of each system of thought or artistic genre they encountered. A sense of national crisis mandated their borrowing, and they approached their task with a keen sense of urgency, believing that China's future rested on the models they chose.

Of the terms that Lu Xun mockingly defines in the passage quoted above, *realism* came to carry the profoundest burden of hope for cultural transformation. And realism generated the largest body of literature in the years that followed, a corpus that has since been recognized as the crowning achievement of twentieth-century Chinese literature both by Chinese critics and by such scholars in the West as Jaroslev Průšek and C. T. Hsia. No other term has had such a decisive influence on modern Chinese criticism and fiction. As I shall detail in chapter 1 of this study, many of the dominant figures of the May Fourth movement were advocates of realism, and during the 1920s the reformist literati split into two factions, one characterized as realist, the other as romanticist. Late in that decade this rift evolved into a violent clash between realist and romanticist leftists, a skirmish that in many ways set the stage for the various literary controversies of the 1930s and 1940s. And these controversies in their turn determined the literary policies of the People's Republic when it was established in 1949. As a result the term *realism* continues to have considerable rhetorical—and political—bite in China today: the literature of each major period of political thaw (including the Hundred Flowers campaign of 1956–57 and the post–Cultural Revolution period) has been applauded as a salutary return to the "realist" tradition of preliberation fiction.[5]

In the West, the word *realism* has a very different recent history. For Western critics it has become one of those embarrassing critical terms that seem to invite typographical alteration; more often than not they set off the word with quotation marks, capitalization, or italics, thereby hoping to dissociate themselves from the now thoroughly discredited epistemology the term assumes. Where critics speak easily of classicism, expressionism, or even romanticism without arousing suspicions that they have fallen into an uncritical endorsement of the mode and the theoretical presuppositions that support it, recent discussions of realism invariably open with a defensive qualification of terms.[6] Contemporary criticism, with its base in linguistic philosophy, has effectively undermined realism's pretense that a literary text may constitute a direct representation of the material or social world: a work of fiction, readers are reminded, is a linguistic construct whose semiotic status must never be forgotten. More radical critics, regarding language as a closed system perpetuated by its internal differences, throw into doubt even the notion of linguistic referentiality. Critical practices that once were standard in treating realist fiction now seem lamentably inadequate: too often they involve a reductive view of the text as mere social documentation or, in the didactic tradition of Marxist criticism, as an illustration of the tenets of social ideology.

5. See the discussion of the new realism of the post-Mao period in Lee Yee, *The New Realism*, pp. 3–16.
6. George Levine, for example, begins his recent book on English realism with a quotation from Thomas Hardy: "Realism is an unfortunate, an ambiguous word, which has been taken up by literary society like a view-halloo" (Levine, *The Realistic Imagination*, p. 3). Levine goes on to argue that, although the concept of realism seems incompatible with the antireferential bias of contemporary criticism, realists in fact anticipated modernism by giving representation in their fiction to profoundly disruptive social and psychological forces. See especially pp. 3–22.

Recent Western critics of modern Chinese literature, sensitized to the philosophical difficulties attending discussions of literary mimesis, have grown loath even to discuss realism. Since the work of Hsia and Průšek the most ambitious Western treatments of May Fourth literature have focused on other, more marginal currents in the period's literary history.[7] Edward Gunn, in his survey of literature written in occupied zones during the Sino-Japanese war, goes so far as to invent a critical term, *antiromanticism*, that he defines so precisely by traits commonly associated with realism (specifically, a concern with the familiar and a tendency to dramatize the failure of certain "individuals' pretensions and their ill-conceived, unreflective ambitions")[8] that I can only assume it was formulated to allow the circumvention of the more familiar but now suspect term *realism*.

The special treatment Westerners accord to the word may be the sign, however, not of their overmastering realism, but of their continued susceptibility to its spirit. In spite of their reservations, realism still exerts a powerful normative hold over the Western literary imagination. Even such contemporary experiments as *le nouveau roman* and American documentary fiction, it could be argued, struggle to escape from the formal problems associated with realism and end defining themselves by it, if only negatively. Moreover, as George J. Becker has observed, the twentieth century has seen several cases of "the resurgence of realism in countries long subject to repressive intellectual and artistic forces."[9] However convincing the refutations of nineteenth-century realist theory may be, they in the end fail to explain either the continued historical productivity of the mode or the lingering rhetorical power of the term itself. Particularly in a case like China, where debate about realism has played such a crucial role in the development of a major literary genre, we are not served by suppressing the term but rather by confronting and critically examining the complex of associations surrounding it. My intention in undertaking here a reconsideration of modern Chinese fiction from the perspective of its most ubiquitous ism, is not, however, to further augment the weight of dogma that beset Lu Xun or to create a sterile taxonomy of the

7. Major examples would be Leo Ou-fan Lee's *Romantic Generation of Modern Chinese Writers*, Perry Link's *Mandarin Ducks and Butterflies*, and Edward Gunn's *Unwelcome Muse*.
8. Edward Gunn, *The Unwelcome Muse*, p. 271.
9. George J. Becker, *Documents of Modern Literary Realism*, p. 20.

period's literary products. I will instead begin by performing a kind of archaeological investigation of the term's usage from its introduction into China at the turn of the century through 1942, when Mao Zedong 毛澤東 established a new literary orthodoxy with his "Talks at the Yan'an Forum on Literature and the Arts." I will not propose a normative definition of *realism*, for it is the ambiguity of the term, its protean quality, that accords it durability and power, enabling it to continually accrue new meanings in response to changing cultural and historical conditions. To explore the new connotations the term accumulated as the Chinese took it up will reveal as much about the presuppositions and limitations of realism itself as about modern Chinese literature.

After considering what the term itself meant to the Chinese, I will examine the influence of realism on the writing of several major Chinese authors. Doing so will immediately expose the considerable gap that developed between the logos of May Fourth criticism and the mythos of the period's fiction. The various literary programs shared a view of writing as a simple, willed activity, the directed and manipulable product of certain daylight intentions. But fiction did not prove so tractable to the intentions, whether ideological or literary, of China's authors during its actual composition. They frequently discovered their own inspirations to be troubled and nocturnal and the fate of their fiction in the world, once severed from its creator, to be unexpected, even perverse (a fact brought home to many of the authors discussed here by the belated criticism heaped on their works during the Cultural Revolution). As often as not, works written according to a literary program failed to satisfy the most basic expectations of its promoters, and works that did succeed artistically or rhetorically eluded simple critical categorization. Though an examination of May Fourth literary criticism is useful in exposing the extent of the period's intellectual crisis as well as the nature of the constraints that the resulting literary factiousness exerted on authors—and I proceed with such an examination in chapter 1—an adequate account of the period's fiction must rely on more than the interpretive categories suggested by its criticism. I will attempt to remedy this in part by reference to recent advances in narratology. But relying on theoretical props designed to assist the study of Western literature can carry us only so far, and I propose to turn for more pertinent help to the fictional texts themselves. Reading the oeuvre of any of the major Chinese realists of the

1920s or 1930s, one is struck by their high degree of formal self-consciousness. Again and again authors introduce frankly reflexive elements into their work, often in the form of authorial alter egos or ironical foregrounding of the very techniques that identify their works as realist. In chapters 2 through 4, I will read major examples of May Fourth realism as metafiction in the belief that the works themselves can best instruct us in how they are to be read. Indeed, my premise is that many realist works operate on two levels, one of "objective" social representation and one of self-conscious allegory. At the allegorial level authors explore the resources and the limitations of the form in which they write; by examining this level, we can uncover the works' stresses and faults, the pitfalls that authors must dodge as they accommodate their material to specific formal restrictions. If allegory, understood in this way, may be said to inform all realist fiction, it asserts itself most insistently in the works of writers like those of the May Fourth period, who were self-consciously adapting an alien artistic form to cultural and historical needs substantially different from those that inspired the form's invention.

Such an interpretive strategy does not simply view realism as a set of positive characteristics but attends instead to its contradictory, problematic features, that is, to the questions that the project of realism raises. This strategy also takes us beyond the traditional focus of critical attention in discussions of realism, the text's claim to mirror an extraliterary reality. Clearly this claim cannot be ignored: all realist fiction gives itself authority by asserting a privileged relationship with reality. Yet the claim is not simply a passive, a priori assumption but also a formal determinant whose operation is discernible in all examples of the mode. Each new work must reproduce the claim in its own right, thereby affirming its singular command over reality. It should therefore be possible, while suspending intractable epistemological questions, to examine the act of representation as a kind of intellectual labor (or, in linguistic terms, as a motivated speech-act) whose characteristic traces may be discovered in the text. The real may, at least provisionally, be viewed simply as an effect of the fiction. This perspective on the Real (whose emblematic rather than essentialist value I will signify through capitalization) frees us from a narrow consideration of the text's relationship to the world (mimesis), allowing exploration as well of the creative generation of the fiction (poiesis) and of its reception and its social use (which, we shall see, is best approached in the case of realism through the Aristotelian notion of catharsis).[10]

It is through a careful examination of these last two categories, I will argue, that we can free ourselves from the epistemological blinders of realism's claim to truth and begin to understand its operation as an aesthetic form. In the rest of this introduction I will take up each of these categories in turn, with the object of constructing a model of realism that accounts for the full range of the aesthetic experience; I will then consider which aspects of this model coincide with, and which conflict with, the presumptions of traditional Chinese criticism. This project is fraught with risk because it requires a high level of abstraction and generality, and I must ask the indulgence of readers who feel toward contemporary literary theory much as Lu Xun felt in 1928 about his extremist critics. Theoretical abstractions in literary studies justify themselves by enriching our understanding of individual works, and my observations are intended only as a preparation for the readings that follow. But scholars have increasingly recognized the continued relevance of deep strains of traditional culture to the modern Chinese experience: to appreciate the unique promises, as well as the unique obstacles, that realism presented to modern Chinese writers we must first explore the internal operation of realism (not just its theoretical rationale) and then identify the points of resistance to the Western mode implicit in China's rich and sophisticated aesthetic tradition.

POIESIS: THE GENERATION OF THE
LITERARY EXPERIENCE

If one takes both of its elements at face value, the term *realist fiction* verges on being an oxymoron: *fiction* connotes the world of the imagination, which authors evoke through the active exercise of their powers of invention, whereas *realism*, by asserting an optimal equivalency of the text and the real world, implies the effacement of the author as creator. The ambiguity of the term is more than a linguistic accident, as the history of the realist novel demonstrates. Particularly in the early years of the genre's development, novels were regularly

---

10. See the discussion of these three "fundamental categories of the attitude of aesthetic enjoyment" in Hans Robert Jauss, *Aesthetic Experience and Literary Hermeneutics*, especially pp. 34–35 and chapters 6–8 of Part A.

prefaced by the author's denial of a role in the tale's composition: the texts were presented to the world as documents *trouvé* (Samuel Richardson's *Pamela*), as journalistic reports (Aphra Behn's *Oroonoko*), or as transcriptions of factual oral accounts (Daniel Defoe's *Moll Flanders*). Authors introduced themselves as a work's editor or publicizer but never as the story's inventor. Such ruses served to create a distance between author and text that accorded the works a powerful sense of autonomy and legitimacy (and at the same time, of course, helped protect the authors from accusations that they were simply spreading malicious or frivolous lies). As the reading public became more sophisticated, authorial disavowals became conventionalized, and only the most naive of readers could have mistaken their intention. They persisted as a formal element, however, because they reflected the fundamental ambivalence of realist fiction, its uncertain relationship to both fact and fiction. Lennard J. Davis has, in fact, called the early English novel a "factual fiction," at once "a report on the world and an invention that parodies that report."[11] From this we may deduce a general rule: realism's claim of pure referentiality involves repudiating a work's origins in the imagination of the author— a denial, that is, of the work's fictionality. This claim is always, however, slightly disingenuous; sophisticated readers never accept it at face value but enjoy the work precisely because of its ambiguous status vis-à-vis the Real.

Realist fiction assumes a gap not only between text and author but also between individual texts and all earlier literature. Crucial to the truth claim of realism is the proposition that the work is directly imitative of life rather than derivative of other texts. This means that a realist text must not only deny its origins in the imagination of the author but disavow as well its indebtedness to traditional literary models; it must assert a fundamental novelty. This claim too is somewhat disingenuous; in fact readers approach a novel with fixed assumptions about the genre and recognize in individual works the influence of earlier writers. But to the extent that references to the literary tradition consciously surface in realist texts, they often do so in a satirical or parodic context. What is often termed the first true novel, *Don Quixote*, for example, may be read in large part as a travesty of the chivalric

11. Lennard J. Davis, *Factual Fictions*, p. 212. Davis discusses "authorial disavowals" in early English fiction at some length; see especially chapters 6, 8, and 9.

romance, and many later works explicitly deconstruct the false ideals promoted by less "realistic" literature (Madame Bovary's life, for example, is a disastrous attempt to imitate the adventures she reads about in romantic novels). Harry Levin has written that realistic "fiction approximates truth, not by concealing art but by exposing artifice,"[12] and in an important sense realism's truth claim is dependent on this denunciation of other, more artificial genres. This affinity for parody and satire betrays, of course, a high level of artistic self-consciousness: though realism may appear to turn its gaze exclusively on the extra-literary world, it is not innocent of the literature that precedes it. But at least at the level of its theoretical rationale, realism would break its ties both with the imagination and with tradition and discover its origins in the author's critical, observing intellect.

The celebrated image of realist fiction as a mirror, though generally read as a metaphor for the direct translation of extraliterary reality into fictional material, is perhaps more interesting for what it shows us about the creation of the author's critical persona and the resultant indirectness of authorial expression in realist fiction. According to the metaphor, composition is merely the disinterested hoisting of the mirror; in Stendhal's famous passage in *Le rouge et le noir* the novel is compared to a "mirror walking down the road," reflecting everything—both the good and the bad—in its path.[13] But a mirror image at best marks off a discrete fragment of the real world with an artificial frame; this fragment then shifts with the perspective of the viewer. So too, the metaphor suggests, artistic representation of the world must be staged from a determinate perspective. This perspectiv-ism, the *point d'appui* of such realist notions as "focalization" (or "point of view") and "authorial objectivity," is a philosophical and aesthetic stance unique to the modern West. Medieval and non-Western artistic traditions generally permit the creative imagination to range freely over the totality of culturally generated images. The tradi-tional Chinese *fu* 賦 ("rhyme-prose" or "rhapsody") for example, often characterized as a predominantly "descriptive" form, ap-proaches the object described (or rather, celebrated) in the work from every possible perspective, enumerating its every feature and comparing any number of similar objects to it by analogy. Realist

12. Harry Levin, *The Gates of Horn*, p. 51.
13. Stendhal, *Le rouge et le noir* (Paris: Éditions Gallimard, 1972), p. 414.

perspectivist descriptions, however, fix the object in a particular relationship with the observing subject, a relationship that is bound by
strict temporal and spatial limitations. For the authorial voice to ex-
ceed these limitations is to stagger the mirror and thereby relinquish
the authority of the critical observer.

Realism's high estimation of the critical observer's stance is
anchored in Enlightenment faith in the capacity of human beings to
free themselves from superstition and prejudice through the exercise
of their faculty of reason. As Hans-Georg Gadamer has said, the
fundamental "prejudice" (or prejudgment) of the Enlightenment is the
prejudice against prejudice itself.[14] As an epistemological exercise,
realist fiction might be viewed as an exploration of the process
through which the mind assimilates external reality to the linguistic
structures or prejudices by which it apprehends the world or, more
potently, as an exploration of the process through which external reality forces a reconsideration of those prejudices. But the observing
mind can discover its independence, can feel the power of its freedom,
only at the moment of disengagement, when it sets itself in opposition
to tradition. Realism's supposedly disinterested investigation of the
external world thus reveals itself to be an internal struggle to free the
mind from its dependence on the received tradition. Just as subjects
can establish their integrity only through a critical gesture of some
kind, so too the truth claim of realist fiction is dependent on its self-
presentation as a critique of cultural prejudices. This manifests itself in
the work as an act of demystification: the realist plot invariably
dramatizes the disappointment of conventional pretensions, desires, or
ideals. The objectified real world, as the agent of these disappointments, plays a crucial role in the discrediting of cultural prejudices,
thereby liberating the mind from the stranglehold of tradition. In the
process the mind is divided into a rationalist objective element that
aligns itself with an ahistoric higher consciousness (or, in the Marxist-
Hegelian tradition, with the full consciousness of a "higher historical
stage") and an opposing subjective element, which is heir to the un-
reasoned biases of tradition. The objectivity of realism thus somewhat
paradoxically elevates the subject (as an independent platform of
observation) while censoring those emotions and prejudices that we
usually think of as an individual's subjectivity.

14. Hans-Georg Gadamer, *Truth and Method*, pp. 239–40.

Authorial disavowal of subjective involvement in the creative process has the effect of focusing attention on the literary artifact itself, divorcing it from the circumstances of its production, and according it a unique substantiality. As an art *object*, the work may be compared with and finally set in a hierarchical relationship to the reality it purports to copy. Approached in this way, a work of art cannot but appear dubious, for however expertly it mimics reality, it can never truly replace that reality. Plato's suspicion of the arts, which necessitated the later Western formulation of a defense of poetry, follows from this elemental sense of art as imitation of the real world. Traditional Chinese aesthetics, which never developed a theory of mimesis like the one that has dominated Western discussions of the arts,[15] did not hypostatize the art object in this way. For the Chinese a work of literature was not a copy of the natural world but one of many manifestations of the fundamental patterns that underlie both the natural and social worlds. This view was most forcefully expressed in the writings of the sixth-century theorist Liu Xie 劉勰, who employed a neatly circular argument to explain the origins of literature, relying on the polysemy of the character *wen* 文, which can mean both "pattern" and "writing," to equate literature with the fundamental structure of the universe. *Wen* (pattern) is "born together with Heaven and Earth," and human beings, the only element of the universe endowed with consciousness, are its mind or heart (*xin* 心). With the birth of the human mind, "the way of nature" is for language to emerge, and with language, *wen* (writing) appears.[16] As Stephen Owen suggests in his discussion of this passage, for Liu Xie "literature thus stands as the entelechy, the fully realized form, of a universal process of manifesta-

15. For a discussion of the lack of mimetic theories of literature in China see James J. Y. Liu, *Chinese Theories of Literature*, pp. 49–73. William F. Touponce, in a spirited critique of Liu's book ("Straw Dogs: A Deconstructive Reading of the Problem of Mimesis in James Liu's *Chinese Theories of Literature*," *Tamkang Review*, no. 1 [Summer 1981]: 359–90) takes issue with Liu's claim that mimesis has not played a significant role in Chinese literary thinking, but his argument confuses René Girard's fundamentally anthropological concept of mimesis (Girard argues that sacrifice is the miming of the original act of violence that underlies all culture) with Plato and Aristotle's concept of literary mimesis (which takes Poetry as an imitation of the phenomenal world). A connection might, no doubt, be drawn between the two (and Girard unquestionably believes his to be related to Plato and Aristotle's), but this connection needs to be carefully articulated. Touponce is forced finally, in an unobtrusive concessional phrase, to concede that "China may be said not to have produced any mimetic theory of literature" (p. 384). This is, of course, precisely Liu's point.

16. Liu Hsieh (Liu Xie), *The Literary Mind*, pp. 9–10.

tion. . . . The writer, instead of 're-presenting' the outer world, is in fact only the medium for this last phase of the world's coming-to-be."[17]

Liu Xie's argument confounds the notion of an origin of writing by suggesting that writing / pattern in some sense precedes and yet is derived from human consciousness. His argument amounts, in fact, to suggesting an equivalency between writing and consciousness, which Liu goes on to make yet more explicit: "'Words with Pattern' [i.e. writing] are the mind of the universe."[18] The literary work, a manifestation of human consciousness and of universal pattern, can never be reduced to a mere shadow of the real world, as it was for Plato; its ontological sufficiency is never open to doubt. Chinese aesthetic philosophers thus concerned themselves little with the mimetic relationship of art object to real world but instead directed their attention to the affective and didactic capacities of art, its power either to awaken in readers the range of emotions that motivated the work's composition or to reveal to readers the network of "principles" that were thought to support both the natural and social worlds. However, Chinese were not uninterested in the creative process as experienced by the individual author: indeed, expressive theories of literature (epitomized by the endlessly repeated maxim "*Shi yan zhi*" 詩言志, "Poetry expresses the mind's intent") played a vital role in Chinese aesthetic philosophy from early times (and remained influential in the twentieth century, as I will show in chapter 1).[19] Even according to expressive theories, however, the author was understood less as an autonomous creator than as a vessel or channel through which the patterns of nature and society manifest themselves.

If the Chinese tradition did offer an intellectual framework with which to consider questions of the artwork's relationship with the external world, it was provided by the neo-Confucian concept of the

17. Stephen Owen, *Traditional Chinese Poetry and Poetics*, p. 20. Andrew H. Plaks also discusses this passage and its relevance to the development of fiction in "Towards a Critical Theory of Chinese Narrative," in Plaks, ed., *Chinese Narrative*, pp. 309–52; see pp. 311–16.

18. Liu Hsieh, *The Literary Mind*, pp. 9–10. Wen 文 as writing/pattern offers some interesting similarities to the Derridean notion of *archi-écriture*, which similarly confounds conventional Western ideas about the origins of writing in the transliteration of speech (see Jacques Derrida, *Of Grammatology*, p. 60).

19. For a discussion of expressive theories of literature in China see James J. Y. Liu, *Chinese Theories of Literature*, pp. 67–87.

"investigation of things" (*gewu* 格物), which is often cited in discussions of the history of Chinese science as the closest point of similarity in Chinese philosophy to Enlightenment notions of the individual as an objective platform of observation.[20] In its early formulation by the philosopher Shao Yong 邵雍, who distinguishes "observation from the perspective of things" and "observation from the perspective of the self," the concept does appear to resemble Western rationalism. But on closer examination, it becomes clear that Shao Yong was not advocating analytical observation of the material world but a meditative use of the external world in the process of self-cultivation: "By viewing things is not meant with one's physical eyes, but with one's mind; nay, not with one's mind, but with the principle inherent in things."[21] The discovery of principle in the objects of the external world helps subjects discover reflexively how principle operates within themselves, to differentiate their nature (*xing* 性), which is balanced and impartial, from their emotions (*qing* 情), which are egotistical and biased. In the thinking of later neo-Confucian philosophers, the affinity between this concept and Western notions of scientific observation seems even weaker: Cheng Yi 程頤 and Zhu Xi 朱熹 increasingly directed the critical spirit of *gewu* away from the investigation of nature and the external world toward ethical speculation and philology, and later Wang Yangming 王陽明, opposing the assumption that principles were located in things external to the mind, redefined *gewu* in strictly moral terms to mean "rectification of the mind."

Though sometimes thought to reveal a commitment to objectivity or realism, such literary applications of the concept of *gewu* as that in Jin Shengtan's 金聖嘆 commentary on *Shuihu zhuan* 水滸傳 (The water margin) are also dominated by this ethical concern. Jin credited the remarkable individuation of character in Shi Naian's 施耐庵 novel to his years of disinterested investigation of people but argues that "the door to the investigation of things" is the pair of Confucian virtues, fidelity (*zhong* 忠) and magnanimity (*shu* 恕).[22] Through the

---

20. The term *gewu* 格物 was originally used in the *Daxue* 大學 (Great learning) and has been the subject of much interesting philological speculation: it has variously been interpreted to mean "to ward off or resist things," "to rectify things," "to take the measure of things," and "to arrive at things." The neo-Confucians accepted the last interpretation, taking "to arrive at" to mean "to investigate the underlying principles of." See Wing-tsit Chan, *A Source Book in Chinese Philosophy*, p. 487.

21. Shao Yong 邵雍, "Supreme Principles Governing the World," in ibid, p. 487.

22. Jin Shengtan 金聖嘆, "*Diwu caizi shu Shi Nai'an Shuihu zhuan* xu san"

exercise of these virtues one recognizes that all things, even the low-liest thief or rat, spontaneously express the inner necessity of their being; if that being, the creature's nature, can be grasped, the artist's finished work will achieve an air of authenticity. Jin's argument is clearly less a call for scientific observation of the external world than for spiritual identification with the objects and beings that inhabit it, that is, for a kind of negative capability. In a manner typical of Chinese criticism, Jin Shengtan focuses on the interaction between author and world prior to composition rather than on the relation-ship of the work's content, once realized, to the external world. Meta-phorical use of the mirror in Chinese aesthetic philosophy illuminates this fundamental difference from Western aesthetics: in Chinese writ-ings the mirror is never equated with the work itself as a reflection of the Real, but with the mind of the author, who through contemplation rids himself (or herself) of a clouded subjectivity and opens himself as a free channel to the Dao (Tao).[23]

CATHARSIS: THE EFFICACY OF LITERARY COMMUNICATION

As is often observed, Western realism is a bourgeois art form that succeeds by appealing to its readers' sense of historical and social identity. René Wellek has noticed, in connection with the nineteenth-century realist novel, the importance of such historical upheavals as the industrial revolution, which brought a new awareness of history—

《第五才子書施耐庵水滸傳》序三 (Third preface to *Five Works of Genius: Shi Nai'an's Water Margin*), in Ma Tiji, ed., *Shuihu ziliao huibian*, pp. 25–29, here pp. 26–27. For further discussion of these passages see Chen Wanyi, *Jin Shengtan de wen-xue piping kaoshu*, pp. 28–31.

23. See the discussion of the mirror metaphor in James J. Y. Liu, *Chinese Theories of Literature*, pp. 50–53. The Chinese *locus classicus* of the metaphor is a passage in *Zhuangzi* 莊子: "The mind of the perfect man is like a mirror. It does not lean forward or backward in its response to things. It responds to things but conceals nothing of its own" (*Zhuangzi*, chap. 7; translated in Wing-tsit Chan, *A Source Book in Chinese Philosophy*, p. 207). The Ming critic Xie Zhen 謝榛 takes up the mirror metaphor in his discussion of poetry as a fusion between emotion (*qing* 情) and scene (*jing* 景). Through this fusion the mind functions like a mirror, faithfully reflecting the external world; the composition of poetry is one means of achieving this perfect union between subjective self and external reality and is therefore valued as an act of self-cultivation. Chinese use of the mirror metaphor describes a mental state, not of objectifying scien-tific discrimination, but of calm receptivity; the subject's response to the object is not exclusively intellectual but encompasses emotional identification as well.

"the far greater consciousness that man is a being living in society rather than a moral being facing God"—as well as a "change in the interpretation of nature which shifts from the deistic, purposeful, even though mechanistic world of the eighteenth century to the far more unhuman, inhuman order of deterministic nineteenth-century science."[24] At the most fundamental level, realist fiction assumes a shared sense of historical progression: both author and reader conceive of the events related in the text as particular, discrete occurrences plotted on a linear temporal course—that same temporal course, in fact, that encompasses all our lives and that we call history. This particularity of events is no more than a pretense, as the theorists of realism themselves concede in their discussion of "typicality," where they indirectly acknowledge the conventionalized and even allegorical nature of realist fiction. Through the notion of types, realism is opened to the transmission of general truths (i.e. ideology) and the encyclopedic portrayal of social reality. Realist fiction, like all narrative art forms, thus presents itself in part as a kind of instruction or teaching,[25] yet unlike a fable, parable, or religious allegory, it is never the transparent vessel of its message. To read a work of realism as a straightforward *roman à thèse*, reducing the text's content to its schematic ideological message, is to overlook the unique creative tensions that inform it. Realist fiction is forever at pains to distinguish its use of language from more dogmatic or discursive usages, often through slighting references to such language and the texts that embody it (we shall examine some of these as they occur in May Fourth fiction, but examples from Western realism are equally abundant). For however conventionalized the events portrayed in realist fiction, the text's claim to capture and relay a specific, unrepeatable slice of life remains crucial to its effectiveness: the text refers its authority to the external world by this means, thereby appearing not to be applying its structures of meaning to the world, but to have discovered them there.

One way that realism persuades us of the particularity of its content is the inclusion of apparently nonfunctional details that contribute descriptive richness to the work but seem to contribute nothing to its instructional purpose. Roland Barthes, in his essay on the "reality effect," cites a passage in Flaubert's "A Simple Heart" in which a piano

24. René Wellek, *Concepts of Criticism*, p. 254.
25. On narrative as instruction see Julia Kristeva, *Le Texte du roman*, pp. 21–22.

is described as supporting "under a barometer, a pyramidal heap of boxes and cartons." The barometer appears to be a "futile" detail, telling us nothing of relevance to the human drama for which we read the story. Even such details, however, are not purely mimetic but serve as signs enunciating the text's desire to align itself with the category of the Real. They communicate a sense of tangible reality, Barthes argues, because of their "resistance to meaning," which "confirms the great mythic opposition of the *true-to-life* (the lifelike) and the *intelligible*." In the ideology of the modern age "reference to the 'concrete'. . . is always brandished like a weapon against meaning."[26] Details like Flaubert's barometer are therefore pivotal to our understanding of realism's truth claim: although they may appear random or arbitrary, their opacity invites our indulgence in the "pure fascination of the image"[27] and thereby persuades us of the authenticity of the world represented in the fiction.

But if the Real made itself felt in the text at no more than this local level, it would be experienced only as a supplement to the thematic intentions of the work. The Real has instead a more powerful formal role to play in the text as the *agent of demystification*. Like the mimetic details discussed above, the demystifying agent resists orderly absorption into the world of the fiction, and its irruption signifies the destabilizing presence of chaos, chance, and the arbitrary. Certain recognizable *topoi*, consisting largely of those unassimilable elements of nature that confound the efforts of the imagination to reorder the world, may be recognized as the primary demystifying agents in realist fiction: hunger, violence, disease, sexual desire, death. All exert powerful constraints on the subject and significantly operate directly on his or her physical being. In realist metaphysics it is always the body that is accorded substantiality, and as the list indicates, it is above all those features of the natural world that invasively trespass the imagined autonomy of the body that achieve status as emblems of the Real. Since their very materiality empowers them, all such agents appear in their essence to be closed off to language, which is powerless to avert the threat they represent to the body. In a sense, the text itself, as a linguistic construct, is helpless before them; perceived as external to language, the Real and its agents are finally unrepresentable and can

26. Roland Barthes, *The Rustle of Language*, p. 146.
27. Pierre Macherey, *A Theory of Literary Production*, p. 58.

at best be pointed to. Not their direct representation, but their effect on the world of the fiction—the spectacle of demystification—constitutes the work. The Real is thus experienced in the text on one level as resistance and limitation and on a more profound level as the threat of indeterminacy of meaning—as the "unnameable."[28]

While the introjection of the Real into the world of the fiction serves the necessary function of prying the critical mind loose from the hold of tradition and thus creating a privileged platform of observation, its presence as the unnameable would appear to threaten disrupting the work's formal stability. The spectacle of demystification is, after all, one of pure negativity, which unchecked could lead only to self-destruction and the dissolution of the aesthetic experience. But the production of an art work is an assertive act, however disguised or hesitant, that entails the creation of an objectively binding meaning; pure negation can never serve as the sole support of a creative act.[29] The use of the Real to induce disillusionment must therefore be seen as only the critical first part of its role in realist fiction. The text would, in the strategic rhetoric of the mode, go on to capture the Real, to contain or domesticate it. But such terminology suggests that internalization—and hence domination—of the Real may better be understood as its banishment; at moments of closure the text projects the Real, with its threat of indeterminacy and chaos, back into the external world and thus reconstitutes itself as a stable system of meaning. Doing so amounts to the text's reestablishing a linguistic reign over the world, to its redefining the Real as the benign product of human endeavor, as determinate language. But in fact, with this gesture of banishment the text revives the distinction between the internal world of the fiction and the external world of the Real and its agents.

With the expulsion of the Real, the aesthetic response generated by realism reveals its similarity to the experience of catharsis that Aristotle believed tragedy instilled in its audience. Realism, like tragedy, performs a ritualistic purgation of the reader's emotions, specifically sympathetic identification with the figures portrayed (pity) and revulsion from the events represented (terror). Certainly much of the aesthetic satisfaction to be derived from realism depends on the arousal

---

28. George Levine takes the creation of Frankenstein as the model of realism's flirtation with the "unnameable." See *The Realistic Imagination*, especially pp. 28–29.

29. In this connection see Hans Robert Jauss's critique of Theodor Adorno's "aesthetics of negativity" in *Aesthetic Experience and Literary Hermeneutics*, pp. 13–21.

and subsequent evacuation of these powerful emotions. But in the reception of the mode, what use is made of this experience? Rousseau was perhaps the first to complain that the cathartic capacity of art operated to maintain the status quo, that its effect was "limited to intensifying and not changing the established morals."[30] Like an act of sacrifice, the ritualistic rehearsal of the subdual of chaos and the inauguration of social order serves only to reaffirm that order and excuse the violence of its creation. Unlike more didactic forms of narrative, which may end with a moral injunction to alter one's actions and thereby change the world, realism would appear to lead only to a private experience of reconciliation with inalterable realities.

Aristotle developed his doctrine of catharsis, it will be remembered, in response to Plato's condemnation of Poetry as mere imitation of the world of appearances. Poetry, in Plato's view, inevitably gravitated toward the "imitation of calamity and recollection of sorrow," thereby stimulating an irrational pity that spreads from poet to audience as if by contagion.[31] In his defense of the arts, Aristotle argues that Poetry, through the cathartic purging of pity and terror, in the end serves to reinstate the higher claims of reason (and philosophy) in the human community.[32] Chinese aesthetic philosophers, lacking a theory of mimesis, likewise found the defense implied in the notion of catharsis unnecessary. Just as the literary artifact stands in a different relation to the referent in the Chinese tradition, so too is the work's connection to the emotional life of both author and reader perceived differently. Poetry is for the Chinese not a mediated objective correlative that, however skillfully the author employs the technique of his or her art, remains the weak shadow of a private subjectivity; it is rather a clear vessel through which stream emotions that are thought to be essentially shared and public. As the manifestation of communal and univer-

30. Jean-Jacques Rousseau, "Politics and the Arts. Letter to M. D'Alembert on the Theatre," quoted in ibid., p. 105.

31. Calamity is, for Plato, the natural subject of imitation, since "the wise and calm temperament, being always nearly equable, is not easy to imitate or to appreciate when imitated." See *The Dialogues of Plato, The Republic*, book 10, p. 481.

32. It is worth observing that both Plato and Aristotle discuss mimesis in an essentially ethical context. In fact, for Aristotle the actions imitated in a work of literature are the object of a priori ethical judgments: "The objects the imitator represents are actions, with agents who are necessarily either good men or bad—the diversities of human character being nearly always derivative from this primary distinction" (*The Poetics*, p. 224). With this ethical concern Plato and Aristotle show a stronger kinship with early Chinese theoreticians than do later Western thinkers, who generally discuss the problem of mimesis in purely epistemological terms.

sally available human emotions rather than private, antisocial passions, poetry is thought to tap directly the fundamental human instincts, which, at least in the dominant Mencian branch of Confucianism, are believed to be benign and social. No contradiction follows from the simultaneous advocacy of the investigation of principle in things and an emotive theory of literature because emotion (*qing*) and principle (*li* 理), unlike the Greek opposition of reason and passion, were generally perceived to function as a complementary, not antithetical, pair. In a chapter titled "Emotion and Literary Expression," Liu Xie argues that emotion and principle are interwoven in a fine piece of literature: "Emotion is the warp of literary pattern, linguistic form the woof of principle."[33] Where Plato associated Poetry with passion in a condemnatory fashion, Chinese literary theory could accommodate the role of both emotion and principle in the generation of a literary work. As a result, literature's capacity to stir the emotions of its audience did not carry the subversive potential Plato feared and that caused him to expel the poetic arts from his republic.

The high value accorded poetry in the Chinese tradition is evidenced in Confucius's high praise for the *Shi jing* 詩經 (Book of poetry), a volume whose study would, he believed, have a salutary effect on the body politic. Like the other forms of literature that Confucius is said to have edited (discursive prose and historical writings), poetry served the fundamental purpose of transmitting cultural values. This emphasis on the dissemination of values is a hallmark of Confucius's teaching (Confucius himself denied having discovered or invented anything new and claimed he simply transmitted the way of the ancients) and is at the heart of the didactic or pragmatic theories of literature that have been by far the most influential ones in Chinese criticism.[34] According to pragmatic theories, literature should, to use the common platitude, serve as "that by which one carries the Way" (*wen yi zai Dao* 文以載道). The eleventh-century philosopher Zhou Dunyi 周敦頤, who was the first to use this phrase, wrote: "Literature and

33. Liu Hsieh, *The Literary Mind*, pp. 246–47.
34. James J. Y. Liu writes:

The pragmatic concept of literature remained practically sacrosanct, so that critics who basically believed in other concepts rarely dared to repudiate it openly, but paid lip service to it while actually focusing attention on other concepts, or interpreted Confucius's words in such a way as to lend support to nonpragmatic theories, or simply kept silent about the pragmatic concept while developing others. (*Chinese Theories of Literature*, p. 111)

rhetoric are skills; the Way and virtue are realities."[35] As the vehicle of the Dao, literature was not a tool for the creation or discovery of new truths but a channel for the transmission of "realities," by which is meant the fundamental moral principles that underlie civilization.

In the West, classical mimetic theories, post-Cartesian epistemological attitudes, and nineteenth-century ideas about history combined to forge an evolutionary view of artistic development, which was endorsed by the promoters of realism and is still current today: new artistic forms are continuously generated in an effort to more nearly approach an ever-elusive external reality. Lacking a theory of mimesis, Chinese aesthetics developed a tenacious classicism; at least within the dominant Confucian tradition, the literati universally proclaimed the canon defined by Confucius to be the final repository of human wisdom and judged later works by the degree to which they approximated the spirit or form of the classics. From this classicism followed a taste for textual hermeneutics, which placed the burden on the interpreter to complete through study the meaning suggested by the text. The object of such study was to recover comprehension of the expressive situation that produced the text or, more profoundly, of the network of principles that operate through the text and of which it is a manifestation. Where an interpretive disturbance was recognized, it was imputed not to a representational inadequacy inherent in the text but to the inability of the interpreter to fully apprehend the significance of an abundantly sufficient text.[36]

Later generations of critics have accorded respectability to those genres of literary production modeled on the Five Classics. Of the

35. Quoted in ibid., p. 114.

36. It will rightly be objected here that both the Western and Chinese traditions are more complex than my argument allows, that I have limited my argument to Greek and Confucian schools of thought, ignoring Christian and Taoist alternatives within the two traditions. It is true that Christianity encouraged a hermeneutical tradition in some ways similar to Confucian classicism and that Chinese Taoists often showed a suspicion of language and linguistic attempts to grasp reality that seems at odds with my characterization of Chinese faith in linguistic manifestations of reality. But Christian thinkers share with the Greeks the notion of an ideal world behind or beyond the phenomenal world and transcending it; the arts, since their media are irredeemably a part of the phenomenal world, can at best hope to mimic what small part of the transcendent world is available to human understanding. Neither Taoists nor Confucians, however, sought to repudiate the phenomenal world through transcendence: for both, truth was immanent in the world. Confucians sought to live according to the principles that patterned the world, whereas Taoists sought a holistic perception of the world as it existed before it was differentiated into patterns by language. Language was suspect to the Taoists precisely because it was the instrument of that differentiation.

canonical works, only the historical writings, of which there are two, raise issues of narrativity and the representation of human actions in time. The first of these, *Shu jing* 書經 (Book of documents) is a record of verbal pronouncements (speeches, admonitions, and so forth) attributed to ancient rulers; the second, *Chunqiu* 春秋 (Spring and autumn annals), is a chronicle of actions and events thought to have significance for the state. The individuation of these two types of history shows a perceived distinction between simply transmitting (or copying) verbal historical material on the one hand and representing (or chronicling) human activity on the other. But neither form can be considered purely mimetic; whether through the selection of materials to be included (in the former case) or through the choice of actions to be recounted (in the latter), other concerns, specifically the ethical responsibility to "allocate praise and blame," generally overwhelmed mimetic interests in Chinese historiography.[37] Historical events were worthy of literary representation for their exemplary value, not in their own right. If history served above all the function of ensuring the continuation of the state, it did so primarily by confirming the cultural values exemplified in its chronicles. Historians thus owed their fidelity first to an ethical, discursive truth and only secondarily to the reality of the particular events they recorded.

Aristotle in his *Poetics* disparages the historian as nothing more than an imitator of the particular phenomena of the world of appearances, or "the thing that has been," while defending the poet, who calculates what is probable given certain universal truths and describes instead "the thing that might be."[38] As we have seen, in China history itself served the exemplary function Aristotle attributes to epic and

37. The Han dynasty historian Ban Gu 班固, in the "Yiwen zhi" 藝文志 (Treatise on literature) chapter of his *Han shu* 漢書 (History of the former Han dynasty), wrote that Confucius used the *Chunqiu* to "allocate praise and blame, respect and condemnation" (*Han shu* 6:1701–84, here p. 1715). In similar passages in the Gongyang 公羊 and Guliang 穀梁 commentaries to the *Chunqiu* Confucius is credited with initiating the historiographical practice of appropriate concealment, that is, the purposeful omission of events that would cast a negative light on otherwise worthy individuals; see Lien-Sheng Yang, "The Organization of Chinese Official Historiography," in Beasley and Pulleyblank, *Historians of China and Japan*, pp. 44–59, especially pp. 49–51. This practice was apparently not seen as compromising the principle of truthful recording celebrated elsewhere in the early histories (in, for example, the tale told in the *Zuo Zhuan* 佐傳 of three brothers, all historians, who are executed when they refuse to conceal a tyrant's act of regicide; see James Legge, trans., *The Ch'un Ts'ew, with the Tso Chuen*, pp. 514–15).

38. Aristotle, *The Poetics*, pp. 234–35.

drama and as a result an independent raison d'être was never generated for fictive narrative forms. China's lack of an epic tradition[39] and the shackling of the Chinese mythmaking imagination, for which Confucian rationalism is frequently blamed,[40] left history the only indigenous model for narrative writing; not until the Tang dynasty (and then only after the arrival of extensive cultural influences from India) did fiction become fully differentiated from history. The uncertain bibliographical treatment traditionally accorded *xiaoshuo* 小說 (literally "small talk," the term now translated as "fiction") gives a clear indication of the fundamental ambivalence Chinese felt toward works of this sort. The earliest categorization of *xiaoshuo*, in Ban Gu's 班固 *Yiwen zhi* 藝文志 (Treatise on literature), treated fiction as defective history, differentiated from the higher historical tradition either by its focus on arenas of life less significant than state affairs or by its questionable factuality.[41] A bibliographical tradition almost as ancient, Wei Zheng's 魏徵 *sibu* 四部 (four-category) system, categorized *xiaoshuo* with philosophy (*zibu* 子部).[42] Their classifications suggest a dual perception of fiction in traditional China, on the one hand emphasizing its narrative (or quasi-historical) characteristics and on the other promoting its value as moral instruction or as an adjunct to philosophy. In either case fiction remained a poor shadow of modes of writing that tradition accorded the highest esteem.

Despite this taint of spuriousness and triviality, Chinese fiction became increasingly autonomous and sophisticated over the course of the centuries and even found its champions. Yet in the eyes of most critics, Chinese fiction never shed the didacticism of its historiographical and philosophical models. C. T. Hsia, for example, has frequently observed the moralistic strain in Chinese vernacular literature

39. See Jaroslev Průšek, "History and Epics in China and in the West," in Průšek, *Chinese History and Literature*, pp. 17–34.

40. See Zhang Haishan, "'Zi bu yu guai, li, luan, shen' pingyi."

41. Ban Gu's criteria continued to be applied as late as the Qing dynasty, when Ji Yun 紀昀, in his preface to the *Si ku* 四庫 (Four treasuries), defined his category of *xiaoshuo* 小說 precisely by the texts' dubiousness as history. If a work could be shown to be patently false, it should be dismissed as valueless, and if no question arose as to its truth value, it should be reclassified as real history; only works that appeared to present a "mixture of truth and falsehood" were to be included in the *xiaoshuo* category, their use to be left to the discretion of the reader. See the discussion by Maeno Naoaki, "Ming Qing shiqi liang zhong duili de xiaoshuo lun." See also Andrew H. Plaks, "Towards a Critical Theory of Chinese Narrative," especially pp. 316–29.

42. See Kenneth J. Dewoskin, "The Six Dynasties *Chih-kuai* and the Birth of Fiction," in Andrew H. Plaks, *Chinese Narrative*, pp. 45–66.

and lamented the failure of traditional criticism to discover "the therapeutic value of popular fiction in providing a vicarious outlet for a reader's repressed desires."[43] But as Hsia has also pointed out, some works of traditional fiction explore "repressed desires" with remarkable sophistication,[44] and it could further be argued that some, particularly from the late Ming and after, achieve powerful cathartic effects through the evocation of Taoist and Buddhist notions of transcendence. It is beyond the scope of this study to consider such works, but we may observe that where cathartic effects are achieved, they generally coexist with more secular, instructional aims. The ending of Gao E's 高鶚 continuation of the *Honglou meng* 紅樓夢 (Dream of the red chamber), where the protagonist Jia Baoyu 賈寶玉 transcends the world of the "red dust" only after first discharging his worldly responsibilities by passing the civil-service examinations, is perhaps the most obvious example of this blending of cathartic and didactic effects. If, then, it would be too hasty to suggest that the experience of catharsis is never elicited in traditional Chinese narrative works, I may at least assert with Hsia that the Chinese tradition never used that experience as an independent rationale for fiction.

In summary, there are several points of marked contrast between the internal operation of realism and traditional Chinese aesthetic assumptions. Realism predicates for the author an autonomous platform of objective observation, a station that in theory is similar to that of the social scientist, and it operates on its readers through catharsis, by arousing and then purging the unpleasant emotions of pity and terror from their minds. In contrast, traditional Chinese literary theory was dominated by a notion of literature as the spontaneous expression of the author's emotional life; even when a place for observation was found in literary composition, it was understood as only a stage in a process of ethical cultivation. Moreover, the Chinese had no notion of catharsis and generally assumed that fiction (if not all literature) should serve didactic purposes. At both the creative and receptive ends, then, realism presented the Chinese with a fundamentally new model of aesthetic experience.

The term *realism* was introduced into China in two stages, first in

43. C. T. Hsia, "Yen Fu and Liang Ch'i-ch'ao," p. 226.
44. C. T. Hsia, "Society and Self in the Chinese Short Story," in his book *The Classic Chinese Novel*, pp. 299–321, especially pp. 307–8.

the context of the late Qing crusade for national restoration (*jiuguo* 救國) and later as part of the May Fourth campaign for enlightenment (*qimeng* 啓蒙). As I have suggested, Chinese intellectuals endorsed the call for a new literature, not for intrinsic aesthetic reasons, but because of the larger social and cultural benefits literary innovation seemed to promise. Realism seemed the most progressive of Western aesthetic modes, in part because of its scientism, in part because realist works took as their subjects a far wider range of social phenomena than earlier, more aristocratic forms did. The Chinese assumed that, once successfully transplanted, realism would encourage its readers to actively involve themselves in the important social and political issues confronting the nation. That Chinese reformers credited realism with this kind of social efficacy was understandable, since theorists in the West (including those from whom the Chinese first learned about realism)[45] had themselves frequently credited the mode with this power. But in its actual operation, as I have described, realism is more given to encouraging an aesthetic withdrawal than an activist engagement in social issues. Indeed, many of the greatest practitioners of realism in the West (one thinks of Chekhov, Flaubert, James, and the early Joyce) consciously placed the interests of art above politics and pursued in their works a highly rarefied aesthetic detachment. It is therefore not surprising that in its practice realism proved to be other than the socially transitive medium Chinese reformers first saw it to be. Their gradual discovery of the true nature of realism and their eventual relinquishment of the mode is the story of this book.

Before going on to consider the theoretical arguments advanced both for and against realism by Chinese intellectuals, it is worth stopping to consider for a moment Lu Xun's facetious definition of the

45. In *The Introduction of Western Literary Theories*, Bonnie McDougall has identified the Western and Japanese secondary works through which the Chinese were introduced to contemporary Western literary currents; see especially chapter 2, "Modern Literary Movements and Currents in the West," pp. 54–84, and chapter 4, "Realism and Naturalism," pp. 147–89. In the case of realism, the Chinese relied on the following works, among others: Richard Green Moulton, *The Modern Study of Literature* (Chicago: Chicago University Press, 1915); George Brandes, *Main Currents in Nineteenth-Century Literature* (6 vols., first published in Denmark in 1871–89; translated by Diana White and Mary Morison; London: Heinemann, 1923); and Shimamura Hōgetsu 島村抱月 "Bungeijō no shizenshugi" 文芸上の自然主義 (Naturalism in literature and art; first published in 1908; reprinted in *Gendai Nihon bungaku zenshū* 現代日本文学全集 [Compendium of modern Japanese literature] 59:150–60 [Tokyo: Chikuma shobō, 1958]).

term in "The Tablet": "To write largely about others [*duo jiang bieren* 多講別人] is realism." This modest formulation is more suggestive than it first appears. Through it, Lu Xun reduces the dispute over literary isms to an elemental question of social relationships. The choice of a literary mode, Lu Xun implies, fixes in a particular configuration the parties who share a literary experience—i.e. the author of the fiction, its "I"; the reader, its "you"; and the "he," "she," or "they" that constitutes the work's protagonist. As I have suggested, realism appealed to the Chinese in part because of the attention it directed on the "others" (*bieren*) of Chinese society, those disenfranchised groups that had historically been overlooked. To draw these neglected groups into the compass of serious literature was in some sense to fundamentally redefine social relations in China. At the same time, however, this new scrutiny risked polarizing literate authors and their subject, the now visible but still mute *bieren*. New questions were raised. Should the relationship of author and subject be understood in a humanistic way, as a proferring of pity to the disadvantaged, or ideologically, as a warning to the powerful and a lesson in self-determination for the underclass? Was the realist authors' disavowal of self a sign of their modesty, or did it disguise a kind of arrogance—that is to say, was their real reason for writing about others a desire to help them or to distance themselves by labeling and defining them? As we discuss how these issues were explored both in the theoretical debates and in the fictional experimentation of the 1920s and 1930s, it will be useful to remind ourselves occasionally of their consequences for the new social definitions that the new literature was intended to create and to reflect. For even the abstractions of the Revolutionary Literature debate, to be examined in the following chapter, can be understood in the simplest of terms as a battle of pronouns, as a contest between the romanticist *wo/women* (I/we) and the realist *ta/tamen* (he/they).

2

"A Literature of Blood and Tears"
May Fourth Theories of Literary Realism

REALISM AND THE PROMISE OF
CULTURAL TRANSFORMATION

"Sincere, progressive, activist, free, egalitarian, creative, beautiful, good, peaceful, cooperative, industrious, prosperous for all"—with this cumbersome list of adjectives the young intellectual Chen Duxiu 陳獨秀 described the new society he and others involved in the May Fourth movement hoped to create. A contrasting set of terms described the old society that was to be replaced: traditional China was "hypocritical, conservative, passive, constrained, classicist, imitative, ugly, evil, belligerent, disorderly, lazy, and prosperous only for the few."[1] The heterogeneity of these lists attests not simply to Chen's bent for rhetorical excess but to the comprehensive nature of the changes he envisioned and to a certain confusion of priorities. With his jumbled adjectives, Chen sketched the fault lines of the coming revolution; along with objective social changes, the moral complexion of the Chinese people was to be transformed.

Literature was to play an important role in this transformation, as Chen made clear in another article, where he imagined an "army of the literary revolution" advancing with banners unfurled. On these banners he saw imprinted the literary equivalents of the above lists: "Down with the ornate, obsequious literature of the aristocrats; up with the plain, expressive literature of the people! Down with the stale, ostentatious literature of the classics; up with the fresh, sincere literature of realism! Down with the pedantic, obscure literature of the

---

1. Chen Duxiu 陳獨秀, "*Xin qingnian* xuanyan" 新青年宣言 (*New Youth* manifesto), *Xin qingnian* 7, no. 1 (1 December 1919); reprinted in Chen Duxiu, *Duxiu wencun* 2:365–68, here p. 366.

recluse; up with the clear, popular literature of society!"[2] In his call for a people's, or national, literature (*guomin wenxue* 國民文學), a realist literature (*xieshi wenxue* 寫實文學), and a social literature (*shehui wenxue* 社會文學), Chen was employing words that resonated with meaning for the young revolutionaries of the time, words that were the building blocks of a new national identity. *Guomin* connoted the recent adjustment in the Chinese world order whereby the once-supreme Middle Kingdom was redefined as a nation-state among others; *xieshi* marked a break with the superstition and entrenched classicism of traditional intellectual life; *shehui* signified the displacement of Confucian bureaucratic and familial relations that, it was hoped, would make possible the birth of a modern, democratic society. These words have been used so insistently to describe the Chinese experience in the decades since Chen wrote that they have grown stale, but one senses from context how fresh and potent they must have seemed to the young Chen Duxiu.

Chen was not the first Chinese intellectual to use the term *xieshi* (or the synonymous *xianshi* 現實) in his prescription for a new literature. The word was in fact a Japanese invention, one of many neologisms created by Meiji intellectuals as they translated works of Western literature and philosophy into Japanese. The compound was then adopted by Chinese students, for many of whom Japanese textbooks and translations provided their first exposure to Western ideas. The reformer Liang Qichao 梁啟超, who fled to Japan after the failure of the Hundred Days' Reform of 1898, was one such student of the West, and his writings contain the first significant Chinese use of the term *xieshi*. In his 1902 essay "On the Relationship between Fiction and the Government of the People," Liang adopted a distinction, originally made by the Japanese critic Tsubouchi Shōyō 坪內逍遙, between works belonging to the idealistic school of fiction (*lixiang pai* 理想派), which draw readers out of the present environment into a better world of the imagination, and those of the realistic school (*xieshi pai* 寫實派), which reveal to readers facets of the present world generally suppressed or ignored.[3] As we shall see, this distinction was to characterize

2. Chen Duxiu, "Wenxue geming lun" 文學革命論 (On literary revolution), *Xin qingnian* 2, no. 6 (1 February 1917); reprinted in Chen Duxiu, *Duxiu wencun* 1:135–40, here p. 136.
3. Liang Qichao 梁啟超, "Xiaoshuo yu qunzhi zhi guanxi" 小說與群治之關係 (On the relationship between fiction and the government of the people), in *Zhongguo jindai wenlun xuan* 1:157–61.

much of the discussion about fiction in the years to follow, though more often than not the term *romanticist* (*langman* 浪漫) was to replace *idealistic*.

Liang's essay was seminal not only for its introduction of these terms but for its forceful advocacy of literary reform. Like Yan Fu 嚴復, another major figure of the late Qing reform movement, Liang had been struck by the esteem accorded to fiction in the West; in Yan Fu's words, Western countries had "time and again benefited from the assistance of fiction" as they became "enlightened or civilized."[4] Whereas fiction had traditionally been viewed in China as an immoral, or at best frivolous, pastime, the nineteenth-century Western example showed that it could serve as a powerful tool for social persuasion. Particularly after the failure of the 1898 reforms, many progressive intellectuals came to believe that a revolution in popular opinion, a cultural transformation, was necessary before political innovations could be attempted in China; both Yan Fu and Liang Qichao saw fiction as a promising instrument for such change. In his 1902 essay Liang went so far as to suggest that the reform of fiction was the primary task then facing the intellectuals: "If you want to revitalize a country's populace, you must first revitalize that country's fiction."[5] Serious fiction such as that popular in the West had the power to awaken commoners' aspirations for a better life and so served the high moral purpose of encouraging them to work for their own and for society's betterment. Liang's ideas were quickly taken up by other reform-minded intellectuals. Wang Zhongqi 王鍾麒, for example, wrote: "What our people lack most is public spirit; only fiction can instill patriotic, communal, and caring feelings in people who completely lack such a spirit."[6] Di Chuqing 狄楚卿 reiterated Liang's estimation of fiction as the Mahayana, or great vehicle, of literature, calling it an "X-ray of society" with an extraordinary power to "guide humanity."[7]

---

4. Yan Fu 嚴復, "Benguan fuyin shuobu yuanqi" 本館附印說部緣起 (Announcing our policy to print a supplementary fiction section), *Guowen bao* 國聞報, 16 October and 18 November 1897; reprinted in Qian Xingcun (A Ying), *Wan Qing wenxue congchao: xiaoshuo xiju yanjiu juan*, pp. 1–12, here p. 12.

5. Liang Qichao, "Xiaoshuo yu qunzhi zhi guanxi," p. 157.

6. Wang Zhongqi 王鍾麒 (Wang Wusheng 无生, pseud.), "Lun xiaoshuo yu gailiang shehui zhi guanxi" 論小說與改良社會之關係 (On the relationship of fiction to social reform), in *Zhongguo jindai wenlun xuan* 1:223–25, here p. 224.

7. Di Chuqing 狄楚卿 (Di Pingzi 狄平子, pseud.), "Lun wenxue shang xiaoshuo

What was original about these arguments was not their apparently exaggerated claims for the power of literature to transform society. The Chinese had always viewed their written heritage, in particular their long philosophical and poetic traditions, as the primary embodiment of their culture, and would-be reformers had frequently ascribed social disintegration to a poor choice of literary models. But in searching for new literary forms to substitute for the offending ones, reformers had traditionally looked to well-established native models and represented their own innovations as the reinstitution of classical manners and customs. Liang and the other late Qing reformers broke this mold by promoting a vernacular rather than classical model and, even more radically, by looking abroad for prototypes. In fact late Qing and early May Fourth thinkers had only a very rough knowledge of Western fiction (Chen Duxiu's list of model writers included such diverse figures as Wilde, Hugo, and Dickens),[8] but they were impressed by how broad an influence fiction exerted over society and by the dynamism they associated generally with Western cultural products.

This dynamism, which was to become one of Chen Duxiu's major themes, had first been observed and analyzed by Yan Fu in his essays of the mid-1890s. While introducing Spencer and Darwin to Chinese readers, Yan Fu had written that whereas the West was forward-looking and welcomed change, China "loves the ancient and despises the new."[9] In 1915, when Chen Duxiu began editing the journal *Xin qingnian* 新青年 (New youth), which was to become the primary forum for discussion of the new literature, he must have thought that history had once again demonstrated the truth of Yan Fu's remarks: the 1911 revolution, though it brought an end to imperial rule, had clearly failed to solve China's underlying social and cultural problems. Once again China had proven resistant to change, and reformers of Chen's generation were stricken with a despondency even more crushing than the one their predecessors had suffered after the failure of the 1898 reform effort. Chen resolved to counter his generation's disheartenment with a passionate drive to instill in Chinese society the

zhi weizhi" 論文學上小說之位置 (On the position of fiction in literature), in *Zhongguo jindai wenlun xuan* 1:234–37, here p. 234.
    8. Chen Duxiu, "Wenxue geming lun," p. 140.
    9. Benjamin Schwartz quotes this line from "Lun shibian zhi ji" 論時變之亟 (On the speed of world change) in *In Search of Wealth and Power*, p. 55.

"power to resist," to move and change.[10] Always given to thinking in dichotomies, Chen Duxiu played heavily on the contrast between East and West in his May Fourth essays, praising the West for its "history of liberation" while lamenting Chinese "ignorance of the function [of revolution] in the improvement of civilization."[11] Chinese timidity was evident not only in political matters but in cultural ones as well, and Chen went on to apply Darwinian notions of evolutionary change to literature. He accepted Liang's division of literature into two schools, the realistic and the idealistic or romanticist, but whereas Liang had found value in both schools, Chen did not give them equal standing. Borrowing freely from contemporary Western accounts of literary history, which portrayed Western literature—and by hegemonic extension, world literature—as having passed from classicism to romanticism to realism in ever-ascending linear progress, he argued the evolutionary superiority of realism.[12] Though classicism and romanticism remained predominant in China, he wrote, it was inevitable that in the future Chinese literature "would move in the direction of realism."[13] As the culmination of a long evolutionary process, realism was for Chen the literary embodiment of the scientific and democratic spirit that he believed characterized the contemporary West. His advocacy of the mode was thus a natural extension of his campaign to rid China of traditional cultural constraints and thereby make way for a general social revolution.

Hu Shi 胡適, an equally influential if somewhat more moderate advocate of reform, joined Chen Duxiu in instructing writers to pay more attention to "meaning and reality" in their works than to matters of style.[14] In an important essay on Ibsen published in 1918,

10. Chen Duxiu, "Dikang li" 抵抗力 (The power of resistance), in Chen Duxiu, *Duxiu wencun* 1:27–34, here pp. 31–32. Cf. Luo Jialun 羅家倫: "The glory of the May Fourth movement lies precisely in getting China to move" (quoted by Vera Schwarcz in *The Chinese Enlightenment*, p. 7).

11. Chen Duxiu, "Jinggao qingnian" 敬告青年 (Call to youth), in Chen Duxiu, *Duxiu wencun* 1:1–10, here p. 1.

12. Chen recaps the development of Western literature from classicism to realism and naturalism (two terms that he did not clearly distinguish) in his article "Xiandai Ouzhou wenyi shi tan" 現代歐洲文藝史譚 (Discussion of the history of modern European literature), *Xin qingnian* 1, nos. 3–4 (15 November and 15 December 1915). He seems to have been primarily influenced by Georges Pellisier's *Le mouvement littéraire contemporain*, Paris: Plon-nourrit, 1901. See the discussion in Bonnie McDougall, *The Introduction of Western Literary Theories*, pp. 147–49.

13. Chen Duxiu, letter to the editor, *Xin qingnian* 1, no. 4 (15 December 1915): 2.

14. Hu Shi 胡適, letter to the editor, *Xin qingnian* 2, no. 2 (1 October 1916): 1–3.

Hu Shi went further, examining the actual operation of realism (or what he called Ibsenism) in far more detail than Chen Duxiu had done. Like other progressive intellectuals of the period, Hu was impressed with the influence that literary works such as Ibsen's plays appeared to exert in Western society. In Hu Shi's view this influence resulted above all from Ibsen's refusal to cater to the greatest human weakness, people's inherent reluctance to confront the truth about themselves and their society. Ibsen defies this natural predilection for escapism and bravely discloses the truth; in particular he forces his readers to observe the many ways in which society and the family work to stifle individual conscience. Yet Hu is careful to insist that though Ibsen's work is critical in spirit, it is never purely negative in effect:

> Ibsen described actual social and familial conditions in order to move readers, to make us feel how dark and corrupt our families and society are and to make us understand that our families and society must be reformed—this is what is meant by Ibsenism. On the surface, it seems destructive, but in fact it is entirely healthy. . . . Ibsen knows that society's diseases are many and complex and that there is no panacea, so he can only take a blood test, describe the illness, and let each patient seek out his or her own medicine.[15]

Astutely, Hu recognizes that in Ibsen's world the positive effect of realistic description is achieved by polarizing the individual and the social order; progress comes only through the lonely struggles of a few extraordinary people against society. Again Hu applies the disease metaphor, suggesting such individuals play a vital role in society's survival: "The health of the society and the nation depends on a few tenacious, unrelenting white blood cells who battle the wicked and depraved elements of society; only through them is there hope of reform and progress."[16] In recognizing that for Ibsen heroism consists of the courage "forthrightly to attack social corruption," Hu Shi evokes, without explicitly naming it, another important theme of the May Fourth enlightenment, that is, the pursuit of *zijue* 自覺, "autonomy" or "self-consciousness."[17] May Fourth thinkers used this term

15. Hu Shi, "Yibushengzhuyi" 易卜生主義 (Ibsenism), *Xin qingnian* 4, no. 6 (15 June 1918); reprinted in Zhao Jiabi, *Zhongguo xin wenxue daxi* 1:179–92, pp. 188–189.

16. Ibid., p. 192.

17. Chen Duxiu first argued the importance of autonomy in 1915. See the discussion in Vera Schwarcz, *The Chinese Enlightenment*, p. 38.

to denote the state of intellectual and spiritual independence that they wanted to see replace the "slavish" mentality inculcated in the Chinese people by Confucianism. Like Chen's notion of perpetual revolution, *zijue* was associated positively with the West: only freethinkers, liberated from the strictures of tradition, could produce the kind of cultural criticism that another frequent contributor to *New Youth*, Luo Jialun 羅家倫, called "the creative force in Western civilization."[18]

Mao Dun 茅盾, the critic and author most responsible for the propagation of a Western-style realism in China, built largely on the work of these late Qing and early Republican reformers when he began to systematically introduce the theory and history of the mode in the early 1920s. His early criticism makes clear that he fully accepted Chen Duxiu's notion of literary evolution, as well as his equation of realism with science and democracy. Indeed, in an article Mao Dun published in January 1920, entitled "What Is the Duty of Contemporary Men of Letters?" he employed the same terms that Chen had used to describe his ambitions for the new literature: he called on writers and critics to "imbue the literary world with the spirit of democracy, to make literature social, to tear down the mask of aristocratic literature and give free reign to the spirit of popular literature."[19] Realism appealed to Mao Dun because of its emphasis on what he called objective observation (*keguan guancha* 客觀觀察) and because of its unflinching examination of all aspects of society, the lower depths as well as the upper strata, the ugly as well as the beautiful. In an article published in *Xiaoshuo yuebao* 小說月報 (Short story magazine), a house journal of the Shanghai Commercial Press where he worked, Mao Dun went so far as to lay out a plan for the introduction of realism, providing two lists of writers whose works merited study and translation. These lists were dominated by Scandinavian and Russian names (Strindberg, Ibsen, Gogol, Chekhov, Turgenev, Dostoyevski, Gorky) but also included Zola, Maupassant, Shaw, and Wells.[20]

18. Luo Jialun, "Piping de yanjiu: san W zhuyi" 批評的研究：三W主義 (The study of criticism—Three W-ism), *Xin qingnian* 2, no. 3 (April 1920): 601–3; quoted in Vera Schwarcz, *The Chinese Enlightenment*, p. 123.

19. Mao Dun 茅盾, "Xianzai wenxuejia de zeren shi shenme?" 現在文學家的責任是什麼? (What is the duty of contemporary men of letters?), *Dongfang zazhi* 17, no. 1 (10 January 1920); reprinted in Mao Dun, *Mao Dun wenyi zalun ji* 1:3–5, here p. 5.

20. Mao Dun, "Xiaoshuo xinchao lan xuanyan" 小說新潮欄宣言 (Manifesto of the column "New Tide of Fiction"), *Xiaoshuo yuebao* 11, no. 1 (25 January 1920): reprinted in Mao Dun, *Mao dun wenyi zalun ji* 1:6–11.

In December 1920 Mao Dun was given a chance to execute his plan: in that month the Wenxue yanjiu hui 文學研究會 (Association for literary studies) was formed in Beijing, and Mao Dun was entrusted with editorship of its quasi-official publication, the newly revamped *Short Story Magazine*. Although the association was probably conceived by Zheng Zhenduo 鄭振鐸, Mao Dun was one of its twelve founding members and a driving force in its operations. In its charter the new organization called for art "for life's sake" (*wei rensheng* 為人生) and specified three goals: the introduction and study of world literature, the reassessment of traditional Chinese literature, and the creation of a new literature. As its members frequently pointed out in later years, the prescription did not amount to advocacy of any particular literary doctrine, but the foreign writers who were most prominently featured in the early issues of the revised *Short Story Magazine* (and whose works were included in the association's series of translations, the *Wenxue yanjiu hui congshu* 文學研究會叢書) were primarily those on Mao Dun's earlier lists, and the association inevitably became linked with realism in the mind of the literate public.

For those who first advocated its adoption in China realism was thus associated with a whole complex of Western ideas and attitudes, especially with notions of cultural dynamism and intellectual autonomy. Nevertheless, a careful reading of the relevant essays by Chen Duxiu, Hu Shi, and Mao Dun reveals certain reservations, or at least hesitations, about the mode, reservations that become significant when viewed in the light of later Chinese reevaluations of the Western influence. Hu Shi, for his part, while expressing admiration for Ibsen's spirit of struggle, appears somewhat reluctant to prescribe his individualistic anarchism for China: "Societies and nations evolve with time, so one cannot definitively point to a certain medicine as a cure-all. . . . Moreover, each society and nation is different: the medicine that's good for Japan may not be appropriate for China."[21] Indeed, Hu Shi was later to actively campaign against individualism,[22] and the ambivalence he displays even in his essay on Ibsenism was characteristic of Chinese discussions of the subject: as Benjamin Schwartz has

21. Hu Shi, "Yibushengzhuyi," in *Zhongguo xin wenxue daxi* 1:191.
22. In 1920 Hu Shi wrote an article entitled "Fei gerenzhuyi de xin shenghuo" 非個人主義的新生活 (The anti-individualistic new life). See Hu Shi, *Hu Shi wencun* 4:1043–60.

observed, when Yan Fu introduced the writings of John Stuart Mill in the 1890s, he construed Mill's individualism not as an end in itself but rather as "a means to the advancement of 'the people's virtue and intellect,' and beyond this to the purposes of the state."[23] For Hu Shi, Ibsen's egoism is likewise defensible not for its intrinsic value but for its positive effect on society. Even with his blood metaphors, Hu Shi wavers in assigning a place to the individual who dares to form an independent judgment on society: where in the first passage cited the social rebel is seen as outside the body, drawing blood for the purposes of an objective diagnosis, by the conclusion of the essay Hu Shi has found a new place for the rebel within the body, as a white blood cell fighting for the survival not of the self but of the larger organism.

Similarly, Chen Duxiu and Mao Dun were forced to modify their professed faith in the natural evolution of literary forms as they learned more about current Western trends. In his "Discussion of the History of Modern European Literature," Chen conceded that realism had given way to naturalism in the West, but in a letter to the editor written shortly thereafter, he recommended that Chinese writers continue to take realism as their model because the explicit portrayal of violence and social disorder in naturalism would not be accepted by Chinese readers.[24] Mao Dun, writing somewhat later and with a better knowledge of the current literary scene in the West, recognized that varieties of neoromanticism (a term that embraced for him such diverse movements as expressionism, futurism, and symbolism) had

---

23. Benjamin Schwartz, *In Search of Wealth and Power*, p. 141. Cf. Chow Tse-tsung, *The May Fourth Movement*, p. 360:

> To many young Chinese reformers, emancipation of the individual was as much for the sake of saving the nation as upholding individual rights. The value of individual and independent judgment was indeed appreciated more in the May Fourth period than ever before, yet the individual's duty to society and the nation was also emphasized.

Also cf. Lin Yü-sheng, *The Crisis of Chinese Consciousness*, pp. 67–68:

> The stress placed on the importance of the individual by Ch'en Tu-hsiu [Chen Duxiu] and by iconoclastic intellectuals in general at this time cannot, from our historical perspective, be identified with the Western concept of individual liberty based on an ethical conviction of the worth of the individual, which evolved mainly through a secularization of religious faith, but rather represented an aspect of the revolt on the part of these intellectuals against the traditional suppression of the individual in Chinese societies. . . . When the high tide of iconoclasm ebbed, the May Fourth individualism waned.

24. Chen Duxiu, letter to the editor, *Xin qingnian*, p. 2.

supplanted realism; indeed, for a short time in mid-1920 Mao Dun
lost his faith in both science and realism and wrote glowingly of the
"revolutionary, liberating, and creative spirit" of romanticism.[25] By
the time of the association's founding later that year, however, he
had come to the conclusion that realism, if no longer at the cutting
edge of international literary developments, was nevertheless "good
for China at this time in its history."[26] Realism met certain local and,
he suspected, temporary needs; in particular, he hoped the practice
of realism would encourage writers to systematically examine the
broader currents of social history and not use their fiction simply to
vent private complaints.

Throughout the period, then, specific Western concepts were
initially embraced because of their potential contribution to China's
cultural rejuvenation, but they were later subjected to reinterpre-
tation when they appeared not to be entirely suited to this larger
goal. These second thoughts suggest that May Fourth thinkers did
not entertain Western concepts out of a disembodied intellectual conviction; they saw them as pieces of a developing solution to one overriding question: from what source could China find the strength to
free itself from the shackles of tradition and establish a new cultural
order? This was above all a question of origins and of will, and in their
effort to forge a literary response to it, May Fourth writers turned to
Western literature. In doing so, however, they were not looking simply
to replace the authority of their own tradition with that of a foreign
one; nor were they looking for formal patterns to copy. Most May
Fourth critics at one time or other warned against the dangers of
imitating other works, whether Western or Chinese. Western literature served Chinese intellectuals primarily as a lever with which they
could pry themselves free of their own tradition. It was admired not so
much for its specific formal qualities but because in the West individual works, especially works of fiction, appeared to emerge from the
fresh and original observations of individuals responding directly to

25. Mao Dun, "Wei xin wenxue yanjiuzhe jin yi jie" 爲新文學研究者進一解
(One more explanation for researchers in the new literature), *Jiefang yu gaizao* 3, no. 1
(1 August 1920): 102. See the discussion of Mao Dun's flirtation with neoromanticism
in Marián Gálik, *Mao Tun and Literary Criticism*, pp. 37–41.
26. Mao Dun, "*Xiaoshuo yuebao* gaige xuanyan" 《小說日報》改革宣言 (Manifesto for the reform of *Short Story Magazine, Xiaoshuo yuebao* 12, no. 1 (10 January
1921); reprinted in Mao Dun, *Mao Dun wenyi zalun ji* 1:19–21, here p. 20.

the stimuli of contemporary social phenomena. May Fourth writers hoped to incorporate into their works a similar authority or essence from outside the traditional province of literature.

The same logic that conditioned the acceptance of such Western ideas as individualism and evolutionism applies to the history of realism and its advocacy in China. Realism was not primarily endorsed by Chinese thinkers for what Westerners associate most closely with it, its mimetic pretense, that is, the simple desire to capture the real world in language. At least in the early years of the New Literature movement, Chinese writers rarely discussed problems of verisimilitude—how the text works to establish an equivalency between itself and the extra-literary world—and little critical attention was given to the technical problems of fictional representation, a preoccupation of such Western realists as Flaubert and James. Instead realism was embraced because it seemed to meet Chinese needs in the urgent present undertaking of cultural transformation by offering a new model of creative generativity and literary reception. Though the thread of both these concerns runs throughout the period under discussion, questions of literary origins generally dominated critical polemics in the 1920s, whereas the issue of literary reception became foremost in the 1930s. In the rest of this chapter, I will take up each of these matters in turn, examining them in the context of the decade in which they received the most discussion.

THE SEARCH FOR
NEW LITERARY ORIGINS

In the introduction we observed the importance of expressive conceptions of literature in traditional Chinese criticism. Given the virulent iconoclasm of much May Fourth thinking, to discover that such theories continued to exert a powerful influence over Chinese literature in the early twentieth century is perhaps surprising. May Fourth intellectuals, as vocal as they were in their opposition to didactic and classicist strains in the critical legacy, never repudiated the notion that literature was above all the articulation of deep human emotions. The familiar Chinese definition of poetry as "the expression of the heart's intent," first recorded in the *Book of Documents* and ubiquitous in later criticism, was cited approvingly by writers as diverse as Guo

Moruo 郭沫若, Lu Xun, and Ye Shaojun 葉紹鈞.[27] In the works of those associated with the romanticist Chuangzao she 創造社 (Creation society), the primary rival of the Association for Literary Studies throughout the 1920s, traditional expressive views were blended with the influence of Western romanticism to promote a self-revelation that was, at least in intention, new in Chinese literature. Even the aggressive self-display of modern Chinese romanticists needs to be distinguished, however, from a Western-style individualism, since it invariably disguises a latent hope that the author's self-expression will somehow contribute to a larger cultural rejuvenation. Lu Xun's early call for a Byronic Mara poetry, for example, was above all motivated by the desire to discover a "warrior of the world of spirit" to "lead us to goodness, beauty, strength, and health."[28] Guo Moruo's early poetry appears at first to be a highly individualistic celebration of his own creative powers, frequently verging on a kind of pure auto-affection, but Guo's pantheism allows a lyric equation of the self with all who might share in the joy of creation; the rebirth he continually celebrates in *Nüshen* 女神 (*The goddesses*) is not just the renaissance of his individual creativity but the renaissance of the Chinese people at large. Even in the confessional fiction of Yu Dafu 郁達夫 the narrator's personal humiliations are pointedly connected with the abased position of the Chinese people in international politics, as if the author's private anxieties could only be healed through a change in the nation's historical fortunes.[29] Once this aspect of their romanticism is understood, the Creation Society members' sudden ideological rebirth in the mid-1920s, after which they denounced individualism and proclaimed their desire to write a *littérature engagé*, does not seem so remarkable: in a typically voluntaristic manner, they simply generalized their individual emotions and, overriding the obvious class distinctions, pro-

27. For favorable references to traditional expressive views see, for example, the following works: Guo Moruo's 郭沫若 letter to Zong Baihua 宗白華 of September 1920 (in Guo Moruo, *Guo Moruo shuxin ji*, pp. 28–35); Lu Xun's "Moluo shi li shuo" 摩羅詩力說 (Power of Mara poetry) (in Lu Xun, *Lu Xun quanji* 1:63–115); and Ye Shaojun's 葉邵鈞 "Wenyi tan" 文藝談 (On the literary arts) in Ye Shaojun, *Ye Shengtao lun chuangzuo*, pp. 3–73.

28. Lu Xun, "Moluo shi li shuo," p. 100.

29. See, for example, the concluding passage of Yu Dafu's 郁達夫 "Chenlun" 沉淪 (Sinking): "O China, my China, you are the cause of my death! . . . I wish you could become rich and strong soon!" (in C. T. Hsia, *Twentieth-Century Chinese Stories*, p. 33).

nounced themselves spokespeople for the masses. Their works continued to display the same heroics of the self, but a self now viewed above all as the progenitor of the coming social revolution.[30]

That we find approving references to traditional expressive theories in the works of writers now classified as realists may seem doubly surprising, but realists too sought a new origin for their literature in the extraliterary world; they too hoped their fiction would speak with the voice of living individuals, that it would be "intimately connected with life."[31] Moreover, May Fourth realists hoped to appropriate for fiction some of the respectability traditionally accorded the expressive art of poetry. If the new fiction was to play an important role in cultural transformation, as they earnestly hoped it would, it must do more than merely amuse or preach; it must engage the affective life of its audience at the deepest level. Only in this way could it be distinguished from traditional didactic fiction and from popular romantic and satirical genres, which the intellectuals belittled as trivial and scandal-mongering. The critic Zheng Zhenduo, in the context of a vehement attack on a popular form of satirical fiction that the literary reformers had dubbed castigatory fiction (*qianze xiaoshuo* 譴責小說), wrote:

> [The writer of fiction] must offer up his own passion, his very viscera. Sometimes he will show a heart overflowing with sympathy for the characters he has created, sometimes he will treat them with the cool attitude of the observer. But he will not go beyond observation to mock, revile, and curse them. . . .
>
> We Chinese have always enjoyed discussing others' secrets. We are pitiless. We scoff, we deride, we curse everyone and everything. Castigatory fiction simply caters to its audience, encouraging them in their bad habits and bad attitudes. If we want China to move forward, it we want

---

30. In the process of their ideological transformation, some Creationists temporarily repudiated the expressive function of literature. Guo Moruo called for writers to be Marxist "phonographs," in this way overcoming their individualism and achieving pure objectivity. This idea was controversial even among other Creationists; Li Chuli 李初梨 agreed that the new proletarian literature must spring from ideology, rather than purely from personal emotions or social observation, but argued that authors had to actively work to unify theory and practice and not simply parrot slogans. See Li's article "Zenyangde jianshe geming wenxue" 怎樣的建設革命文學 (How to build a revolutionary literature), *Wenhua pipan* 2 (15 February 1928): 3–20, and the rebuttal by Guo Moruo, "Liushengjiqi de huiyin" 留聲機器的回音 (The phonograph's echo), *Wenhua pipan* 3 (20 February 1928), reprinted in *Geming wenxue lunzheng ziliao xuanbian* 1:215–27.

31. Ye Shaojun, "Wenyi tan," pp. 33–34.

the Chinese people to become sympathetic, sincere and earnest, we must first rid ourselves of this kind of castigatory fiction.[32]

In passages like these, Zheng associates the expressive potential of the new literature with the inculcation of ethical values, specifically pity (*tongqing* 同情) and sincerity (*cheng* 誠). Ye Shaojun, another founding member of the Association for Literary Studies and one of the most important writers of the 1920s, blended self-expression and moral earnestness in a similar way in his 1921 series of essays *On the Literary Arts*. One of Ye's intentions in these pieces, which were published serially in the literary supplement to *Chen bao* 晨報 (Morning news), was to integrate the critical mission that Chen Duxiu and Hu Shi had assigned to the new literature with his own view of literary inspiration. Impatient with the various isms circulating in contemporary literary circles (including realism), Ye argued that "true literature" is never the product of imitation, theory, or commercial considerations but "originates in the author's deep feelings." Composition itself is a "pure and fleeting" inspiration, "arising from some yearning and for some purpose that [the author] himself does not understand and has not the time to analyze."[33] Prior to this moment of inspiration, however, a writer will have undertaken a comprehensive investigation of the world:

> The writer, like other mortals, is a mere grain floating in a boundless sea, but the scope of his observation is inexhaustibly large; everything that he comes across is material for his observation. The writer's perception, his spirit's vision, turns in all directions, a candle shining round about. Not only is his sight as far-reaching as a telescope and as observant of detail as a microscope but it also delves into the heart of things, into their inner being. There is no optical tool that can be compared to it.[34]

It is only after extended observation that the writer, "having entered into the heart of things and experienced their force of life, involuntarily develops a powerful need to express [what he has experienced]." Understood in full, then, the creative process constitutes self-

32. Zheng Zhenduo 鄭振鐸, "Qianze xiaoshuo" 譴責小說 (Castigatory fiction), in Zhao Jiabi, *Zhongguo xin wenxue daxi* 2:392–95, here pp. 393–94. See also Ye Shaojun, "Wenyi tan," especially sections 17 and 33.
33. Ye Shaojun, "Wenyi tan," p. 23.
34. Ibid., p. 18.

cultivation (*ziji xiuyang* 自己修養); without such cultivation the author's "view of human life, his Weltanschauung, his 'ego'" would remain tentative and unformed.[35]

The similarity between Ye's observation (*guancha* 觀察) of the external world and the neo-Confucian idea of the investigation of things, described in the previous chapter, is evident: observation in this sense is not the coldly analytical examination of the material world that Westerners associate with scientific realism but a stage in the moral tempering of the observer. Composition, likewise, is not a technical rendering of the external world but rather a further stage in this process, when the moral knowledge acquired through observation coalesces and finds spontaneous expression in words. If an author's work emerges from such cultivation, it should offer evidence of precisely those virtues that Zheng Zhenduo wished to see fostered in the Chinese people: pity and sincerity. "Pity for the weak," Ye writes, "is the most universal emotion of artists";[36] it releases the "great power of literature, to break down the barriers that divide person from person,"[37] thus ensuring that the author's work will have both depth and moral substance, that the author's self-expression will not be mere self-indulgence. Similarly, the truth (*zhen* 真) of a literary work is dependent on the sincerity of the emotions expressed in it. This principle is so fundamental for Ye that he divides all authors into two categories according to it: "sincere" writers are those who "profoundly recognize that the aim of literature is to arouse the readers' pity, to increase their understanding, to give them solace and joy," while the "insincere" ground their "soulless" writing in "a mocking, comic spirit" or in "decadent, barbarous self-justification."[38] In this context the perspectivism suggested earlier to be characteristic of realism acquires a moral value: authors prove their sincerity precisely by recognizing, and refusing to overreach, the range of their personal observations. They above all resist the temptation to engage in the epic fabulation of events and characters—what Průšek, following Goethe, calls *Lust zum fabulieren*—and refuse to emulate popular fiction's preoccupation with plot and event at the expense of character and emotion.

Ye Shaojun's overt (if unacknowledged) indebtedness to neo-

35. Ibid., p. 32.
36. Ibid., p. 32.
37. Ibid., p. 50.
38. Ibid., p. 8.

Confucian thought make him—in his role as a literary theorist, at least—something of an anomaly among members of the Association for Literary Studies; certainly his conception of literary inspiration, with its emphasis on self-cultivation and the virtues of pity and sincerity, seems remote from a Western understanding of realism. Yet his preoccupation with the morality of observation—with the ethical questions raised by the social research that all writers of fiction practice—was not unique to him. It may in fact be found even in the theoretical writings of an outspoken advocate of scientific realism like Mao Dun. Indeed, Mao Dun's critical writings of the period 1920–27 are not the unambiguous defense of realism many have thought them. Doubts about aspects of the mode surface repeatedly, particularly in discussions of naturalism, a doctrine Mao Dun began actively propagating in late 1921, drew away from increasingly after 1923, and finally compared negatively with realism in 1927. Mao Dun's gradual disavowal of naturalism was in part a response to mounting criticism of his views by the Creation Society, but it also had its source in his deep-rooted ambivalence about the objectivity naturalism required of its practitioners. As early as 1920 Mao Dun had observed what he called the "excessive" emphasis on objectivity in some kinds of realism, an emphasis that he feared could prove "destructive." He wrote:

> Critical spirit is an advantage of realism, but it is also its imperfection. Realism analyzes thoroughly all social problems and endeavors with all its force to lay open their darker aspects. To use intelligible language in this way to awaken the masses is not bad, but merely to criticize without interpreting can cause melancholy and deep sorrow, and these can lead to despondency.[39]

Even as he campaigned for naturalism in 1921 and 1922 (a period in which he does not seem to have distinguished it clearly from realism), Mao Dun conceded its dangers: an untempered objectivity may lead to a mechanistic view of life, to a determinism that ultimately encourages both author and reader to disengage themselves from society and from life.[40] In fact, as Marián Gálik has observed, Mao Dun not only "failed to follow Zola's naturalistic criticism in its most lucid

39. Mao Dun, "Wenxue shang de gudianzhuyi, langmanzhuyi he xieshizhuyi" 文學上的古典主義、浪漫主義和寫實主義 (Classicism, romanticism, and realism in literature), Xuesheng zazhi 學生雜誌 (Student magazine) 7, no. 9 (September 1920): 19.
40. These doubts about naturalism are expressed most potently in two of Mao Dun's articles written in 1922: "Ziranzhuyi yu Zhongguo xiandai xiaoshuo" 自然

form" but also implicitly refuted naturalism's underlying philosophical premises.[41] In responding to a critic of naturalism, he wrote: "My present opinion, that we should adopt naturalism, does not mean that we should follow it in everything. Perhaps the naturalistic worldview is not entirely appropriate for Chinese youth, but what I want us to take from naturalism is not its worldview but the power of its techniques."[42] Naturalistic techniques encompassed, of course, the objective observation so fundamental to realism, but Mao Dun insists that observation must be tempered by the "imagination" of the author, who constantly analyzes and synthesizes the raw data he or she encounters.[43] As the decade wore on, Mao Dun began to differentiate realism and naturalism, conveniently ascribing to the latter the destructive properties he feared (such as unfeeling objectivity, pessimism, and determinism). In 1927 he expressed his preference for the realism of Tolstoy, who "made fiction out of his life experiences," over the naturalism of Zola, who "experienced life in order to make fiction."[44]

Even when he was most strenuously advocating naturalism, Mao Dun insisted that a successful literary work conveys not just the author's observations but the author's personality (*gexing* 個性) as well.[45] Thus even this most scientific of Chinese realists found a place

---

主義與中國現代小說 (Naturalism and contemporary Chinese fiction) 13, no. 7 and "'Zuolazhuyi' de weixianxing" "左拉主義"的危險性 (The dangers of Zolaism). See Mao Dun, *Mao Dun wenyi zalun ji* 1:83–99, 108–9.

41. Marián Gálik, *Mao Tun and Literary Criticism*, p. 80.

42. Mao Dun, letter to the editor, *Xiaoshuo yuebao* 13, no. 6 (10 June 1922): 3.

43. See Mao Dun, "Xin wenxue yanjiuzhe de zeren yu nüli" 新文學研究者的責任與努力 (The duties and efforts of researchers in the new literature), *Xiaoshuo yuebao* 12, no. 2 (10 October 1921), p. 4; reprinted in Mao Dun, *Mao Dun wenyi zalun ji* 1:27–32, here p. 31.

44. Mao Dun, "Cong Guling dao Dongjing" 從牯嶺到東京 (From Guling to Tokyo), *Xiaoshuo yuebao* 19, no. 10 (10 October 1928); reprinted in Tang Jinhai et al., *Mao Dun zhuanji* 1:331–45, here pp. 331–32.

45. See the discussion in Mao Dun, "Xin wenxue yanjiuzhe de zeren yu nüli," p. 31. Of all May Fourth critics, Mao Dun was the most suspicious of expressive views of literature, but, as this article makes clear, he did not deny them outright. Compare, however, another article of the same year, "Wenxue he ren de guanxi ji Zhongguo gulai duiyu wenxuezhe shenfen de wuren" 文學和人的關係及中國古來對於文學者身份的誤認 (People's relationship to literature and mistaken views on the position of literati in ancient China), in which Mao Dun criticizes traditional literature for its overemphasis on the expression of private subjectivity. Works of literature may be said to express life, he argues, but the emotions they arouse belong "to the people, to humankind, not just to the individual." "Writers exist to serve humankind; they should forget themselves and think only of literature. Then literature will be equivalent to human life itself" (Mao Dun, *Mao Dun wenyi zalun ji* 1:22–26).

for self-expression in his theory of literature. But although both realists and romanticists shared a view of literature as self-expression, they
came to disagree sharply on their definition of the self and on the range
and quality of the feelings whose literary expression they sanctioned.
Whereas the romanticists celebrated the self's affirmative characteristics and its generative powers, for realists the particularity of an
author's viewpoint was not in itself enough to justify a composition.
Realists refused to don the mantle of personal artistic genius in which
the romanticists wrapped themselves and insisted that the personal
emotions expressed in a work of art must first be mediated through
concern for others. For example, Ye Shaojun, by emphasizing pity in
his early literary theory, ensures that his description of the creative
process, while allowing for the spontaneity of artistic expression,
incorporates a sense of the self's relation to others. That is to say, the
literary self, as Ye describes it, is at heart a social construct; unlike the
idlike creative platform of the romanticists, it is a bounded ego, subject to and defined by powerful social and moral constraints. Mao
Dun similarly insists that the author's personality as expressed in a
literary work must be understood in a social context.[46]

There is, then, in the writings of early May Fourth realists a double
sense of fiction as a field for self-expression and for the exploration of
constraining influences on the self. For realists the new fiction could
authorize itself only through authors' rigorous moral efforts to purge
their consciousness of all modes of self-involvement that might inhibit
their capacity for social engagement. The curious blend of liberation
and constraint that resulted from this formulation was given
metaphorical expression in the repeated call by Zheng Zhenduo, Mao
Dun, and others for "a literature of blood and tears":[47] the new fiction
was to possess the palpable reality of fluids exuded by the body. But
significantly the fluids to which the expression refers are released only
when the body is physically wounded (blood) or when the spirit is
bruised by empathy (tears). The metaphor would seem to suggest that
self-expression becomes possible only within a context of injury or
loss.

46. See Mao Dun, *Xiyang wenxue tonglun*, p. 14.
47. See Zheng Zhenduo, "Xue he lei de wenxue" 血和淚的文學 (Literature of
blood and tears), in *Zheng Zhenduo xuanji*, p. 1079.

These assumptions about the self and its literary expression are apparent not only in the literary theory of the 1920s but in the period's creative writing as well; in the next chapter, under the heading "moral impediments to realism," we will examine their effect on the fictional works of Lu Xun and Ye Shaojun. I have chosen the word *impediment* advisedly, not wishing it to imply a value judgment (as though flawed Chinese works were to be measured against a consummate Western model); indeed, I will argue that the mediation of these ethical preoccupations with the formal demands of realism characterizes the originality—and in Lu Xun's case, the genius—of certain works of modern Chinese fiction. But in the eyes of at least some of the period's critics, overemphasis on self-expression did in fact impair the creativity of less talented writers and therefore did function as an impediment (in a fully negative sense) to the development of the new literature. In many cases desire to exhibit sincerity led authors to overuse poorly digested autobiographical materials, while an eagerness to demonstrate pity made them add large dollops of sentimentality. By the mid-1920s some critics were already voicing objections to the highly personal, emotional quality of May Fourth writings and calling for a maturer, more objective fiction. Gan Ren 甘人, a member of the Yu si she 語絲社 (Spinners of words society), complained that overindulgence in "self-expression" amounted to no more than the author's cry "Pity me!" Of May Fourth writers, only what he calls the "purely objective" fiction of Lu Xun escaped his criticism.[48] Mao Dun likewise objected to the limited focus and sentimentality of much May Fourth fiction; he too excepted only Lu Xun from this criticism.[49] When Mao Dun himself took up fiction writing in the late 1920s, he labored to produce a comprehensive and objective portrait of Chinese society. His novels, along with those of Ba Jin 巴金, Lao She 老舍, and several other writers of the 1930s, show an increasing mastery of Western fictional techniques, as well as a new willingness to experiment with (in Jaroslev Průšek's critical terminology) less "lyrical," more "epic"

48. Gan Ren 甘人, "Zhongguo xin wenyi de jianglai yu qi ziji de renshi" 中國新文藝的將來與其自己的認識 (The future and self-perception of the new arts in China), *Beixin* 2, no. 1 (1 November 1927); reprinted in *Geming wenxue lunzheng ziliao xuanbian* 1:56–62, here pp. 58–59.

49. See Mao Dun, "Du *Ni Huanzhi*" 讀《倪煥之》 (On reading *Ni Huanzhi*), *Wenxue zhoubao* 8, no. 20 (12 May 1929); reprinted in Mao Dun, *Mao Dun wenyi zalun ji*, pp. 277–94.

narrative models.[50] But these achievements were hard earned, both for
the aesthetic and moral reasons we have discussed (indeed, as we shall
see in chapter 3, even Mao Dun found it difficult to escape the subjectivity he felt marred earlier May Fourth fiction) and for political
reasons—the atmosphere for experimentation became increasingly
difficult after 1927, when the Creation and Sun societies initiated a
virulent attack on the realists.

The critical exchange that followed this attack, now known as the
Revolutionary Literature debate, was in many ways a watershed in
modern Chinese literary history: an examination of the documents relating to it reveals the nascent formulation of almost all the ideas that
were to dominate leftist literary polemics in the years that followed.
The debate must be understood at least in part as a consequence
of the abortive revolution of 1927, which ended in July when the
Nationalist party broke its alliance with the Chinese Communist party
and expelled its officers from Wuhan. This followed on the heels of the
April massacre in Shanghai, when the Nationalists had slain tens of
thousands of suspected Communist sympathizers. These events temporarily shattered China's left wing, and in the months that followed
the survivors debated intensely what had gone wrong; factional divisions deepened, and mutual recriminations inevitably resulted. On
the cultural front a profound rift had already existed, as we have
observed, between the Creation Society and writers affiliated with the
Association for Literary Studies. Much had changed, however, since
the early 1920s, when the two groups had disagreed over the slogans
"Art for life's sake" and "Art for art's sake." As early as 1923 Guo
Moruo, the guiding force behind the Creation Society, had abandoned
what the realists called his "ivory tower" view of literature and had
started promoting a new view of art as "revolutionary propaganda."[51]

---

50. Průšek takes Yu Dafu as representative of the "lyrical" tendencies and Mao
Dun as representative of the "epic" tendencies that together characterize modern
Chinese literature. See "Mao Tun and Yü Ta-fu," in Průšek, *The Lyrical and the Epic*,
pp. 121–77.

51. The first indication of a change in Guo Moruo's thinking came in May 1923 in
a manifesto entitled "Women de wenxue xin yundong" 我們的文學新運動 (Our new
literary movement) (*Chuangzao zhoubao* 3, nos. 13–15 [27 May 1923]). Later the
same year he developed his theory of art as "revolutionary propaganda" in an article
entitled "Yishujia yu gemingjia" 藝術家與革命家 (The artist and the revolutionary)
(*Chuangzao zhoubao* 18, nos. 1–2 [9 September 1923]). For fuller discussions of Guo
Moruo's intellectual odyssey during this period see David Tod Roy, *Kuo Mo-jo* (especially pp. 134–161) and Marián Gálik, "Studies in Modern Chinese Literary Criticism,"
Part 4.

In the journals the society subsequently established, such as *Hongshui* 洪水 (The deluge) in 1925 and *Chuangzao yuekan* 創造月刊 (Creation monthly) in 1926, Guo and his colleagues assumed increasingly radical positions on political and cultural matters, quickly becoming the most aggressive propagators of Marxist theory in China. In the late 1920s they and members of another like-minded organization, the Chinese Communist party–sponsored Taiyang she 太陽社 (Sun society),[52] confidently declared themselves the standard-bearers of proletarian culture and launched a fervent attack on more moderate factions, whose capitulation to the bourgeoisie was, they felt, one of the reasons for the 1927 debacle.

The Creation Society and the Sun Society were themselves rivals, each group claiming it was the first to have advocated revolutionary literature in China and each vying for a position of leadership.[53] But in their theoretical pronouncements the two groups were not far apart: both were committed above all to the notion of class warfare. Yu Dafu had introduced the idea of "class struggle in literature" in May 1923,[54] but it was not aggressively applied to a review of the new literature until 1928. By that time the concept of proletarian realism was being discussed in the Soviet Union, and Qian Xingcun 錢杏村, the leading theoretical light of the Sun Society, quickly seized on the term as a convenient means both to assert the importance of class stance in literature and to appropriate the word *realist* for the ex-

---

52. The Sun Society was organized by three officers of the left-wing government in Wuhan, Qian Xingcun 錢杏村, Jiang Guangzi 蔣光慈, and Yang Cunren 楊邨人, all of whom fled to Shanghai in late 1927. As Mao Dun observed, "The Sun Society's leading figures were party members who had retreated from the battle line; this was the first time that the Chinese Communist party calculatedly involved itself in literary activities" ("Guanyu 'Zuolian'" 關於左聯 [Concerning the League of Left-Wing Writers], in *Zuolian huiyi lu* 1:150). The Sun Society was short-lived: the first issue of its journal, *Taiyang yuekan* (The sun monthly), was published on January 1, 1928, but it continued publication only through July of that year, after which the Shanghai authorities banned it.

53. The Creationist Li Chuli claimed Guo Moruo had been the first to promote revolutionary literature, in his 1926 article "Geming yu wenxue" 革命與文學 (Revolution and literature), but the Sun Society insisted that honor belonged to one of its founders, Jiang Guangzi, who had published an article entitled "Wuchan jieji geming yu wenhua" 無產階級革命與文化 (Proletarian revolution and culture) in 1925. See the discussion in Amitendranath Tagore, *Literary Debates in Modern China*, p. 81.

54. Yu Dafu, "Wenxue shang de jieji douzheng" 文學上的階級鬥爭 (Class struggle in literature), *Chuangzao zhoubao*, no. 3 (May 1923): 1–5. Yu Dafu was a founding member of the Creation Society but later shifted his loyalties to the Spinners of Words Society.

treme left.[55] In his view proletarian realism (*puluo xianshizhuyi* 普羅現實主義), or what he sometimes called new realism (*xin xianshizhuyi* 新現實主義), was to be distinguished from bourgeois realism (naturalism) largely by its refusal of class compromise; while naturalists falsely assumed that authors could transcend their social origins and assume a lofty, disinterested objectivity, proletarian realists recognized that all literature was class-bound and hence took their stand "on a fighting proletarian platform."[56] Moreover, whereas the old realism was individualistic and stagnant (*jing* 靜), proletarian realism was communal and activist (*dong* 動).[57] Another critic who raised a strong voice against bourgeois realism at this time was the Creationist Li Chuli 李初梨: in a 1928 article he specifically rejected the currently fashionable definitions of literature as self-expression or social description. Art, he insisted, should instead be understood either as an expression of the proletariat's "will to live" or as a reflection of "class practices." Deriding the realist call for "a literature of blood and tears," he demanded in its place a literature of "machine-guns and trench mortars."[58]

The members of the Creation and Sun societies were not content with general attacks on realism, however, and proceeded to denounce by name several of the best-known authors of the 1920s. In particular Lu Xun, Mao Dun, Ye Shaojun, and the now renegade Creationist Yu Dafu were admonished, in part for their continued focus on the problems of intellectuals and the middle class, in part for failing to offer a

---

55. The Japanese literary critic Kurahara Korehito 藏原惟人 was responsible for introducing the term *proletarian realism* into Japan with his April 1928 article "Puroretariya riarizumu e no michi" プロレタリアリアリズムえの道 (The road toward proletarian realism), which appeared in the first issue of the magazine *Senki* 戰棋 (Battle flag). His article was promptly rendered into Chinese by Qian Xingcun, who published his translation in the July 1928 issue of *Taiyang yuekan*. In an article on Qian Xingcun, Marián Gálik discusses the origins of the term in the Soviet Union and then shows how its meaning shifted slightly when it was adopted first by the Japanese and then by the Chinese; Gálik's major finding is that both Chinese and Japanese advocates of proletarian realism disregarded the emphasis on psychology that characterized Russian definitions of the term. See Gálik's article "Studies in Modern Chinese Literary Criticism," Part 3.

56. Qian Xingcun, "Cong Dongjing hui dao Wuhan" 從東京回到武漢 (From Tokyo back to Wuhan), in Fu Zhiying, *Mao Dun pingzhuan*, pp. 255–314, here p. 313.

57. See Qian Xingcun, "Zhongguo xinxing wenxue zhong de jige juti de wenti" 中國新興文學中的幾個具體的問題 (Several concrete problems concerning China's new literature), *Tuohuangzhe* 1, no. 1 (10 January 1930): 341–82; reprinted in *Geming wenxue lunzheng ziliao xuanbian* 2:915–46. See especially pp. 930–31.

58. Li Chuli, "Zenyangde jianshe geming wenxue," pp. 15–17.

positive message of hope to the workers and peasants. Theorists from the Sun Society (especially Qian Xingcun) were the most vocal in their attacks on individual authors. Qian accused Lu Xun not only of blindness to the class base of literature but of a failure to show a sense of historical change in his fiction. Lu Xun's work, he wrote, was obsessed with the past and stagnant; it offered at best an "empty pity" for the downtrodden. Literature should do more than simply describe life—it should create new life, that is, actively propel society into the future. While grudgingly conceding that Lu Xun had made contributions in the area of fictional technique, he insisted the contributions were achieved at the expense of "political ideas."[59] Qian similarly censured Mao Dun's work for its exclusive focus on the dark side of life, for its retrospective tone, and for its failure to communicate a sense of the future.[60] In Qian's view, Mao Dun was obsessed with out-of-date literary forms and failed to recognize the necessity of inventing new forms to give expression to the concerns of a new age.[61]

The Creationists' criticisms were most passionately refuted not by the writers they singled out but by theorists and critics associated with two other literary organizations, both of which had been established to encourage greater "freedom of thought" in literary matters: the Xinyue she 新月社 (Crescent society), founded in 1923 by the poet Xu Zhimo 徐志摩,[62] and the Spinners of Words Society, founded in 1924 by Lu Xun's brother, the essayist Zhou Zuoren 周作人.[63] Two members of

59. All these criticisms are advanced in Qian Xingcun's article "Siqu le de A Q shidai" 死去了的阿Q時代 (The bygone age of Ah Q), published in the March 1928 issue of *Taiyang yuekan*; reprinted in *Geming wenxue lunzheng ziliao xuanbian* 1:180–94, here pp. 183–84.

60. See Qian Xingcun, "Mao Dun yu xianshi: du le *Ye qiangwei* yihou" 茅盾與現實:讀了《野薔薇》以後 (Mao Dun and reality: after reading *Wild Roses*), *Xinliu yuebao* 4 (15 December 1929); reprinted in Fu Zhiying, *Mao Dun pingzhuan*, pp. 159–216.

61. See Qian Xingcun, "Zhongguo xinxing wenxue zhong de jige juti de wenti," *Geming wenxue lunzheng ziliao xuanbian* 2:945.

62. In its manifesto the Crescent Society called for the "free" and "dignified" pursuit of "healthy" ideals through literature (a formulation that amounted to a concealed reproach of the Creationists, who, Crescent Society members felt, were guilty both of an obsession with sexual matters in their literary works and of petty factionalism). One member of the Crescent Society who jumped eagerly into the fray of the Revolutionary Literature debate was Liang Shiqiu 梁實秋, who in an essay entitled "Wenxue yu geming" 文學與革命 (Literature and revolution) wrote: "Proletarian literature or literature for the masses is an impossibility because literature fundamentally depends upon human personality and does not recognize any class distinction" (quoted in Amitendranath Tagore, *Literary Debates in Modern China*, p. 109).

63. The Spinners of Words Society was well known for Zhou Zuoren's 周作人 dictum that artists should pursue their personal interests (*quwei* 趣味) in literary mat-

the latter group, Gan Ren and Han Shihang 韓侍桁, mounted a strong
defense of realism in 1928, in the process specifically addressing the
problem that had earlier concerned Ye Shaojun and Mao Dun, that is,
how to integrate the critical and expressive functions of literature. Gan
Ren directly challenged the Creationists' frequently reiterated premise
that "All art is propaganda": true literature, he wrote, should be
understood as "an outflow of pure emotion." As such, it was "disinterested and above all classless."[64] Han Shihang decried all utilitarian
views of artistic production and elaborated a sophisticated reassessment of the artist's role in society. In an article entitled "Confession,
Criticism, and Creation," Han argued that confession—the unbridled
expression of the author's inner being—is a characteristic feature of
modern literature. This unburdening of the author's psyche should
always be undertaken in a "realistic spirit" and should never be self-
indulgent; if these conditions are met, confession leads to a transcendence of the self. There is thus no contradiction between realism and
self-expression; indeed, "criticism and confession are one and the
same thing." In this light, Han Shihang joins Ye Shaojun in defining
realist fiction in terms of personal ethical cultivation: "Realism," Han
wrote, "teaches us humility and sincerity."[65] In another article, "Individualistic Literature and Other Matters," Han suggests that the
whole question of individualism revolves on how "self" is defined.
Ideally the self should be understood in relation to the environment:
the ego is a receptor, responding sympathetically to the outside world,
and is thus inevitably involved in the larger issues of society and

---

ters; in making this advocation, Zhou was in fact recommending that authors follow
their private muses rather than march to the impersonal step of a particular literary or
social doctrine. See the discussion of *quwei* in David E. Pollard, *A Chinese Look at
Literature*, pp. 72–84. Lu Xun was loosely affiliated with the Spinners of Words Society
and published in their journals, but he did not fully ascribe to his brother's ideas on
literature.

64. Gan Ren, "Laza yipian da Li Chuli jun" 拉雜一篇答李初梨君 (A page of
confusion in reply to Mr. Li Chuli), first published in *Beixin* 2, no. 13 (6 May 1928);
reprinted in Li Helin, *Zhongguo wenyi lunzhan*, pp. 77–78. "All art is propaganda" is,
of course, Upton Sinclair's dictum from *Mammonart*; it won wide acceptance in left-
wing circles in China in the mid-1920s. For a full discussion of Gan Ren's and Han
Shihang's responses to the Creation and Sun societies see Amitendranath Tagore, *Literary Debates in Modern China*, pp. 80–123.

65. Han Shihang 韓侍桁, "Gaobie yu piping yu chuangzao" 告別與批評與創造
(Confession, criticism, and creation), *Beixin* 2, no. 22 (1 October 1928): 27–32, here
p. 30.

life. "When writers express themselves, they give voice to modern society, to modern trends of thought, to all aspects of modernity!" Though an artistic work may appear "purposeless" and egocentric, it can in fact serve as a guiding light for society at large.[66]

Significantly Mao Dun, Lu Xun, and most of the other writers singled out for criticism by the Creation and Sun societies did not join forces with Gan Ren and Han Shihang to champion an independent role for the artist in modern society. As we have seen, many of them had at one time or other publicly expressed misgivings about the pessimistic and deterministic tendencies of realist fiction, so the allegations now directed against their own work may have resonated too deeply with their own doubts to permit a spirited defense. Mao Dun's major contribution to the Revolutionary Literature debate, for example, the two essays "From Guling to Tokyo" and "On Reading *Ni Huanzhi*," though moving and elegantly written, constitute a lame defense of realism. Among other matters they address Qian Xingcun's scathing estimation of Mao Dun's trilogy *Eclipse* as containing "nothing but the sick and bewildered attitudes" of young intellectuals.[67] In his own defense Mao Dun suggests that his trilogy is in some sense more faithful to the times than the "sloganeering" literature of the romanticists-turned-revolutionaries, but he does not defend realist techniques of objective observation or argue the closer equivalence of realist fiction to the extraliterary world. Rather, he pleads the greater sincerity of his own literary effort. He implies that he foresaw criticisms like those of Qian Xingcun: "I knew that if I had written more bravely, more positively, my work would have been better received. But it seemed shameful to sit in my study writing brave things . . . so I elected to express freely my sense of disillusionment."[68] Through this formulation, Mao Dun defends his personal candor but also, of course, implies a profound doubt about the social efficacy of his fiction and indeed of all writing produced during a revolutionary period. What seems to irk Mao Dun about the Creationists is not so much their ideological

---

66. See Han Shihang, "Gerenzhuyi de wenxue ji qita" 個人主義的文學及其它 (Individualistic literature and other matters), *Yu si* 4, no. 22 (28 May 1928); reprinted in *Geming wenxue lunzheng ziliao xuanbian* 1:461–65.

67. Qian Xingcun had made this accusation in the article "Cong Dongjing hui dao Wuhan," in Fu Zhiying, *Mao Dun pingzhuan*, pp. 264–65.

68. Mao Dun, "Cong Guling dao Dongjing," in Tang Jinhai et al., *Mao Dun zhuanji*, p. 334.

stance, nor their denigration of his and his colleagues' artistic efforts, but their refusal to concede their own limitations, to acknowledge for themselves the "shame" of the study. He pointedly reminds the Creationists that it was they who, by preaching "art for art's sake" in the early 1920s, had most egregiously hindered Chinese literature from engaging social issues.[69] Writers dubbed bourgeois realists, he suggests, at least recognize the true nature of their class background and reject the fantasy that one can override one's personal history and become one of the masses by simply spouting slogans. Moreover, realists at least know who constitute their audience and do not pretend to be addressing the illiterate masses in books whose circulation will never extend beyond the middle class.

The terms of Mao Dun's defense thus conceded crucial elements of the critique that had been launched against him. In fact his receptivity to some of the Creationists' ideas was evident as early as 1925, when he composed an essay on proletarian art espousing the notion of class struggle in literature; Marián Gálik has suggested (with perhaps a degree of exaggeration) that from that point on, "the literary platform ceases for him to be a universal and national one . . . but turns into a class platform."[70] A similar change seems to have occurred in Lu Xun's thinking around then, and several of his essays from the years 1925–27 seem to foreshadow the themes of the Revolutionary Literature debate. Most striking in this regard is his famous talk "Literature in a Revolutionary Period," which was delivered at the Huangpu Military Academy on 8 April, 1927, several months before the most strident of the Creationists' essays were published (and, one notes, just four days before the Shanghai massacre). On reading it, one is left with the impression that Lu Xun had already internalized much of the criticism that was to be directed against him. Referring to his small output of short stories, Lu Xun goes far beyond his critics in depreciating them and even denies that he should be accorded the title "author." The "complaining" about social conditions in his and similar works, he declares, is finally powerless: the strong "do not talk—they kill." At the same time, however, Lu Xun refuses to accept the arrogant claim of the Creationists that their own works constitute a truer contribution to the revolution. In fact, Lu Xun turns the Creationists' own

69. Mao Dun, "Du *Ni Huanzhi*," in Mao Dun, *Mao Dun wenyi zalun ji*, p. 284.
70. Marián Gálik, *Mao Tun and Literary Criticism*, p. 90.

arguments against them by calling into question the role of literature itself in a revolutionary period. Evoking the traditional expressive view of literature (but without crediting its origins in the Chinese tradition), Lu Xun argues that writing should "flow naturally from the heart with no regard for consequences"; only writing produced in this way by the common people themselves could constitute a true revolutionary literature. The works of intellectuals who choose to style themselves the people's representatives "lack vigor" and merely "voice the sentiments of onlookers." China has no people's literature because the people remain illiterate; their true emotions are expressed through revolutionary actions rather than words. "During a great revolution, literature disappears and there is silence."[71]

Mao Dun and Lu Xun both clearly resented the Creation and Sun societies for assuming that they alone fathomed the inner truths of radical literary theory. After all, both writers had labored conscientiously for years to introduce progressive literary opinion (including Marxist and Soviet perspectives) from the West—Mao Dun through his work at the *Short Story Magazine* and Lu Xun through, among other things, his editorship of a series of translations, the *Weiming congshu* 未名叢書 (Unnamed series). By 1927 Mao Dun and Lu Xun had already accepted many of the tenets of revolutionary literature: they agreed with the Creation and Sun societies that literature could serve as a tool of radical politics,[72] and shared their opponents' concern about the individualism fostered by bourgeois realism.[73] But they were not convinced that the belligerent theorizing and sloganeering of the Creationists constituted a satisfactory solution to the dilemma in

71. Lu Xun, "Geming shidai de wenxue" 革命時代的文學 (Literature in a revolutionary period), in Lu Xun, *Lu Xun quanji* 3:417–24, here p. 420.

72. Lu Xun accepted the notion that "all art is propaganda," although he subjected the slogan to a characteristic twist in a 1928 letter to Dong Qiufang 董秋芳, later published as "Wenyi yu geming" 文藝與革命 (Literature and revolution): "All literature becomes propaganda once you show it to someone else. . . . Indeed, the only way to avoid propaganda is by never writing, never opening your mouth. This being so, literature can naturally be used as a tool of revolution" (in Lu Xun, *Lu Xun quanji* 4:77–86, here p. 84).

73. In his "*Benliu* bianjiao houji" 《奔流》編校後記 (Afterword to *Currents*) (*Benliu* 1, no. 3 [20 August 1928]), for example, Lu Xun recalls Hu Shi's 1918 article on Ibsen, observing that it did not have as great an effect on the literary world as one might have expected. This was in part the result of Ibsen's dedication to individualism, which did not meet China's needs. Lu Xun then calls for a critique of Ibsen's work from a "collectivist"standpoint (concluding on a satirical note, however, by suggesting that "for that, we'll have to await the revolutionary intelligentsia and their leaders") (in Lu Xun, *Lu Xun quanji* 7:162–65.

which the new literature found itself. Indeed, they felt about the creative efforts of the Creation and Sun societies (which were rather sparse to begin with) much as their opponents felt about theirs: they were superfluous verbiage, the product of mere onlookers of the revolution, of no measurable use to the present struggle. As the debate progressed, the accusations traded between the two factions began to take on an oddly specular quality for, despite their mutal disregard, both sides shared a common set of standards in which questions of literary origins and the utility of literature held pride of place. In the minds of both parties a literary work could justify itself only by the purity of its affective origins or by its salutary effect on the revolutionary cause as a whole. And by that standard, the new literature—like the revolution it was to have succored—had failed.

By the end of the 1920s, in the face of increased Nationalist persecution and the impending Japanese invasion, leftist intellectuals recognized the need to turn away from internal squabbles and concentrate their energies on outside opponents. Indeed, at its Sixth Party Congress in 1928 the Chinese Communist party resolved to consolidate all revolutionary forces in a new "united front from below." In 1930 members of the various factions of leftist literati met to create an institutional expression of this united front in the *Zuoyi zuojia lianmeng* 左翼作家聯盟 (League of left-wing writers), which served in the years that followed as the principal forum for radical literary opinion in China.[74] The platform approved at the first meeting called for a progressive literature that would serve as a "weapon in the battle for liberation": "Our art will oppose feudalism and capitalism, and also combat the bourgeois ambition to secure one's position in society."[75] Despite its highly emphatic tone, however, the platform carefully refrained from making specific aesthetic recommendations. This

74. The most thorough history of the league in English is Anthony James Kane's dissertation, *The League of Left-Wing Writers and Chinese Literary Policy*. The appearance of harmony cultivated by the league in fact concealed fierce internal discord, which finally erupted in the famous "two slogans" debate upon the league's disbanding. For accounts of the league's internal conflicts see Tsi-an Hsia, "Lu Hsün and the Dissolution of the League of Leftist Writers," in Hsia's *Gates of Darkness*, and Maruyama Noboru, "The Appraisal of the Literature of the Thirties in the People's Republic of China: Aspects of the Ideological Background to Contemporary Chinese Literature," in Wolfgang Kubin and Rudolf G. Wagner, *Essays in Modern Chinese Literature*.

75. "Zhongguo zuoyi zuojia lianmeng de lilun gangling" 中國左翼作家聯盟的理論綱領 (Theoretical platform of the League of Left-Wing Writers), *Mengya yuekan* 1, no. 4 (April 1930): 166–67.

restraint was inevitable, since the league, though committed to an appearance of unity, constituted a rather unstable alliance of factions and since league members continued to hold different views on practical aesthetic matters. As Mao Dun observes, in selecting a name for the association the organizers specifically chose the term *left-wing writers* rather than *proletarian writers* to indicate that the left had "purged itself of the errors of the proletarian literature movement of the last two years."[76] Nevertheless, the platform specifically states: "We will do all we can to promote the production of proletarian art."[77] Such compromises were necessary to the league's establishment and continued functioning, a fact that is nowhere more obvious than in the many new definitions of realism that emerged in the early years of its existence.

Qu Qiubai 瞿秋白, the league's most influential theorist, clearly saw his own role as that of mediator between the two factions that had quarreled so vehemently in the late 1920s but that now shared membership in the league. He was a close personal friend of such Creation and Sun society members as Qian Xingcun and Jiang Guangzi 蔣光慈, and clearly sympathized with their political ambitions.[78] At the same time, however, he warmly defended Lu Xun and Mao Dun, whose works he admired and whom he felt had made important contributions to the progressive cause. In his book on Qu Qiubai, Paul Pickowicz discusses his opinion of several Soviet theoreticians of the arts, concluding that Qu had reservations about both the "mechanistic" (or "deterministic") view of the relationship of art and society associated with Plekhanov and the "idealistic" views of Bogdanov and Chernyshevsky; he had most in common with Lunacharsky, who occupied a middle ground between the deterministic and idealistic viewpoints.

76. Mao Dun, "Guanyu 'Zuolian,'" p. 151.
77. "Zhongguo zuoyi zuojia lianmeng de lilun gangling," p. 167. It is clear from Mao Dun's memoirs that "left extremists" had the upper hand in the league during its early years. Mao Dun records his irritation when he learned that his old friends from the Association for Literary Studies Zheng Zhenduo and Ye Shaojun were not invited to join the league, and his impatience with the attitude of many league members, who valued "organizational" and propaganda work more than the literary endeavors of practicing authors. During the first months of the league's existence Mao Dun even pretended to be ill much of the time to avoid being enlisted in the league's political busywork—thus allowing time for his own writing. See Mao Dun, *Wo zouguo de daolu* 2:55–58.
78. Paul Pickowicz quotes Qu Qiubai 瞿秋白 as having once written that he was "born a romantic, who always wanted to transcend environment and accomplish some

So too in his writings about realism did Qu take an intermediate position. While he was attracted to the "materialist" underpinnings of realism, he shared the romanticists' reservations about the excessive scientism and determinism of naturalism. He recommended that writers start from a base of realism but work to introduce more positive, forward-looking elements into their fiction; he hoped in this way to remedy realism's passivity and negativity without entirely abandoning the model of critical independence that it assumed.[79]

Qu's views on realism must be understood in the context of his critique of the European influence that had dominated Chinese culture in the 1920s. As he saw it, realism and romanticism both had dubious aspects as they were practiced in the West; he wanted to extract the positive qualities from them in order to delineate a new literary mode more appropriate to China's needs. This notion of conjoining realism and romanticism became an oft-repeated theme of leftist literary theory in the 1930s. Zhou Yang 周揚, the Communist theoretician who was later to become the "literary czar" of the People's Republic, frequently argued that to see the two artistic modes as antagonistic was a mistake; just as an individual's subjectivity should ideally be brought in line with objective reality, so in the end romanticism should be integrated with realism.[80] The realism that Qu, Zhou, and other league members continued to advocate was thus very different from what Mao Dun had understood by the term in the early 1920s: their new realism, also described as proletarian realism, activist realism (*dong de xianshizhuyi* 動的現實主義) or, after Zhou Yang's introduction of the Soviet term in 1933, socialist realism (*shehuizhuyi de xianshizhuyi* 社會主義的現實主義),[81] was defined largely by conjoining terms that had previously been held in ideological opposition, terms

---

miraculous deed, which would amaze and move the people" (*Marxist Literary Thought in China*, p. 113). Pickowicz also points out (p. 113) that some sources indicate Qu helped launch the Sun Society, although Qu himself never refers to his role in this regard.

79. Ibid., pp. 128ff.

80. Zhou Yang 周揚, "Xianshizhuyi shilun" 現實主義試論 (A tentative discussion of realism), *Wenxue* 6, no. 1 (1 January 1936); reprinted in *Wenxue yundong shiliao xuan* 2:334–43, especially p. 343.

81. Zhou Yang introduced the term in an article entitled "Guanyu 'shehuizhuyi de xianshizhuyi yu geming de langmanzhuyi'" 關於"社會主義的現實主義與革命的浪漫主義" (Concerning socialist realism and revolutionary romanticism), published in *Xiandai* 1, no. 4 (1 November 1933); reprinted in *Wenxue yundong shiliao xuan* 2:314–27.

that in many cases had been the bywords of opposing sides in the Revolutionary Literature debate. According to the formula, literature was to reflect and describe reality but also to direct and propel reality.[82] Literature was to be the subjective expression of the masses' class interest but was also to be an active force in organizing the masses and in systematizing their worldview.[83] Literature was to stand at the level of the masses but was at the same time to raise their cultural level.[84] Literature was to constitute the author's objective observation of and research into reality but only from the perspective of a correct worldview, specifically that of the workers and peasants.[85]

That such authors as Lu Xun and Mao Dun felt themselves in general agreement with the league's approach to literature, if not with the theorists' specific definitions of realism, is evident from their active participation in the debate over third-category (*di san zhong ren* 第三種人) literature in 1932. The primary advocates of third-category literature—that is, literature written from the perspective of neither the gentry nor the proletariat but from an independent critical standpoint—were Hu Qiuyuan 胡秋原, a critic well versed in Marxism and originally himself a member of the league, and Su Wen 蘇文, the editor of the literary journal *Xiandai* 現代 (*Les contemporaines*). Their call for the separation of literature from politics built on the earlier writings of independent critics like Gan Ren and Han Shihang. Hu Qiuyuan had himself contributed to the 1928 debate by publishing

---

82. See Ai Siqi 艾思奇,"Xin de xingshi he wenxue de renwu"; 新的形勢和文學的任務 (New forms and the mission of literature), *Wenxue jie* 1, no. 2 (July 1936): 1–8; also see Lu Ding 路丁, "Xianshi xingshi he minzu geming zhanzheng de dazhong wenxue" 現實形勢和民族革命戰爭的大眾文學 (Realist forms and mass literature of the people's revolutionary war), *Xianshi wenxue*, no. 1 (1 July 1936).

83. The first call to "systematize" the masses' worldview was probably Liu Jianheng's 劉劍橫 "Yishi de yinglei yu geming de zhishifenzi" 意識的營壘與革命的智識分子 (The barracks of consciousness and revolutionary intellectuals), *Taidong yuekan* 2, no. 7 (1 March 1929); reprinted in *Geming wenxue lunzheng ziliao xuanbian* 2:783–97 (see especially p. 792). It became a recurrent theme in 1930s' criticism; Zhou Yang was particularly fond of invoking it. See, for example, Zhou Yang, "Guanyu wenxue dazhonghua" 關於文學大眾化 (On the massification of literature), *Beidou* 2, nos. 3–4 (20 July 1932); reprinted in *Wenxue yundong shiliao xuan* 2:410–13, especially p. 412.

84. Qu Qiubai, "Puluo dazhong wenyi de xianshi wenti" 普羅大眾文藝的現實問題 (Practical problems of proletarian mass literature), *Wenxue* 1, no. 1 (25 April 1932); reprinted in *Wenxue yundong shiliao xuan* 2:371–90, here p. 373.

85. See Zhou Yang, "Guanyu 'shehuizhuyi de xianshizhuyi yu geming de langmanzhuyi,'" and Zhu Xiuxia 祝秀俠, "Xianshizhuyi de kangzhan wenxue lun" 現實主義的抗戰文學論 (On realist War of Resistance literature), *Wenyi zhendi* 1, no. 4 (1 June 1938): 115–19.

an article that passionately made the case for a liberal view of art and of the artist's role in society; it was imperative, he wrote, to distinguish true literary efforts from propaganda and to allow artists the freedom to seek out their own "spiritual adventures." He also argued, however, that literature should play a designated role in society, that of "exposing social evils and corruption."[86] Literature should thus serve as a kind of disinterested *Kulturkritik*, but for it to do so the authors had to distance themselves from the political arena. In December 1931 Hu Qiuyuan and several sympathizers founded a journal entitled *Wenhua pinglun* 文化評論 *(Cultural criticism)*, in whose pages he developed these ideas in polemical essays that targeted the Nationalist-sponsored movement for a national defense literature together with the League of Left-Wing Writers. In the opening issue's "Statement of Purpose" the editors proclaimed themselves "free intellectuals" who served no master but the truth; their role, as they saw it, was to analyze and interpret society with "complete objectivity." In succeeding issues, Hu published articles with such provocative titles as "On the Literature of Dogs" and "Hands Off Art," in which he opposed all attempts to restrict the natural development of the arts.

The league perceived Hu's attack as a serious threat, in part because Hu bolstered his arguments with quotes from Plekhanov and other Marxist theorists but also because his criticisms raised crucial questions about the legacy of the May Fourth movement. Hu's position amounted to a vigorous defense of precisely those strains of May Fourth thought that theorists within the league, such as Qu Qiubai, wished to put to rest. While Qu still recognized the value of some aspects of the May Fourth legacy (specifically its antifeudalism, anti-imperialism, scientism, and nationalism), he impugned the individualism and uncritical infatuation with the West that had also characterized it. These he saw as evidence of the movement's essentially bourgeois values, which could only inhibit the development of a true proletarian revolution in China.[87] Qu wrote that Hu Qiuyuan, by denying the class basis of literature, undervalued art's capacity to exert a direct and positive influence over society. Hu's position, therefore, was

86. Hu Qiuyuan 胡秋原, "Geming wenxue wenti" 革命文學問題 (The question of revolutionary literature), *Beixin* 2, no. 12 (16 April 1928); reprinted in *Geming wenxue lunzheng ziliao xuanbian* 1:330–44, here pp. 343–44.

87. Qu Qiubai, "Wusi he xin de wenhua geming" 五四和新的文化革命 (May Fourth and the new cultural revolution), *Beidou* 2, no. 2 (20 May 1932): 359–62.

another example of sterile bystanderism (*pangguanzhuyi* 旁觀主義), which wrapped what was ultimately a defense of bourgeois liberalism in high-sounding appeals for objectivity.[88] In Qu's mind, Hu's notion of an independent critique differed little from the old romanticist doctrine of "art for art's sake."

The debate between Hu Qiuyuan and the league was considerably broadened when the brilliant prose stylist Su Wen published an account of it in his highly influential journal, *Les contemporaines*. Although Su Wen was later to be forced into an unwilling association with Hu, in the beginning he rejected both sides of the debate, which he saw as a sterile exchange between "academic" and "partisan" Marxists. Su Wen took the side of practicing authors against the theorists, pointing out the impossibility of producing literature according to the league's dictates. The "proletarian literary culture" that the league promoted was far too rudimentary to offer viable creative models, and Chinese authors, as members of the petty bourgeoisie, were by definition incapable of producing proletarian literature. "At the present time, it is fortunate to be blind and wise to fall silent."[89] He proposed a "way out" of this dilemma: writers should recognize their identity as members of a "third category" and pursue the truth rather than political rectitude in their fiction. They should write for posterity, for those future readers who would be capable of appreciating the true value of literature.

Intriguingly, Su Wen's arguments repeated many of Lu Xun's own observations about the difficulty of writing in a revolutionary period, but with a difference. Whereas Lu Xun, in his address at the Huangpu Military Academy, had cynically advised silence for all but the true proletarian writer, Su Wen was above all concerned with keeping writers productive. Although Lu Xun's own patronage of young writers from diverse class backgrounds suggests that his recommendation of silence was a rhetorical exaggeration, it vividly communicated his refusal to give art (or the concerns of artists) priority over life. That he

88. These ideas are developed in the greatest detail in Qu's "Wenyi de ziyou he wenxuejia de buziyou" 文藝的自由和文學家的不自由 (Literary freedom and the slavery of writers), *Xiandai* 1, no. 6 (1 October 1932); reprinted in Su Wen, *Wenyi ziyou lunbian ji*, pp. 77–99.

89. Su Wen 蘇文, "Guanyu *Wenxin* yu Hu Qiuyuan de wenyi lunbian" 關於《文新》和胡秋原的文藝論辨 (On the literary debate between *Literary News* and Hu Qiuyuan), *Xiandai* 1, no. 3 (1 July 1932); reprinted in Su Wen, *Wenyi ziyou lunbian ji*, pp. 62–76, here p. 76.

saw third-category literature as a dangerous inversion of priorities is clear from his comments on the debate:

> To live in a class society yet to be a writer who transcends classes, to live in a time of wars yet to leave the battlefield and stand alone, to live in the present yet to write for the future—this is sheer fantasy. . . . To try to be such a person is like trying to raise yourself from the ground by tugging at your own hair—it can't be done.[90]

Lu Xun in fact denies the possibility of a third category. The literary despotism of which Hu Qiuyuan and Su Wen accused the league could thus be dismissed as imaginary: their criticisms simply exposed a personal refusal to accept the class nature of literature.

In a 1933 book of essays related to the third category Su Wen declared an end to the debate, reporting that the league, through Lu Xun, had conceded its sometimes mechanical approach to literary theory. But some members of the league, especially the theorist Zhou Yang, refused to let the matter lie. Through sporadic attacks Zhou succeeded in turning the squabble to the league's benefit and in the process further polarized Chinese writers along strictly defined political lines.[91] ("Ally or enemy" went the slogan that the league borrowed from the All-Russian Association of Proletarian Writers, or RAPP.)[92] The equation of literature with a truly independent social critique was never again to be argued so baldly. The question of the origins of literature had found a new answer: literature was still understood as the "expression of the heart's intent," but that heart was now defined by class rather than individual interests.

THE SEARCH FOR A NEW AUDIENCE

The question of the nature of literary invention that had been so intensely discussed in the early years of the May Fourth movement gave way to a new concern in the early 1930s. Particularly after the establishment of the League of Left-Wing Writers, more and more Chinese intellectuals turned their attention to matters of literary consumption:

90. Lu Xun, "Lun 'di san zhong ren'" 論"第三種人" (On the third category), *Xiandai* 2, no. 1 (10 October 1932); reprinted in Lu Xun, *Lu Xun quanji* 4:438–44.
91. For an example of Zhou Yang's subsequent criticism of Su Wen see "Wenxue de zhenshixing" 文學的真實性 (Truth in literature), *Xiandai* 3, no. 1 (1 May 1933); reprinted in *Wenxue yundong shiliao xuan* 3:204–19.
92. Marián Gálik, *Mao Dun and Literary Criticism*, p. 115.

who was the audience for the new literature, and by what mechanism did it influence its readers' lives? Such questions had, of course, not been overlooked by earlier advocates of literary reform; late Qing thinkers like Liang Qichao had originally been impressed by the wide audience that fiction attracted in the West and by its evident power to alter the consciousness of its readers. In describing how literature exerted this power, Liang borrowed from traditional expressive theories: a work of literature, he wrote, influences its readers above all by stirring their emotions. The didactic and expressive functions of literature were thus, in Liang's view, complementary rather than opposing forces. A genuinely popular and social fiction of the kind he advocated should inspire the masses' active participation in the campaign for national restoration—not, however, by preaching at them, but by awakening their instinctive longing for a better world. Later reformers, as we have seen, did not abandon this belief in the social efficacy of fiction (even Lu Xun's darkest expressions of doubt seem to betray his continued susceptibility to it), and the May Fourth movement saw an intensified struggle for literary democratization. In the years that followed much was achieved: scholars began to take an active interest in popular art forms and folklore,[93] and most significantly, the spoken language (*baihua* 白話) won widespread acceptance as the primary medium for all forms of written communication.

But the success of the language reform movement did not result in the expanded audience for fiction that had been anticipated. The reformers soon discovered that the new literature appealed to an even smaller audience than traditional vernacular literature had, and they could not but observe the irony of a literature's seeming closed off from the very people whose needs it purported to address. In the early 1930s Qu Qiubai pointed out that by concurrently promoting *baihua* and introducing a wide range of Western terminology, Chinese writers had created a new hybrid language that the illiterate masses found just as incomprehensible as classical Chinese (*wenyan* 文言). Moreover, the literary forms that had been introduced from the West were, it was now recognized, fundamentally bourgeois in nature and therefore had little persuasive power with the lower classes. League members hoped that they could solve these problems through

93. For a full treatment of the folklore movement see Chang-tai Hung, *Going to the People.*

their propaganda work and through their theoretical expositions of mass literature and the new realism. The results, however, were not immediately encouraging. As we have seen in our discussion of Su Wen, many felt the new prescriptions for literature posed insurmountable difficulties for authors, and even such architects of the new realism as Qu Qiubai recognized that few contemporary works actually met the requirements of theory.

The deteriorating military and political situation of the late 1930s made this situation even more difficult, increasing as it did the pressure on writers to produce literature that would directly benefit the war effort. When the league disbanded in 1936 amid the famous Battle of the Slogans, a new group, the Zhongguo wenyijia xiehui 中國文藝家協會 (Union of Chinese writers and artists) was promptly formed with the stated purpose of mobilizing the cultural field to the defense of the nation. The union's manifesto, like the platform of the league before it, provided stirring political rhetoric but no concrete aesthetic directives. Although the ultimate goals of the new literature were unmistakable, their implementation remained problematic. Writers continued to struggle with the unwieldy demands of the new realism, hoping somehow to create a literature that simultaneously offered a realistic critique of society and served immediate political ends. In particular, writers whose sensibilities had been formed in the heyday of the May Fourth movement (and this included many who first came to prominence in the early 1930s) found themselves in an agonizing dilemma. On the one hand, they sincerely desired to demonstrate their patriotism by producing a politically useful literature; on the other, their literary instincts recoiled from the schematization of the literary product that their cultural generals prescribed. The anguish of writers in the face of this predicament haunts the successive critical debates of the late 1930s, especially those concerning formulism, satire, and national forms.

Formulism (*gongshizhuyi* 公式主義) was the term by which critics referred to fiction that advanced its ideological message in an overly mechanical or schematic fashion. The debate over it was the one major critical exchange of the late 1930s that was initiated not by Communist party–based ideologues but by practicing writers and their sympathizers. Though formulism was not widely discussed until 1937, several issues relevant to it were broached in a 1936 altercation be-

tween Hu Feng 胡風 and Zhou Yang over the issue of typicality.[94]
Their disagreement significantly emanated from conflicting interpreta-
tions of the protagonist of Lu Xun's famous novella "The True Story
of Ah Q." Hu Feng, in a piece that he prepared for a general collection
of essays entitled *One Hundred Questions about Literature*, praised
Ah Q as fully satisfying the requirement that fictional characters
exhibit both individuality and typicality; he repeated the common
observation that Ah Q, through a distinctive and colorfully developed
character, clearly embodies general truths about Chinese peasantry.[95]
Zhou Yang took issue with this notion in an essay that was published
shortly thereafter. Although characters like Ah Q were common
among Chinese peasants before the 1911 revolution, he wrote, Ah Q
could not be said to be representative of all Chinese, nor even of all
Chinese peasants. "He has his unique individual experience, his
unique life-style, his unique psychological makeup."[96]

This disagreement about Ah Q may seem innocuous enough, but it
in fact reopened some old wounds. One of Qian Xingcun's most belli-
cose contributions to the Revolutionary Literature debate of 1928 had
been an essay entitled "The Bygone Age of Ah Q," in which he had
accused Lu Xun of creating in Ah Q a negative model that failed to
convey the innate heroism of the Chinese peasantry and indicated no
potential for positive change. Zhou Yang intended no such condemnation of Lu Xun, but implicit in his argument was the suggestion that
Ah Q may be called typical only of a former and now fading reality,
not of a present or future one. In a more general sense Zhou Yang
questioned the way in which Hu Feng associated typicality with
observation in his description of the creative process. According to Hu
Feng, authors must begin their work with the careful scrutiny of real
people and events; through such investigation they uncover the historically determined general truths that underlie the existence of people
and events and give them meaning. It is these truths that they then com-

94. The relevant articles of the debate were reprinted in Hu Feng, *Miyun qi fengxi xiaoji*, pp. 19–62.
95. Hu Feng, "Shenme shi 'dianxing' he 'leixing'" 什麼是典型和類型 (What are "type" and "model"?), in Zheng Zhenduo with Fu Donghua, *Wenxue baiti*, pp. 216–20, here p. 217.
96. Zhou Yang, "Xianshizhuyi shilun," in *Wenxue yundong shiliao xuan* 2:342.

municate in their writings.[97] Zhou Yang, on the other hand, believed that characters in literature are valued for their individuality, not simply because they represent allegorical types, but he went on to insist that artistic representation of reality should stem from a "subjective honesty" that is ideally guided by a "correct worldview." Zhou Yang's position on this subject is somewhat difficult to assess: he wants both to insist on the uniqueness of all fictional phenomena and to argue the importance of ideological rectitude ("correct worldview") over observation. Although Zhou Yang tries to find a place for self-expression in the creative process with the phrase "subjective honesty," it is clear that in his view an author's subjectivity must first be brought into line with an objectively sanctioned worldview (for which one may here read "Marxism").[98] Hu Feng believed that general truths should not be arrived at theoretically but should be uncovered through observation, that is, that one should move from the specific to the general rather than vice versa. Despite the somewhat equivocal nature of Zhou Yang's position, Hu Feng's view was perceived as the more liberal, for it allowed individual authors a measure of latitude to discover their own worldview through observation.

Hu Feng was attracted to the notion of typicality because it helped resolve for him the apparently conflicting demands of realistic and ideological integrity in fiction. The same concern may be discovered in the articles on formulism, or all-the-same-ism (*chabuduozhuyi* 差不多主義), that started to appear the following year. In 1937 the disagreement arose not from theory but from dissatisfaction with the new fictional product. A critic writing under the pen name Dong Zhi 烔之 was the first to apply the expression *all-the-same-ism* to recent Chinese fiction. "Of late," he wrote, "new Chinese literary works all

97. See Hu Feng, "Xianshizhuyi di yi 'xiuzheng'" 現實主義底一"修正" (Realism: an emendation), *Wenxue* 6, no. 2 (1 July 1936): 301–8. Hu Feng's emphasis on the importance of observation must be understood in the context of his frequent attacks on objectivism (*keguanzhuyi* 客觀主義), by which he referred to the detached scientism characteristic of naturalism. See the discussion of his theory of subjectivity (*zhuguan lun* 主觀論) in Su Guangwen, *Kangzhan wenyi jicheng*, pp. 268–70.

98. Zhou Yang had long concerned himself with the dialectics of subjectivity and objectivity. In his 1933 article "Wenxue de zhenshixing" he wrote that authorial subjectivity is always in dialectical conflict with objective reality but insisted that subjectivity is not in the end distinguishable from "class consciousness." He went on to equate "proletarian subjectivity" with "historical objectivity." "Truth in literature" is thus not a matter of artistic technique, nor even of the artist's sincerity (as Ye Shaojun had maintained), but of an author's class standing. That is to say, one can only objectively understand the world if one looks at it through proletarian eyes.

seem to proceed from a formula and thus easily give the impression of being all the same." He blamed this development primarily on the authors' slavish following of political guidelines, which had the effect of curtailing independent thought.[99] Later that year the critic Wang Renshu 王任叔 directly countered Zhou Yang's argument that a correct worldview was the fundamental condition for all artistic activity; an author, he wrote, should be capable of drawing "close to reality," even its dark side. In an obvious reference to the Creationists, he pointed out that ideological rectitude had in the past served as a screen that writers used to hide themselves from reality. Wang insisted that the "realism" of modern Chinese fiction—its authentic representation of the nation's plight—was not the achievement of the theorists but of practicing writers like Lu Xun, whose stories served both to reflect the truth about Chinese society and to instruct readers in how to implement change.[100] Another critic, Lu Digen 鹿地亘, echoed this opinion, asserting that focusing too exclusively on a work's propaganda value was self-defeating: great artistry was itself the most persuasive of tools.[101]

In his theoretical essays of the late 1930s Mao Dun sometimes defended the "temporary immaturity" of the new literature,[102] but he clearly agreed with the critics' underlying assessment—that much of the new literature treated contemporary events in an ideologically acceptable, but dry and methodical, manner. In a discussion of the new war literature, Mao Dun observed that works with a military theme, if written without the benefit of observing soldiers in action, for example, were invariably schematic and undifferentiated.[103] The simple

---

99. Dong Zhi 烔之 first made this argument in an article entitled "Zuojia jian xuyao yizhong xin yundong" 作家間需要一種新運動 (We need a new movement among authors), published in early 1937 in the *Wenyi fukan* 文藝附刊 (Literary and arts supplement) of *Dagong bao* 大公報. Dong Zhi further developed his ideas in a later essay, "Zai lun chabuduo" 再論差不多 (More on all-the-same-ism), *Wenxue zazhi* 1, no. 4 (August 1937): 34–40. I quote here from page 34 of the latter essay.

100. Wang Renshu 王任叔 [Ba Ren 巴人], "Xianshizhuyizhe de lu" 現實主義者的路 (Road of the realist), *Zhongliu* 2, no. 6 (5 June 1937): 293–96.

101. Lu Digen 鹿地亘, "Guanyu 'yishu he xuanchuan' de wenti" 關於"藝術和宣傳"的問題 (On the literature and propaganda problem), *Kangzhan wenyi* 1, no. 6 (28 May 1938): 50–53.

102. See especially Mao Dun's reply to Dong Zhi, "Guanyu 'chabuduo'" 關於"差不多" (Concerning all-the-same-ism), *Zhongliu* 2, no. 8 (5 July 1937); reprinted in Mao Dun, *Mao Dun wenyi zalun ji* 1:660–62.

103. See Mao Dun, "Bayue de ganxiang—kangzhan wenyi yinian de huigu" 八月的感想—抗戰文藝一年的回顧 (Reflections in August: a look back at one year of

way to remedy this tendency toward formulism, in Mao Dun's opinion, was to recognize the centrality of characterization (rather than theme or plot) in the composition of a story. He wrote of his own fiction:

> To my mind, character is the most important element in constructing a short story. In my own experience, I first let a character ripen in my mind, let him or her come alive so that when I close my eyes, it is as though a real human being were before my eyes. Then when I begin writing I discover that I can move right along without laying down my pen—the story simply flows out.[104]

A similar emphasis on characterization can be discovered in the critical writings of many other May Fourth realists during the late 1930s and 1940s. In his debate with Zhou Yang over typicality, Hu Feng had repeatedly underscored the importance of character over events in fiction,[105] and the writers Wu Zuxiang 吳組緗 and Zhang Tianyi 張天翼 both wrote substantial treatises on character description in the early 1940s.[106] Clearly all these writers were concerned that the ideological emphasis of the new literature somehow neglected a crucial element of fictional composition as they understood it. As we have seen, earlier realists, such as Ye Shaojun, had been preoccupied with the place of pity in fiction, that is, with the humanistic relationship of author to character inherent in the Western model of realism. The realists' sudden growth of interest in the technical problem of characterization at this late stage of the national crisis would appear to represent a nonpolemical reassertion of those values. At the very least, it implied a distaste for the ideological posturing that increasingly characterized literary debate among Chinese leftists.

Although realists continued to explore the problem of characteriza-

---

War of Resistance literature), *Wenyi zhendi* 1, no. 9 (16 August 1938); reprinted in Mao Dun, *Mao Dun wenyi zalun ji* 2:762–71, here p. 765.

104. Mao Dun, "Guanyu xiaoshuo zhong de renwu" 關於小說中的人物 (On fictional characters), *Kangzhan wenyi* 7, nos. 2–3 (20 March 1941); reprinted in Mao Dun, *Mao Dun wenyi zalun ji* 2:887–89, here p. 887.

105. See, for example, Hu Feng, "Xianshizhuyi di yi 'xiuzheng,'" p. 307.

106. Wu Zuxiang 吳組緗, "Ruhe chuangzao xiaoshuo zhong de renwu" 如何創造小說中的人物 (On creating fictional characters), *Kangzhan wenyi* 7, nos. 2–3 (20 March 1941); and Zhang Tianyi 張天翼, "Tan renwu miaoxie" 談人物描寫 (On character description), *Kangzhan wenyi* 7, nos. 4–6 (10 November 1941 and 15 June 1942).

tion in fiction, polemical objections to formulism were heard less often after 1938, when late in that year a campaign was launched to criticize literature "not related to the War of Resistance" (*yu kangzhan wuguan* 與抗戰無關). Once again the demonstrated commitment of authors to immediate political goals became the touchstone by which their literary output was judged. But even literature that clearly did concern itself with matters of importance to the national political agenda was liable to being attacked for the mode in which its author chose to treat the subject. Satire in particular was viewed with suspicion. A full-blown debate on satire erupted following the discovery in 1938 that a translation of Zhang Tianyi's short story "Hua Wei xiansheng" 華威先生 (Mr. Hua Wei), which pointedly satirized the ineffectual wartime bureaucracy, had been used by the Japanese in the course of a propaganda campaign. Lin Lin 林林, for example, argued that such works, however true a picture of social ills they painted, were detrimental to the national morale; at the very least, they should not be disseminated abroad or to Hong Kong, where they might fall into unfriendly hands.[107]

The critical, pessimistic nature of satire had in fact been noticed years earlier, during the Revolutionary Literature debate, in connection with Lu Xun's satirical stories.[108] The essayist Lin Yutang 林語堂 had also broached the subject in the early 1930s, when he declared his preference for a rational, humanistic humor (*youmo* 幽默) over an embittered, restrictive satire.[109] Lin's suggestion that authors adopt a tone of amused detachment had infuriated Lu Xun, who in 1935 wrote two short essays in which he defended the satirist as possessed of both the "good intentions" and the "warm feelings" of wanting to change the world. Moreover, he wrote, satire served the purpose of calling attention to "irrational, ridiculous, disgusting, or even detestable" truths that are commonplace but frequently passed over. Typically, however, Lu Xun took a less-than-sanguine view of the actual capacity of satirical literature to effect change: "By the time a satirist

---

107. Lan Hai discusses the satire debate in *Zhongguo kangzhan wenyi shi*, pp. 338–42.

108. In this connection see, for example, the defense of Lu Xun's satire written by Cheng Wenying 成文英, "Fengci wenxue yu shehui gaige" 諷刺文學與社會改革 (Satirical literature and social reform), *Mengya yuekan* 1, no. 5 (May 1930): 121–28.

109. See Lin Yutang 林語堂, "Lun youmo" 論幽默 (On humor), Parts 1–2, *Lunyu*, 論語 (The analects), no. 33 (1934): 434–39; 34 (1934): 522–25.

appears in a group, that group is already doomed; certainly writing cannot save it."[110]

Many of Lu Xun's arguments (though not his cynical afterthought) were repeated by critics and authors who spoke in defense of "Mr. Hua Wei." Most vocal of these was Mao Dun, who defended both exposure literature (*baolu wenxue* 暴露文學) and satire as the expression of a passionate moral purpose; despite the critical nature of their content, he wrote, such works have an overwhelmingly positive influence on readers. "If a writer writes exposés out of anger and hatred for all that is vile, the result is activist, as has been proven by the twenty-year history of the new literature."[111] Moreover, as more than one critic pointed out, only by exposing evils does one prepare the way for their removal.[112] The satire debate continued until the latter part of 1940, ending with a weak consensus that literature has a double role: to extol and to expose. Fiction could accommodate some critical treatment of social issues, but the present imperative was for the creation of greater numbers of "positive types."[113] Ideally, any work of literature that portrayed negative social phenomena should give equal time to the positive social influences that could serve as their antidote. This formula in effect called for writers to curtail the independent critique of satire and to substitute for it a clear-cut didactic or social message.

The debate that had the most widespread effect on the course of Chinese fiction, however, finally directing it away from May Fourth cosmopolitanism, was over national forms (*minzu xingshi* 民族形式), or what was sometimes called old forms (*jiu xingshi* 舊形式). This debate, though initiated by the theorists, would not have been possible without the work of folklorists and literary scholars in the 1920s who, as part of a general reassessment of Chinese cultural history, had described and reclassified the popular arts. Yet in the years following

110. Lu Xun, "Shenme shi fengci?" 什麼是諷刺? (What is satire?), in Lu Xun, *Lu Xun quanji* 6:328–30, here p. 329; see also "Lun fengci" 論諷刺 (On satire), in *Lu Xun quanji* 6:277–79.

111. Mao Dun, "Bayue de ganxiang," p. 766.

112. Wang Renshu, for example, in "Minzhu yu xianshi" 民主與現實 (Democracy and reality) makes this argument and then insists, "To tell lies is not the business of writers" (*Wenyi zhendi* 4, no. 2 [16 November 1939]: 1255–59).

113. For one formulation of this argument see Huang Sheng 黃繩, "Kangzhan wenyi de dianxing chuangzao wenti" 抗戰文藝的典型創造問題 (The problem of creating types in War of Resistance literature), *Wenyi zhendi* 3, no. 6 (1 July 1939): 997–1001.

the May Fourth demonstrations few had endorsed these arts as relevant to the contemporary struggle. Lu Xun, for example, though a highly erudite and original scholar of traditional vernacular literature, had written in 1927 that since popular literature was formally and ideologically tainted by exposure to the high culture, it was decadent and could not be called a "true people's literature."[114]

In the early 1930s, however, concern about questions of literary reception sparked a movement for the popularization—or what might in the Chinese context more accurately be called the "massification"— of the arts. Yu Dafu first introduced the term *dazhong wenyi* 大衆文藝 (mass literature) as the title of a journal he founded in 1928; in the opening statement of the first issue, he pointed out the term's origins in Japan, where it referred primarily to popular romances and martial arts fiction. He insisted, however, that his intention in using the term was not to promote such fiction but to "make literature the possession of the masses."[115] We can observe in Yu's comments the same ambivalence about popular culture that had troubled Lu Xun. While theoretically interested in reaching out to the masses, reformers like Lu Xun and Yu Dafu remained wary of traditional forms of popular expression. As a consequence, the massification campaign in its initial stages focused rather narrowly on questions of language and content and failed to have any appreciable effect on the form of the literature then current.

With the gradual discrediting of Western fictional models in the late 1920s and 1930s, however, more and more critics came to believe that only a revolution in form could close the gap between the new literature and the masses. Zhou Yang, following the Soviet model, advocated the use of various agitprop small forms, such as sketches, reports, and brief political poems.[116] Others called for a "mass fiction" that would take the crowd itself as both theme and protagonist and heralded Ding Ling's 丁玲 short story "Shui" 水 (Water, 1933) as the first successful work of this kind.[117] Finally some theorists, Qu Qiubai

114. See Lu Xun, "Geming shidai de wenxue," p. 422.
115. Yu Dafu, "'Dazhong wenyi' shiming" "大衆文藝"釋名 (Explanation of the term "mass literature"), *Dazhong wenyi* 1, no. 1 (20 September 1928); reprinted in *Geming wenxue lunzheng ziliao xuanbian* 2:657–58.
116. Zhou Yang, "Guanyu wenxue dazhonghua" 關於文學大衆化 (On the massification of literature), *Beidou* 2, nos. 3/4 (20 July 1932); reprinted in *Wenxue yundong shiliao xuan* 2:410–13, here p. 410.
117. Feng Xuefeng 馮雪峯 hailed Ding Ling's 丁玲 story as marking the birth of a

the most vocal among them, began to suggest that writers reexamine traditional artistic forms to discover the source of their popularity. Oral storytelling, opera, and popular songs, unlike elite Western forms, could win immediate acceptance with the masses and thus could prove useful in forging a truly populist culture.[118] Qu was not suggesting uncritical appropriation of the old forms, however, as the following warning makes clear: "One should avoid the kind of opportunism that would consist of blindly imitating old forms. Here our efforts should be twofold: first, in emulating old forms we should make our own revisions; second, we should forge new forms out of the elements of the old."[119] Lu Xun was one of those persuaded by Qu's argument. In 1934 he wrote an essay in which he acknowledged the need for artists to concern themselves with the interests of the general public and conceded that much could be learned from the old forms. But he reiterated Qu's caution that "when old forms are adopted, certain things must be removed while others must be added, resulting in a new form, a change."[120]

In 1938, however, in the context of the wartime effort to mobilize the masses through the arts, a much more aggressive effort, supported by such Communist party theorists as Zhou Yang, Ai Siqi 艾思奇, and Chen Boda 陳伯達, was made to advance the slogan "National forms." This time the slogan clearly entailed the rejection of certain May Fourth values, particularly the cosmopolitanism and critical independence that May Fourth authors had employed to divorce themselves from tradition. One author even suggested that May Fourth intellectuals had carried their interest in the West so far that it colored their life experiences; while granting that their compositions were a faithful record of life as they lived it, he said their works still remained

---

new kind of fiction, characterized by a true understanding of class conflict and a focus on collective action rather than individual psychology. See "Guanyu xin de xiaoshuo de dansheng: ping Ding Ling de 'Shui'" 關於新的小說的誕生—評丁玲的《水》 (On the birth of a new fiction: on Ding Ling's "Water"), *Beidou* 2, no. 1 (20 January 1932): 235–39.

118. Qu Qiubai, "Dazhong wenyi de wenti" 大衆文藝的問題 (The problem of mass literature"), *Wenxue yuebao*, no. 1 (10 June 1932); reprinted in *Wenxue yundong shiliao xuan* 2:391–99, here p. 397.

119. See Qu Qiubai, "Puluo dazhong wenyi de xianshi wenti" 普羅大衆文藝的現實問題 (The real problems of proletarian mass literature), *Wenxue* 1, no. 1 (25 April 1932); reprinted in *Wenxue yundong shiliao xuan* 2:371–90.

120. Lu Xun, "Lun 'jiu xingshi de caiyong'" 論"舊形式的採用" (On the adoption of old forms), in his *Lu Xun quanji* 6:24.

totally irrelevant to China and the Chinese people.[121] In discussing the important achievements of modern Chinese fiction since the May Fourth movement, Zhou Yang and Chen Boda calculatedly downplayed the Western impact, emphasizing instead modern fiction's indebtedness to traditional vernacular literature. Their attitude toward Lu Xun, who after his death in 1936 had rapidly been elevated to an unassailable position in the Chinese Communist pantheon, is revealing in this regard: in stark contrast to the Creationists, who had berated Lu Xun for his slavish imitation of bourgeois Western forms, Zhou Yang and Chen Boda now hailed Lu Xun above all as a creator of national forms.[122]

Not surprisingly, May Fourth realists and their sympathizers, while outwardly approving the slogan "National forms," treated it with much caution. They were clearly reluctant to entirely repudiate Western fictional models and resented the theorists' attempts to rewrite the history of modern Chinese literature. Hu Feng insisted (as did Guo Moruo) that Western literature and thought had played a decisive role in the May Fourth period and specifically cited Lu Xun as an example of an author who took his inspiration primarily from foreign literature.[123] Hu went on to warn that by obscuring the true nature of the May Fourth rebellion, advocates of national forms ran the risk of simply catering to the superstitions of the readers rather than educating or challenging them. The end result would, he feared, be the reinstatement of traditional prejudices.[124] Mao Dun shared many of Hu Feng's reservations: he insisted that in the course of its development modern Chinese literature had borrowed from both Chinese and foreign literatures and that to see either influence as exclusive was a mistake.[125] In discussing a slogan frequently used by the national-

---

121. See Pan Zinian 潘梓年, "Lun wenyi de minzu xingshi" 論文藝的民族形式 (On national forms in literature), *Wenxue yuebao* 1, no. 2 (15 February 1940).

122. For a discussion of Chen Boda's 陳伯達 and Zhou Yang's attitudes on national forms see Marián Gálik, "Main Issues in the Discussion on 'National Forms,'" especially pp. 100–104.

123. See Hu Feng, "Duiyu wusi geming wenyi chuantong de yi lijie" 對於五四革命文藝傳統的一理解 (An interpretation of the revolutionary literary tradition of the May Fourth movement), in Hu Feng, *Lun minzu xingshi wenti*, pp. 33–44.

124. For a fuller discussion of Hu Feng's position on the national forms debate see Theodore D. Huters, "Hu Feng and the Critical Legacy of Lu Xun," in Leo Ou-fan Lee, *Lu Xun and His Legacy*, pp. 143–46.

125. See Mao Dun, "Jiu xingshi, minjian xingshi, yu minzu xingshi" 舊形式、民間形式與民族形式 (Old forms, folk forms, and national forms), *Zhongguo wenhua* 2, no. 1 (25 September 1940); reprinted in Mao Dun, *Mao Dun wenyi zalun ji* 2:860–69.

forms advocates, "New wine in old bottles," he suggested that perhaps only 1 percent of the "old bottles," i.e. traditional literary forms, actually merited study.[126] Moreover, he reiterated Lu Xun's and Qu Qiubai's warnings of the mid-1930s: "When we say 'use,' of course we don't mean unqualified acceptance. At this time we need to do research to discover to what extent old forms may be used and experiment to discover how to make something new of the old."[127] Zhang Tianyi, in an essay specifically devoted to the subject of national forms, recognized a temporary need for the existence of two levels of literature, one "advanced," one "popular," each appealing to a different audience in forms that audience would understand. As literacy spread, however, he expected that the two levels would merge, since ideally literary form should be determined solely by content.[128] But Zhang's two-level view of contemporary literary needs was rejected outright by most advocates of national forms,[129] and his "form follows function" argument was criticized by others as abstruse and theoretical when the times demanded direct cultural intervention in the lives of the people.[130]

In his 1942 "Talks at the Yan'an Forum" Mao Zedong specifically addressed the issue of national forms, as well as the other issues of contention among leftist writers that we have touched on, in the hope of unifying all cultural workers behind a policy of massification. Although his reasoning in the "Talks" is highly dialectical in form, Mao clearly lent his authority to those who had taken positions of ideological rigidity in each of the earlier literary debates. He affirmed the importance of a correct worldview in fiction over the independent

126. Mao Dun, "Lun ruhe xuexi wenxue de minzu xingshi" 論如何學習文學的民族形式 (How to study national forms in literature), Zhongguo wenhua 1, no. 5 (25 July 1940); reprinted in Mao Dun, Mao Dun wenyi zalun ji 2:843–59, here pp. 845–46.
127. Mao Dun, "Dazhonghua yu liyong jiu xingshi" 大衆化與利用舊形式 (Massification and the use of old forms), Wenyi zhendi 1, no. 4 (1 June 1938); reprinted in Mao Dun, Mao Dun wenyi zalun ji 2:725–26.
128. Zhang Tianyi, "Guanyu wenyi de minzu xingshi" 關於文藝的民族形式 (On national forms in literature), Xiandai wenyi 2, nos. 1–2 (15 October 1940 and 25 November 1940); reprinted in Zhang Tianyi, Zhang Tianyi wenxue pinglun ji, pp. 73–108, especially p. 87.
129. See Huang Sheng, "Dangqian wenyi yundong de yige kaocha" 當前文藝運動的一個考察 (Investigation of the present literary movement), Wenyi zhendi 3, no. 9 (16 August 1938): 1081–86.
130. See Li Lei 李雷, "Lun tongsu duwu de wenyihua" 論通俗讀物的文藝化 (On making popular reading matter into literature), Wenxue yuebao 1, no. 2 (15 February 1940).

observations of the author; he favored a restricted use of satire that would permit a truly adversarial or caustic tone only in works that targeted the enemies of socialism; and he strongly urged the substitution of popular native forms for the Western models that had been introduced in the May Fourth period. The series of "rectifications" that followed Mao's talks quickly bolstered the authority of his opinions. The intellectual Wang Shiwei 王實味 was the first to fall: Mao's political secretary Chen Boda accused him of "denying the creativity of the oppressed masses" by opposing the use of national forms.[131] Shortly thereafter the party theoretician Ai Siqi, in an exchange with the painter Zhang Ding 張丁, lodged a stern warning on the dangers of satirizing those within one's own camp.[132] And finally, such famous authors as Ding Ling, Ai Qing 艾青, and Xiao Jun 蕭軍 were chastised for their unwillingness to surrender their artistic independence and embrace wholeheartedly the party's stance on political and artistic matters. Ding Ling was specifically criticized for continuing to use the techniques of the old realism in her fiction.[133] Mao's "Talks," when read in the context of the fifteen years of polemical debates that preceded them, offered little that was new, but they effectively marshaled the dissatisfactions many had long felt with May Fourth views of literature as an independent *Kulturkritik*. The "Talks" established a new orthodoxy of opinion on art and literature and are the inescapable basis for all later theory and criticism in China.

The introduction of realism into China in the early twentieth century was motivated by a profoundly iconoclastic ambition: with it and other tools Chinese intellectuals hoped to completely remake an ancient and highly developed culture. As May Fourth writers were themselves to discover, however, dramatized iconoclastic gestures do not in themselves constitute real change. The cultural field is not so easily molded, and traditional prejudices often govern even the manner in which the appurtenances of tradition are overturned. In elevating fiction to the domain of high culture, May Fourth writers continued to rehearse traditional notions of what constituted that culture,

131. See Chen Boda, "Xie zai Wang Shiwei 'Wenyi de minzu xingshi duanlun' zhi hou" 寫在王實味《文藝的民族形式短論》之後 (Written after Wang Shiwei's "Short discussion of national forms in literature"), *Jiefang ribao*, 解放日報, 3 and 4 July 1942.
132. Ai Siqi, "Tan fengci" 談諷刺 (On satire), *Jiefang ribao*, 24 May 1942.
133. See the discussion in Merle Goldman, *Literary Dissent in Communist China*, pp. 42–43.

if only from the necessity of distinguishing their own works from such popular—and, they believed, damaging—genres as "black screen" (*heimu* 黑幕) and "mandarin ducks and butterfly" (*yuanyang hudie* 鴛鴦蝴蝶) fiction. May Fourth criticism generally, for all its aggressive introduction of theories from the West, approaches those theories with the aesthetic priorities of traditional criticism. Specifically, May Fourth critics continued to focus, not on techniques of representation, but on questions of the work's origin (i.e. on the basis of what authority is the work generated?) and of its reception (i.e. what is the work's effect on society at large?).

Realism, as we have described its operation in the West, is a fundamentally epistemological exercise, which involves testing the capacity of language to capture and communicate the Real. Realism served an indisputable purpose in China as long as it was being used to question the underlying principles of traditional Chinese culture, but once this goal was accomplished, its status became increasingly problematic. As we have seen, writers who adopted realism defined it in terms of its moral and pragmatic limits, whereas the times seemed to call for an activist art that could serve as a tool to unify and organize the Chinese people. These writers did not expect, or desire, that their literature would achieve the purgation of antisocial passions that, I have argued, characterizes its operation. But with the increasing politicization of the literary scene in the late 1920s and 1930s the actual effect on readers of the new literature came under closer scrutiny. The Western literary models Chinese writers had so eagerly adopted, realism in particular, became suspect, their impact now appearing more conformist than radical. Once the limitations of realism were observed, the notion of literature as *Kulturkritik* came to be understood as a function of individualism and thus as part of a larger ideological webbing that the Chinese associated with the hegemonic intentions of the West. The Western equation of critique with a superior grasp of the Real, independent of the context from which the work emerged and the audience to which it returned, was suppressed, if indeed it may be said to have ever taken a very firm root in China. Critical realism, which had been adopted in China as a tool for revolution, became suspect precisely for its failure to advance the communal ends of that revolution.

Theodore D. Huters has written that "the essence of Lu Xun's critical thought must be sought in the uncertain space left by his avoidance of the pitfalls of system on the one hand and of self-complacency on the other."[134] Something similar might be said about the many writers who continued to practice critical realism in China in the late 1920s and 1930s. While disabused of the individualistic (and therefore in Chinese eyes self-indulgent) tendencies of some forms of realism, they continued to hope that the mode's emphasis on observation and critique could counterbalance the increasingly presumptuous demands of ideological dogma. In the chapters that follow, we will consider the creative works that emerged from the "uncertain space" occupied by critical realists. In examining the works of individual authors we will address two primary questions, which parallel Chinese preoccupations with the creative origins of literary works and their reception. The first concerns the nature of the self-imaging that accompanies any attempt to give representation to the external world.[135] As I have suggested, the desire to fully describe Chinese society, to make its elements separate and signifiable, obliged Chinese authors to construct a new and independent sense of self. The process of fashioning the self left its traces in the form and style of individual works, which we will work to uncover. The second question we will broach is that of literary transitivity: what imprint does the authors' concern with the utility of their work leave on their fiction? In particular we will explore authorial discovery of and resistance to the consolatory effect of catharsis as it operates in realist fiction.

134. Theodore D. Huters, "Hu Feng and the Critical Legacy of Lu Xun," p. 130.
135. Jacques Lacan has observed that the image a child sees of itself in a mirror is the prototype for all objects it later distinguishes in the world. From this notion we may speculate that representation of the external world involves a projection of the ego onto the objects that make up that world. See the discussion in Julia Kristeva, *Powers of Horror*, pp. 46ff.

3

Lu Xun, Ye Shaojun, and the
Moral Impediments to Realism

LU XUN: THE VIOLENCE OF OBSERVATION

The preeminent position that both Chinese and foreign critics of modern Chinese literature accord to the few short stories in Lu Xun's two collections *Nahan* 呐喊 ("The outcry," also translated as "Call to arms," 1923) and *Panghuang* 徬徨 ("Hesitation," also translated as "Wandering," 1926) is certainly not due to the quality of their author's narrative imagination. Judged purely as exercises in storytelling, many of Lu Xun's stories are unsatisfactory performances: some, like "Yijian xiaoshi" 一件小事 (A trifling affair, 1919) and "Guduzhe" 孤獨者 (The misanthrope, 1925) offer plot lines that are oddly truncated or that never achieve their full dramatic potential, while others, including the highly acclaimed "Zhufu" 祝福 (New Year's sacrifice, 1924), are so crowded with incident that the plot lines would appear shamelessly melodramatic if they were not mediated by an ironical narration.[1] It is rather to the particular quality of Lu Xun's moral introspection that critics and later writers of fiction in China, including all the other authors to be treated here, have responded so enthusiastically. Lu Xun's stories, like the fiction of the other major realist writer of the 1920s, Ye Shaojun, characteristically highlight not a narrated content but the interpretive procedures through which that content is evaluated. Lu Xun introduces these interpretive concerns into his fiction through a wide array of formal and stylistic innovations, which confer on his fiction an unprecedented degree of aesthetic self-consciousness. Lu Xun justly wrote in the afterword to his essay collection *Fen* 墳 (The grave) that he more frequently used his scalpel to dissect himself than to dissect others,[2] and the scars of this self-

1. Theodore D. Huters makes a similar observation about "New Year's Sacrifice" in his "Blossoms in the Snow."
2. Lu Xun, "Xie zai *Fen* houmian" 寫在《墳》後面 (Postscript to *The Grave*), in Lu Xun, *Lu Xun quanji* 1:282–90, here p. 284.

dissection are evident in the formal experimentation of his fiction. But Lu Xun was not much interested in bringing the details of his personal life into his writings, and the self-dissection he practiced was not that of a frankly confessional writer like Yu Dafu. Instead, what Lu Xun constantly probed with his restless experimentation was his identity and responsibility as a writer. The same moral purpose that dictated the didactic element in his fiction—making it, at least superficially, an outcry against social injustices—at the same time compelled a reflexive examination of his own role as observer of Chinese society and dispenser of its literary representations. Though later writers were to approach the ethical and formal problems he broached with more fertile narrative imaginations, none wrote with the same degree of scrupulous self-examination.

Lu Xun's preface to the short stories collected in *The Outcry* narrates the awakening, deferral, and eventual expression of the moral purpose that informs his fiction. Its narrative form pointedly directs readers' attention away from a simple thematic approach to the stories toward a consideration of the author's personal investment in their composition. The psychological origin of Lu Xun's moral indignation is evoked in the story of his father's death from superstitious medical practices,[3] as a result of which Lu Xun undertook the study of Western medicine. How that indignation was redirected from somatic to spiritual concerns, specifically to literature, is recounted in a scene whose impact is at once political, aesthetic, and personal. In the scene Lu Xun, at the time a young medical student in Sendai, Japan, views a war slide depicting a Chinese bound and about to be hanged as a spy by the Japanese. Lu Xun is interested not so much in the physical brutality of the act depicted in the slide as in its social significance: the execution is performed above all for its informational value, "as a warning" to other Chinese. Regardless of his possible guilt or innocence, the victim's death is intended to symbolically impose a certain order on the social relations of the observers. Lu Xun's attention thus naturally turns to the Chinese audience within the slide whose potential reception of the message conveyed by this act of violence may be said to license it, and he is appalled by their moral obtuseness. Oblivious both to the individual tragedy being played out before them and

3. See the discussion of Lu Xun's psychological makeup in Leo Ou-fan Lee, "Genesis of a Writer: Notes on Lu Xun's Educational Experience, 1881–1909" in Merle Goldman, *Modern Chinese Literature*, pp. 161–88, especially p. 168.

to the significance of their own role as witnesses, they have come simply to "enjoy the spectacle."

Besides the content of the slide, the unique circumstances of its viewing—in a microbiology class after the day's lessons are concluded—disturb Lu Xun. The classroom setting, as well as the coldly reproductive nature of the photographic medium, would seem to encourage Lu Xun to view the projected scene with the distancing, objectifying perspective of scientific observation—as a self-delimited fact, unavailable to the interference of its viewers. But unlike the microbes that are the class's usual viewing matter and which are indeed oblivious of their observers, the execution assumes the observers' presence and is enacted for their sake. Lu Xun is aware of two groups of observers, in both of which he participates but with whose responses to the slide he feels profoundly at odds. While national identity connects him most intimately with the Chinese audience within the slide, his recognition of their spiritual apathy makes him painfully sensible of the distance, both moral and physical, that separates him from his compatriots. Yet his physical presence in the audience of Japanese students compels him to feign pleasure at the sight of the slide ("I had to join in the clapping and cheering in the lecture hall along with the other students"),[4] involving him in a kind of bad faith perhaps even more reprehensible than the curiosity of the Chinese audience he censures. The scene thus encapsulates a double sense of one observer's alienation and complicity: while, as a Chinese, he too is targeted as a receptor of the warning the act is meant to convey, for survival's sake he must share the delight of its authors.

The young Lu Xun has violated the smooth transmission of the slide's message by his affective identification with the victim, but he silences that sympathy, realizing that its immediate expression would be equivalent to offering himself in substitution for the victim, a risk he is unwilling to run. Only at the level of his personal interpretive heresy is Lu Xun's true response registered; his failure to find an outlet for that response condemns him to years of embittered "loneliness," a private agony that Lu Xun wanly hopes the composition of short stories will purge. If this aim is to be accomplished, however, a troublesome aesthetic dilemma must be addressed: lest Lu Xun's own work

4. Lu Xun, "Zi xu" 自序 (Preface), in Lu Xun, Lu Xun quanji 1:415–21, here p. 416. The translations from Lu Xun's stories and essays are adapted from those of Yang Xianyi and Gladys Yang in Lu Xun, Selected Works.

be guilty of further disseminating the spectacle of violence, the narration must, while faithfully rendering scenes of paradigmatic social significance such as that depicted in the slide, disallow the unthinking transmission of their original message. Lu Xun's frequent expression of concern for the "young people" who will constitute his audience is in fact motivated by an awareness of the dangers of transmission; doubtful that his readers will fare better than he has at breaking the chain of violence through which the message of social discipline is perpetuated, he fears that his work will "infect" them with the same lonely, because inoperative, consciousness of social injustice that has embittered his own life. As we shall see, Lu Xun attempts to prevent the possibility of his fiction's spreading such infection by introducing a discursive counterargument (or what might be called an interpretive static) to the violence of the work's *histoire*.

"Shi zhong" 示衆 (A public example, 1925), from Lu Xun's second collection of short stories, *Hesitation*, is the story that most nearly reproduces the scene described in his preface. The brief event recounted in the story is, like the slide Lu Xun saw in Japan, a *Querschnitt*, or "slice of life," self-delimited and cut off from what precedes and follows it. The incident is given little narrative development: even the criminal charge for which the "public example" is punished is suppressed in the text, thus divorcing the exhibition from whatever moral or social justification it might otherwise have carried. The characters painted on the criminal's jerkin, which should provide a narrative clue to his criminal past, are transmitted in the narration only through the illiterate Baldy's unintelligible efforts to read them ("*Weng, du, heng, ba, er . . .*");[5] they mark nothing more than the criminal's singling out as a public example. The reader's instinctive desire to deduce from his exhibition a transferable message and then fix on that message as a kind of reified content is thereby frustrated, and the reader's attention is directed instead to the mechanics of the communicative act itself. The crowd's curiosity, again the focus of Lu Xun's regard, is similarly stimulated not by the content but by the violence of the communication, and the essentially fickle, transferable nature of that curiosity is exposed at the end of the story by its sudden diversion to a nearby rickshaw accident.[6]

5. Lu Xun, "Shi zhong" 示衆 (A public example), in Lu Xun, *Lu Xun quanji* 2:68–73, here p. 69.
6. Cf. the following remarks by Lu Xun, which amount to an outline of the plot of "A Public Example":

In its portrayal of crowd dynamics "A Public Example" employs, as Patrick Hanan has observed, a "cinematic" technique,[7] but this is less a point of similarity with the slide-viewing incident discussed above, as he suggests, than the mark of its difference. Where the slide had presented a static view, here the rapid movement of the narrator's observing eye as he moves among the crowd of onlookers is what one first notices on reading the story. At times, as if trying to follow a complicated sequence of rapidly edited closeups, readers become disoriented: to whom do the red nose, bald head, or straw hat belong? As a result readers, though their quality of observation retains the clinical exteriority of the camera, feel themselves pressed into the crowd, unable to attain the equanimity of a distanced view. The disorienting cinematic technique of "A Public Example" thus forces on readers an unwilling identification with the crowd. To the extent that they resist such identification on ethical grounds, they are compelled to scrutinize their own processes of observation. Readers' complicity in the observation of the criminal has already been suggested by the title, whose literal meaning ("show crowd") could refer either to the narrated exhibition of the criminal or to the act that the story itself represents of putting the crowd on display to its audience of readers.

The most developed treatment of ritual victimization in Lu Xun's works is the final scene of his best-known story, "Ah Q zhengzhuan" 阿Q正傳 (The true story of Ah Q, 1921), which, unlike the above examples, narrates its protagonist's execution from the perspective of the victim. Like the public example and the alleged spy of the slide, Ah Q remains in a fundamental sense an anonymous figure; as is characteristic of sacrificial victims, he is both a part of his community and apart from it.[8] Ah Q's lack of a surname is the first sign of his ambiguous

---

The masses, especially in China, are always spectators at a drama. . . . Before the mutton shops in Beijing a few people often gather to gape, with evident enjoyment, at the skinning of the sheep. And this is all they get out of it if a man lays down his life. Moreover, after walking a few steps away from the scene they forget even this modicum of enjoyment. There is nothing you can do with such people; the only way to save them is to give them no drama to watch." ("Suiganlu sanshiba" 隨感錄三十八 [Random thought 38], in Lu Xun, *Lu Xun quanji* 1:311–16, here p. 311; translation by Leo Ou-fan Lee, *Voices from the Iron House*, p. 72)

7. Patrick Hanan, "The Technique of Lu Hsün's Fiction," p. 89.
8. See René Girard, *Violence and the Sacred*, especially the chapters entitled "The Origins of Myth and Ritual," pp. 89–119, and "Sacrificial Substitution," pp. 250–73.

position in a society where individuals are most powerfully conjoined through familial ties, but his claim, however unreliable, that his surname is in fact Zhao 趙 hints at a possible kinship (moral if not familial) with the most respected family in town. His personal name is also ambiguous: *Ah* is a meaningless prefix, and the Western letter *Q*, which visually proclaims its alien origins every time it is encountered in the Chinese text, at the same time has a culturally specific pictorial value if Zhou Zuoren 周作人 is correct in suggesting that Lu Xun chose the graph because it looked like the drawing of a head with queue dangling.[9] Ah Q's character is in a similar manner at once bound and free. As a transient scavenger, he depends for survival on the odd jobs occasionally offered him by the townspeople, who in turn use him as an all-purpose scapegoat. In this latter capacity, he is frequently made the butt of public ridicule, which is the means by which individuals at all levels of the village society assert their position and bolster their pride. Section 3 of the story dramatizes the reinforcement of social discriminations in the village through a chain of willfully perpetrated acts of humiliation, descending from the local society's top register to its lower depths. In spite of Ah Q's humble place in this society, his eager pursuit of an even more lowly object of ridicule (a defenseless nun) shows clearly that he is no mere victim of the social order but very much a participant in it. Yet, unlike the others, he can be said to harbor no consistent ambitions or desires; he simply adopts the enthusiasms and prejudices of those he encounters.[10] Ah Q's unashamed imitation of the villagers' social jousting (of which the most obvious example is his lice-counting contest with Wang Laihu 王癩胡, "Whiskers Wang") exposes the underlying absurdity of such competitions. The social divisions thus established are revealed as merely formal, empty of underlying values, however self-righteously justified. What separates Ah Q from the other villagers, who, like him, play the role of either oppressor or victim as the occasion allows, is the facility with which he traverses the line at which social discriminations are drawn. He is even adept at "self-belittling," as when "to change defeat into victory" he slaps his own face and feels just as if he had beaten

---

9. See Zhou Zuoren (Zhou Xiashou), *Lu Xun xiaoshuo li de renwu*, p. 41.
10. In this connection see Lin Yü-sheng's discussion of Ah Q's "lack of an interior self" in *The Crisis of Chinese Consciousness*, p. 129.

someone else.[11] By playing both parts at once, Ah Q makes himself his own scapegoat. To the extent that he is a Chinese everyman, Ah Q's behavior typifies the arbitrary and self-divisive modes of social operation that Lu Xun believed characterized Chinese civilization.

If at his execution Ah Q is technically scapegoated for a crime he has not committed, the text is careful to prevent readers from sentimentally identifying with him as a hapless victim. They know he is guilty of similar crimes, and as he disingenuously admits to his accusers, he had wanted to take part in the crime of which he is accused (523); readers also recall how he had once relished the spectacle of another's execution (509). As he is being paraded about as a public example before his execution, Ah Q is wise enough not to protest his innocence ("It seemed to him that in this world it was probably the fate of everybody at some time to have his head cut off" [525]) but to simply try to satisfy the crowd's expectations of his behavior. Again in conformity with the anthropological model of the sacrificial victim, Ah Q, in spite of his very real fear of death, perceives his execution to be an honor. As the primary participant in the ultimate spectacle of social reinforcement, in which the community's reciprocal violence is concentrated on a single victim, he basks in what the narrator has earlier termed "reflected glory": "It may have been like the case of the sacrificial beef in the Confucian temple; although the beef was in the same category as pork and mutton, being of animal origin just as they were, later Confucians did not dare touch it since the sage had enjoyed it" (494–95).

Ah Q faces his execution with aplomb until near the end, when Lu Xun introduces one of his favorite and most extreme images to revive a sense of the execution's cruelty and violence. In the last moments of his life, Ah Q grows dizzy and sees before him only a sea of eyes, which are "eager to devour more than his flesh and blood." The eyes then merge into one, "biting into his soul" (526). The same image was used in "Yao" 藥 (Medicine, 1919), where the men who gather to observe a revolutionary's execution are said to stare with a "famished look"[12] and in "Kuangren riji" 狂人日記 (The Diary of a madman,

---

11. Lu Xun, "A Q zhengzhuan" 阿Q正傳 (The true story of Ah Q, in Lu Xun, *Lu Xun quanji*, vol. 2, pp. 487–532, here p. 494. Page numbers for further citations from this story are given in the text.

12. Lu Xun, "Yao" 藥 (Medicine), in Lu Xun, *Lu Xun quanji* 1:440–49, here p. 441.

1918), where the protagonist senses the cannibalistic desires of relatives and fellow villagers primarily through their gazes. Much of the story "A Public Example" also follows the eyes of the crowd, whose scrutiny of the criminal takes on a particularly vicious quality. But in that story and in "The Diary of a Madman" the victim's own glance meets the gaze of the crowd at moments, with interesting results. At one point in "A Public Example" the character called "Fat Boy" looks up at the prisoner's eyes, which "seemed to be fixed on his head," and then hastily averts his glance.[13] Later Fat Boy notices the criminal staring at his chest and nervously inspects himself to see what is wrong.

The madman in "The Diary of a Madman" also mentions several times how his gaze disturbs those he believes are persecuting him. In the exchange of glances between oppressor and victim the direction of violence is momentarily inverted: however briefly, the observed (the arbitrarily chosen public example) becomes the observer, and the observer (the Chinese crowd, and by extension the readers themselves) becomes the observed. For a moment readers sense that the crowd's violence is rooted in just the feeling of terror their actions arouse in their victim.

Ah Q is not awarded a return glance, but at the crucial moment of his death, a sudden break in the narrative accomplishes a similar bringing-to-consciousness of the nature of his sacrifice and the observer's role in it. Just when Ah Q feels himself consumed by the eyes of the crowd, now conflated into a single monstrous eye, the psychological narration is suddenly broken by the cry "*Jiu ming* 救命! Help!" The narrator then catches himself: "But Ah Q did not utter this" (526). This phantom plea is effectively the climax of the story, replacing the expected description of Ah Q's death. It is presented as dialogue, but its status as such is immediately retracted in the line that follows. Readers are left somewhat uncertain about the plea's origins and its place in the narration: is it perhaps a cry that takes form suddenly in the mind of Ah Q, only to be silenced by his execution? The cry would then represent a belated discovery on Ah Q's part of his victimization. But perhaps, considering the paucity of interior monologue generally in the story, another interpretation can be argued: that for this brief moment the narrator's stance as disinterested storyteller is suspended,

13. Lu Xun, "Shi zhong," p. 69.

allowing him to present his personal plea for Ah Q's salvation. Ah Q is incapable of achieving the degree of self-consciousness implicit in the cry, so the narrator must help him to the thought. If this latter interpretation is correct, the narrative, which to this point has depicted the social order as a seamless web in which all are guiltily enmeshed, is here rent to allow the direct expression of an indignation that originates outside the narrated social world in the critical consciousness of the narrator.

Whether we perceive the thought as originating in the narrator's or Ah Q's mind may in the end matter little, however, considering the particular nature of the relationship between narrator and protagonist in the story. As is clear from the opening chapter, the narrator shares with Ah Q an identification that runs far deeper than the affective bonding of pity. The narrator complains that he has long felt "possessed" by his subject and observes that his own fate as an author is intimately entwined with Ah Q's: the subject of a biography "becomes known to posterity through the writing and the writing known to posterity through the subject—until finally it is not clear who is making whom known." Or more literally translated: "It is finally unclear whether people are made known through writing, or writing is made known through people [*ren yi wen chuan, wen yi ren chuan* 人以文傳，文以人傳] (487). This formulation throws into question the usual assumption of the subservience of a biographical text to its subject: does the text exist to cast reflected glory on the individual, or does the individual exist to corporealize texts and the cultural prescriptions of which they are the vessel? The narration of Ah Q's execution may simply constitute another link in the chain of substitutions (of acts of ritual sacrifice and of the representations of those acts) through which the originary violence at the heart of Chinese society is perpetuated and disseminated. The sudden narrative breakdown at the moment of Ah Q's death, at the expiration of the subject who is to make his writing "known to posterity," attests to Lu Xun's urgent need to break that chain. To save Ah Q would be not simply to rescue the individual from the anonymity of cultural processing but also to preserve the possibility of an independent critical stance unassimilable to such processing and, not incidentally, the possibility of a fiction to express it. The plea not to be cannibalized is thus both the narrator's sympathetic projection into the character Ah Q and a self-defining textual gesture distancing the "true story" of Ah Q's execution (that is, the story as understood through the critical consciousness of the narrator) from a culturally subservient narrative of ritual violence, or what we might call, using an equally likely translation of the term *zhengzhuan*, the "story proper."[14]

Chinese society, as depicted in the stories we have discussed, is a field of arbitrary significations that nevertheless exerts a binding, tyrannical influence over the lives of its individual members. Its oppressive effect is less the result of the willful manipulation of one class—whether defined in sociological or ethical terms—by another than of the impersonal, enmeshing authority of culture and tradition.[15] This authority is consolidated through acts of ritual violence, but perpetuated on a daily basis through textual governance, that is, through the intimidating power of the written word.[16] More frequently than they are made into examples through execution or public display, the characters in Lu Xun's stories are brought to submission through obedience to the written manifestations of Chinese culture: in the story "Kong Yiji" 孔乙己 (1919) the protagonist's stubborn fidelity to the traditional scholarly ideal ends in his total physical and spiritual degradation; Chen Shicheng 陳士成 in "Baiguang" 白光 (The white light, 1922) commits suicide after his failure to pass the examinations; and Ah Q's greatest embarrassment is his inability to sign the confession forced upon him (a fact made doubly ironical by his namelessness). Characters who might be thought to have mastered the art of writing are no less subject to this textual discipline. To ensure their personal survival, the intellectuals in Lu Xun's satirical stories are compelled to continue producing the textual propaganda that upholds the system, despite the obvious inequivalency of its content to the realities of their own lives. In "Shuangwu jie" 雙五節 (The

14. As the narrator points out at the beginning of the story, the term *zhengzhuan* derives from a stock phrase of the traditional novelist: "Enough of this digression, and back to the *story proper*" (488; my italics).

15. The story "Lihun" 離婚 (Divorce, 1925), in which it takes no more than the authoritative manner of Seventh Master as he calls for snuff to quell the indignation of the unusually audacious peasant girl Aigu 愛姑 ("Now she realized the full power of Seventh Master . . . and she repented bitterly" [in Lu Xun, *Lu Xun quanji* 2:152]), is an example of the way power works in Lu Xun's stories: its effect is realized less through its aggressive employment than through the fear it inspires in its victims, assisted by the complacency of bystanders.

16. The disciplinary—or in Lu Xun's favorite metaphor, the cannibalistic—nature of Chinese culture as expressed in its literary corpus is frankly indicated in "The Diary of a Madman," where the madman finds the Confucian classics filled with nothing but the two words *chi ren* 吃人 (eat people).

Double fifth festival, 1922), Teacher Fang Xuanchuo's 方玄綽 complacent acceptance of this inequivalency is expressed in his doctrine of *chabuduozhuyi* 差不多主義 (all-the-same-ism), through which he rationalizes his ethically questionable but lucrative involvement in government affairs. Similarly, the novelist protagonist of "Xingfu de jiating" 幸福的家庭 (A happy family, 1924) abandons "true art" to compose a trivial but marketable account of an ideal family that bears only a negative resemblance to the exasperating conditions of his own home life. Though not guilty of a conscious intention to exploit, such intellectuals are held morally accountable in Lu Xun's fiction because of their function as agents of the social order. Working intimately with the media through which cultural *doxa* is reproduced and disseminated, they are in a position, denied such illiterates as Ah Q, to develop a critical perspective on Chinese society and their role in it. But though an intimation of personal hypocrisy is sometimes thrust on them, as with Fang Xuanchuo, who at the close of "The Double Fifth Festival" suddenly recognizes the similarity between his own intellectual habits and his wife's superstitious behavior, in each case the illumination is resisted and the risks of a full critical consciousness go unassumed.

Clearly Lu Xun hoped that he was not himself guilty of this kind of bad faith and that his own compositions, by serving as a formal vehicle for the dissemination of a critical social consciousness, could avoid contributing to the social oppression whose textual agency they so frequently evoke. But as Lu Xun was acutely aware, representational art risks making the victim into a mere object of the reader's curiosity or pity; in the process of reading, these emotions, which significantly are those of the observer, are satisfied, thereby camouflaging the true nature of the reader's involvement with the victim. We have seen how Lu Xun employed a cinematic technique and the image of the devouring eye to establish an uncomfortable identification between reader and crowd in several of his stories. More commonly in his early stories, however, Lu Xun attempted to counter the purgative effect of representational art by using what in the preface to *The Outcry* he calls *qubi* 曲筆. This term has been translated as "innuendoes"[17] but would be better rendered as "distortions" since the word traditionally

---

17. *Qubi* 曲筆 is rendered as "innuendoes" in the translation of Yang Xianyi and Gladys Yang. See Lu Xun, *Selected Works* 1:38.

referred to deliberate misrepresentations of the truth by historians to avoid the wrath of the powerful. As Lu Xun describes them, these distortions are introduced at the closure of some of his stories to cancel their pessimistic effect. He cites the wreath that appears on the son's grave in "Medicine" and the possibility that Shan Si Saozi 單四嫂子, "Fourth Shan's Wife," dreams of her dead child in "Mingtian" 明天 (Tomorrow, 1919) as examples. One might also note the cry "Save the children!" at the end of "The Diary of a Madman" or the vision of the children's "new life" at the conclusion of "Guxiang" 故鄉 (My old home, 1921). Significantly, Lu Xun sees these as appendages, outside the formal integrity of the stories as such; because of them his works "fall far short of being works of art" (420). He has resorted to these distortions for extrinsic reasons, out of obedience to "my general's orders." Elsewhere Lu Xun makes clear whom he means by "my general": "[*The Outcry*] might also be described as 'written to order.' But the orders I carried out were those issued by the revolutionary vanguard of that time, which I was glad to obey."[18]

Lu Xun's distortions are never integrated into the work's *histoire* but operate only at the discursive or symbolic level of the text. They can indicate hope only if we assent to the intervention of the author's extrinsic symbolic imagination. The willed nature of such significations is apparent, for example, in the symbolic structure of "Medicine," not only with the wreath that Lu Xun mentions but also with the two other images that dominate the story: the blood-soaked bun that is used as a medicine and the crow that also "appears from nowhere" at the grave side. As Milena Doleželová-Velingerová has observed of the crow, these images must be given a dual interpretation: the original superstitious interpretation is replaced at closure with a "hopeful" radical one.[19] To accomplish this hermeneutical inversion, however, the story resorts to a dual strategy involving both the discursive and narrative levels of the text. The superstitious belief that an execution victim's blood will cure a child's body is disabused through emplotment (the child dies), while the hope that the revolutionary through his execution may be proffering a medicine for the country's soul is advanced symbolically. The discursive level of the

18. Lu Xun, "*Zi xuan ji zi xu*" 《自選集》自序 (Preface to *My Selected Works*), in Lu Xun, *Lu Xun quanji* 4:455–59, here p. 456.

19. See Milena Doleželová-Velingerová, "Lu Xun's 'Medicine,'" in Merle Goldman, *Modern Chinese Literature*, pp. 221–32.

story, with its revolutionary symbolism, may be said to resist the pessimism of the plot, in which traditional cultural significations are impugned.

Patrick Hanan has observed that Lu Xun's "pleas" for the future, which we have here analyzed as distortions, are to be found only in Lu Xun's first volume of stories, The Outcry.[20] The stories in his second volume, Hesitation, however, accomplish the same goal in a more sophisticated way, through the use of ironical mediating narrators. As we shall see, these narrators allow Lu Xun to posit the opening of a full critical illumination of the social order and to explore its consequences. The narrators and protagonists who are granted moments of illumination assume a particular role in the social order as it is described in Lu Xun's stories: they are all intellectual onlookers, situated morally between the crowd and its victims. "The Diary of a Madman," one of Lu Xun's earliest stories, had, of course, also taken the bearer of a full critical consciousness as a protagonist, but there the madman had been treated as a full-fledged victim of the social order. The intellectuals who people Lu Xun's later stories represent a third party, who because of their intimation of the true nature of traditional society feel a degree of alienation from it but who also continue to enjoy, however indirectly, the benefits it accords to members of the elite classes. The nature of their alienation is tested in the course of the story, often through direct confrontation with one of society's victims.[21]

The encounter between the narrator of "New Year's Sacrifice" and the character Xianglin Sao 祥林嫂, an impoverished peasant woman who has twice been taken into the narrator's home as a maid, is perhaps the paradigmatic example of such confrontations. During the

20. Patrick Hanan, "The Technique of Lu Hsün's Fiction," p. 93.
21. For another treatment of the alienated loner in Lu Xun's stories and his or her relationship with the crowd see Leo Ou-fan Lee, Voices from the Iron House, pp. 69–88. My emphasis here differs somewhat from Lee's in that I see the fundamental social configuration behind the stories not as a dyadic one (of loner and crowd) but as a triadic one (of intellectual, crowd, and victim). The intellectual feels caught between the crowd and its prey: his sense of alienation (born in part of self-pity) accords him a measure of sympathy for the victim, but as a relatively privileged member of society, he cannot avoid a sense of complicity with the crowd. The alienation that interested Lu Xun was not that of the misunderstood or frustrated individualist but that of the moral coward. All of his loners are intellectuals who achieve a degree of insight into the cannibalism of Chinese society, only to discover that they do not have the courage or wherewithal to act on their ethical instincts.

course of the story Xianglin Sao has been kidnapped and physically abused by peers from her village, but her final ruin is brought on by the symbolic and spiritual abuse more insidiously practiced by the narrator's own family. After she is forced into a second marriage, her employers treat her as contaminated, prohibiting her participation in the family sacrifices, and through idle comments awakening her doubts about an afterlife. In a crucial scene Xianglin Sao shocks the narrator, who has been educated abroad and prides himself on his enlightened thinking, by cornering him and asking, "Do dead people have souls or not?"[22] This question, though apparently superstitious, directly addresses the question of the cannibalized victim's fate: can those sacrificed for the maintenance of an orderly society be simply buried and forgotten, or does the violence of their deaths leave ineradicable scars on the social body? Can such as Ah Q in fact be saved? The intellectual, in evading the victim's question ("I am not sure" [8]), exposes both his intellectual poverty and, more profoundly, his moral cowardice. Xianglin Sao's question, by undermining the authority of the intellectual's social position, which is predicated on both moral and intellectual leadership, momentarily awakens in him an intimation of his complicity in the collective act of violence against her. But the intellectual, as always in Lu Xun's stories, proves unfaithful both to the victim and to his own insight. By pitying Xianglin Sao, he reduces his understanding of her situation to a purely affective involvement, which may then be purged through catharsis. At the end of the story, the narrator is suddenly freed of all the doubts that had plagued him as he considered Xianglin Sao's tragic story: "I felt only that the saints of heaven and earth had accepted the sacrifice and incense and were reeling with intoxication in the sky, preparing to give Luzhen's 魯鎮 people boundless good fortune" (21).

Such moments of purgation, in which the intellectual narrator feels a sudden uplift that is often incongruous with the events related in the story, are common at the conclusions of Lu Xun's later stories. After the narrator of "Zai jiulou shang" 在酒樓上 (In the wineshop, 1924) hears his friend Lü Weifu's 呂緯甫 confession of complete disillusionment, he walks away from the hotel feeling "refreshed."[23] The narra-

22. Lu Xun, "Zhufu" 祝福 (New Year's sacrifice), in Lu Xun, *Lu Xun quanji* 2:5–23, here p. 7. Page numbers for further citations from this story are given in the text.
23. Lu Xun, "Zai jiulou shang" 在酒樓上 (In the wineshop), in Lu Xun, *Lu Xun quanji* 2:24–34, here p. 34.

tor of "The Misanthrope" unexpectedly cries out in "anger and sorrow mingled with agony" upon seeing his friend Wei Lianshu's 魏連殳 corpse laid out, but "then my heart felt lighter, and I paced calmly on along the damp cobbled road under the moon."[24] These passages can only represent the cathartic moment in which the narrator's weighty sense of identification with a victimized friend or acquaintance is exorcised. The response of readers to these moments depends largely on their attitude toward the narrator, who mediates the experience for them. The narrators have to varying extents been equated with Lu Xun himself, but the significant point of resemblance is their shared class status, which allows them access to the written language by which they can give a voice to "silent China." This tool endows them with the power to narrate the life of the other classes and thereby to inscribe meaning on the social body as a whole. But because these narrators and their class have failed in this task of writing, the Chinese people are "like a great dish of loose sand."[25] Although readers share the emotional satisfaction expressed at closure, their awareness of the narrator's moral failure obstructs the story's full cathartic effect and raises questions about the moral utility of such narratives.

These questions are explored in a resonant way in one of Lu Xun's most troubling stories, "In the Wineshop." The narrative heart of the story is the simple tale of a boatman's daughter, Ashun 阿順, who grows ill and dies after learning of the marriage that has been arranged for her. But in the telling of this tale Lu Xun employs multiple narrative levels that substantially distance the discursive level of the text from the central event of the plot. The circumstances of Ashun's death are first told to the narrator's friend, Lü Weifu, by the boatman's neighbor; Lü Weifu then relates them to the "I" of the narrative. None of these narrators has a direct role in Ashun's tragedy, and they are only very tenuously related to each other (Lü Weifu, though a friend— "if such he would still let me call him"—of the narrator, has been out of touch for ten years and runs into the narrator purely by chance). It is as though Lu Xun had set up these narrative layers out of an extraordinary delicacy not unlike that of Lü Weifu, who hesitates to call

24. Lu Xun, "Guduzhe" 孤獨者 (The misanthrope), in Lu Xun, *Lu Xun quanji* 2:86–109, here p. 108.

25. Lu Xun, "Wusheng de Zhongguo" 無聲的中國 (Silent China), in Lu Xun, *Lu Xun quanji* 4:11–17, here p. 12.

on Ashun to bring her the sprigs of artificial flowers she once desired: "You have no idea how I dread calling on people, much more so than in the old days. Because I know what a nuisance I am, I am even sick of myself; so knowing this, why inflict myself on others?"[26] But Lü Weifu's delicacy in fact masks a fear that direct involvement with Ashun will force him to face the moral dilemma that their class separation entails, a confrontation to which he does not feel equal.

The many layers of narration that Lu Xun employs in "In the Wineshop" succeed, finally, not in shielding the narrator from Ashun's tragedy but in extending the range of responsibility for it. The boatman's neighbor ignorantly blames her story on "fate"; Lü Weifu dismisses it as "a futile affair" and returns to giving instruction in the Confucian classics. Both, although touched by Ashun's story, ultimately reinstate it in a system of meaning (superstition in the case of the neighbor, Confucianism in the case of Lü Weifu) that can only continue to reproduce such stories. Both of them are thus touched by the moral contamination that irradiates from the story of her death. But since the primary narrator, the "I" of the narration, walks away from his encounter with Lü Weifu feeling "refreshed," having succeeded in his intention to "escape the boredom" of his stay precisely by being entertained with the story of Ashun, perceptive readers cannot but see that his narrative, the story "In the Wineshop" itself, has not escaped that contamination. It is as much a violation of Ashun as the two narratives that it mediates.

By self-consciously exposing the cathartic operation of realist fiction through his ironical epiphanies, Lu Xun offers in these stories a radical critique of his own method and of the realist project in general. Realism, he implies, risks making authors accomplices to the social cruelty they intend to decry. The realist narrative, by imitating at a formal level the relation of oppressor to oppressed, is captive to the logic of that oppression and ends by merely reproducing it. As the title of his second collection suggests, many of Lu Xun's experiments in the short story form turn in on themselves and hesitate between speech and silence, between the assertive act of fictional creation and a metafictional retraction of that act. This hesitation mirrors formally the emotional vacillation of which Lu Xun frequently complained.

---

26. Lu Xun, "Zai jiulou shang," p. 8.

Though he several times admitted that he found "only darkness and nothingness" to be real[27] and that it was "only by coming down in the world that one learned what society was really like,"[28] he was unwilling in his writings to submit entirely to the "darkness" of reality. In the story "Tomorrow" the narrator observes: "Fourth Shan's Wife was a simple woman who did not know what a fearful word *but* is. Thanks to this *but*, many bad things turn out well and many good things turn out badly."[29] Lu Xun's stories are in fact predicated on this *but*: in "Tomorrow," Fourth Shan's Wife uses the word to express a superstitious hope that fate will spare her child from suffering ("But maybe Bao'er 寶兒 is only bad at night; when the sun comes out tomorrow, his fever may go and he may breathe more easily again" [451]), while the plot of "Tomorrow" uses it to disabuse her of hope and expose the cruelty and ineffectuality of superstition. Finally, however, with the introduction of a distortion (as Lu Xun explains in his preface, "But since this was a call to arms...I did not say that Fourth Shan's Wife never dreamed of her little boy" [419]) the narration employs the adversative a third time to reintroduce a note of hope.

The gate to critical consciousness that Lu Xun's stories wish to open is a revolving door hinged on the adversative *but* from which, once entered, the reader can never escape. Wavering between disillusionment and hope, Lu Xun exposes and obstructs the fictional effects he introduces. His ruthless introspection ends by disturbing the model of realist fiction he adopted from the West by undermining both the assured objectivity of the observer and the complacency of the reader's cathartic response. In his postscript to *The Grave*, Lu Xun asks whether he is building a monument in his essays or digging his own grave.[30] So too his stories appear at once constructive and destructive (or deconstructive) of both the larger cultural heritage and of their own effect on the reader. As other writers inherited the new fictional model Lu Xun's stories presented, they took on as well the profound moral doubts and formal uncertainties that inform them.

---

27. Letter to Xu Guangping 許廣平, 18 March 1925, in Lu Xun, *Lu Xun quanji* 11:19–22, here pp. 20–21.
28. Lu Xun, "Zi xu," p. 415.
29. Lu Xun, "Mingtian" 明天 (Tomorrow), in Lu Xun, *Lu Xun quanji* 1:450–57, here p. 451.
30. Lu Xun, "Xie zai *Fen* houmian," p. 282.

YE SHAOJUN: PITY, SINCERITY, AND
THE DIVISIVE POWER OF NARRATIVE

Lu Xun's short stories constitute a small portion of his literary output and are the product of a brief creative period in the late 1910s and early 1920s, when Lu Xun had already reached middle age. Ye Shaojun, also known by the pen name Ye Shengtao 葉聖陶, was a considerably more prolific writer of fiction. Between 1922 and 1936 he published six volumes of short stories and one of the first Chinese novels in the contemporary colloquial language, *Ni Huanzhi* 倪煥之 (1929). In fact, Ye began publishing fiction as early as 1914, when he was twenty years old; in that year alone nineteen of his stories (all composed in the classical language) appeared in the popular Shanghai magazine *Libailiu* 禮拜六 (Saturday).[31] Although these early stories were written in part because Ye needed the income they provided, Ye insisted that he had approached their composition seriously, that (borrowing a phrase that had from ancient times been used to disparage fictional composition) they were intended as something more than "idle talk of the streets" (*jie tan xiang yu* 街談巷語).[32] The historian Gu Jiegang 顧頡剛, a childhood classmate and lifelong friend, was later to concur with this appraisal, insisting that Ye had from the start "aimed at realism, not at illusion," and thus "had nothing in common with the popular romantic and humorous schools of fiction."[33] Given this earnest attitude toward fiction writing, Ye Shaojun perhaps inevitably became disenchanted with the political and cultural stance of commercial magazines like *Saturday*; in 1917, when the publishers distributed an advertisement whose copy ran "I'd rather subscribe to *Saturday* than take a concubine," Ye was overwhelmed with disgust and discontinued his association with the magazine. He turned his energies instead to his teaching job in the countryside not far from Suzhou and apparently did not write another story until 1919. In that year Gu Jiegang, now a member of the reformist Xinchao she 新潮社 (New tide society) at Beijing University, wrote to Ye, inviting him to

31. Shang Jinlin 商金林, "Ye Shengtao nianpu" 葉聖陶年譜 (A chronology of Ye Shengtao's life), *Xin wenxue shiliao* 1 (1981), pp. 253–67, here p. 258. For a discussion of these early stories see Chen Liao, *Ye Shengtao pingzhuan*, pp. 20–30.
32. Ye Shaojun, letter to Gu Jiegang 顧頡剛, 13 November 1914; quoted in Chen Liao, *Ye Shengtao pingzhuan*, p. 21.
33. Gu Jiegang, "Xu" 序 (Preface) to Ye Shaojun, *Gemo*, pp. 1–17, here pp. 13–16.

join the organization and suggesting that he write some pieces for publication in the society's journal. Ye, who had been eagerly absorbing the ideas of the New Literature movement, responded quickly, submitting the story "Yisheng" 一生 (A life) for publication in the March edition of Xinchao 新潮 (New tide). In the following months he proceeded to publish a series of stories in the vernacular language, as well as several essays on such topics as educational reform and women's issues. These attracted the attention of Mao Dun and Zheng Zhenduo, who late in the winter of 1920 were organizing what was to become the Association for Literary Studies; they invited Ye Shaojun to become one of its twelve founding members and shortly thereafter visited Shanghai to make his acquaintance. By 1921 Ye was thus emerging as one of the most promising figures of the New Literature movement.

Ye's years of apprenticeship as a writer and his fecundity allow us to examine his developmental pattern, which was in fact characteristic of many Chinese realists. Whereas Lu Xun's stories, as the mature product of a rigorously examined life, allow the expression of self and class concerns only in a highly indirect manner, Ye Shaojun's early works are characterized by a high degree of self-reference and sentimentality. As he developed in his craft, Ye Shaojun clearly worked to eliminate these elements from his fiction in the interests of a more objective representation of his social environment. Though he continued to use autobiographical materials, he struggled to achieve greater distance between his life and its mediated expression in his fiction. This process of growth has been applauded as "maturation" toward realism by several critics,[34] but perhaps because of the nature of Ye's early aesthetic philosophy, in his case this maturity may have been achieved at a high cost. In the essays collected under the title On the Literary Arts, which were written in 1921, just as he was coming into his own as a writer of short stories, Ye Shaojun argued that composition should be understood as a kind of self-cultivation through which authors foster in themselves the virtues of pity and sincerity. But as

34. See, for example, Yang Yi 楊義, "Lun Ye Shengtao duanpian xiaoshuo de yishu tese" 論葉聖陶短篇小說的藝術特色 (On the artistic characteristics of Ye Shengtao's short stories) (Zhongguo xiandai wenxue yanjiu congkan 2 [1980], pp. 201–22), and Ren Guangtian 任廣田, "Cong Gemo dao Ni Huanzhi—lun Ye Shengtao ershi niandai de chuangzuo sixiang" 從《隔膜》到《倪煥之》—論葉聖陶二十年代的創作思想 (From Barriers to Ni Huanzhi: on Ye Shengtao's theories of writing in the twenties) (Zhongguo xiandai wenxue yanjiu congkan 4 [1980]: 209–25).

we have seen, realism as an aesthetic form assumes an ambivalent view of both these virtues: because of realism's dual claim to be at once fact and fiction, the voice of the realist narrator inevitably contains a measure of artifice and is therefore not fully "genuine"; moreover, realist works induce the emotion of pity only with the ultimate intention of purging it through catharsis. As we shall see, Ye Shaojun's early commitment to these values as important not only to daily life but to the activity of writing itself, led him to resist certain of realism's formal characteristics and thus influenced in a significant way the development of his art.

Despite his more considerable fictional output, Ye Shaojun was even less of a natural storyteller than Lu Xun was. Discussing the predominant influences on his fiction, he wrote that epic and adventure fiction interested him little. It was the style (literally, the *biqu* 筆趣, or "stylistic allure") of Washington Irving's sketches and Oliver Goldsmith's fiction that most attracted him in his youth.[35] As Jaroslev Průšek has observed, Ye's early fiction is also indebted to traditional Chinese literary jottings (*biji* 筆記) and ballads, as well as the writings of such Western realists as Turgenev and Chekhov.[36] These diverse models all share a preoccupation with locale and mood and generally exhibit a highly restrained use of narrative resources. Emplotment, to the extent that it is allowed, appears always to derive from something close at hand. Ye himself described the source matter of his stories as follows:

> I've lived in cities and in towns; I witnessed some small part of life in those places, so I wrote about what I saw. I've been a teacher and exposed to educational circles, so I wrote about that. I've had some superficial acquaintance with the events of the Chinese revolution as it developed, so that became my subject as well. Almost all the characters in my fiction are either intellectuals or the urban bourgeoisie because those are the groups with which I am familiar; I don't understand workers or peasants any more than I understand wealthy merchants and bureaucrats.[37]

35. Ye Shaojun, "Za tan wo de xiezuo" 雜談我的寫作 (Miscellaneous comments on my writings), in Ye Shengtao, *Ye Shengtao lun chuangzuo*, pp. 149–55, here p. 151.
36. Jaroslev Průšek, "Yeh Shao-chün and Anton Chekhov," in his *The Lyrical and the Epic*, pp. 178–94.
37. Ye Shaojun, "*Ye Shengtao xuanji* zixu" 《葉聖陶選集》自序 (Author's preface to *Selected Works of Ye Shengtao*), in Ye Shengtao, *Ye Shengtao lun chuangzuo*, pp. 194–98, here p. 195.

As a consequence of Ye's reluctance to go beyond the part of life that he had personally observed, the narrative situations in his stories tend to be grounded in domestic or local life, and his use of plot tends to be highly restrained (as we have observed, Ye associated contrived plot machinations with popular fiction, which he felt catered shamelessly to the audience's predilection for sensation and scandal). Even when Ye does treat significant historical or political events in his fiction, he does so indirectly: the story "Ye" 夜 (Night, 1927), for example, which concerns Jiang Jieshi's 1927 massacre of Communist sympathizers, views that calamity through the eyes of an old woman and a child as they come to terms with the death of their family members. Similarly, in Ni Huanzhi, Ye Shaojun avoids a direct portrayal of the revolutionary events of 1927, presenting them only through fragmented allusions in the protagonist's memory; as Mao Dun was to complain, this indirectness has the effect of robbing Ye's novel of a sense of historical immediacy.[38]

The downplaying of plot in Ye Shaojun's fiction results in an increased focus on psychological and emotional realities. At the center of many of the stories in Ye's first collection, Gemo 隔膜 (Barriers, 1922), is a lyric epiphany, for which the narrative workings appear no more than a staging. Characters too are not so much developed as sketched in as necessary adjuncts to the emotional elevation of the epiphany; often they are nameless and designated only by pronouns. A work such as "Bukuai zhi gan" 不快之感 (An unhappy feeling, 1920), in which the narrator struggles to overcome a vague, inexplicable sense of discomfort, is little more than an exercise in emotional hermeneutics. If in such works Ye risks descending into solipsism, that danger is offset somewhat by the nature of the emotional epiphany that is attained or sought. The stories invariably dramatize the presence or absence of tongqing, "fellow feeling" or "pity." Tongqing figures most forcefully—and sentimentally—in the relationship of mother and child in such stories as "Mu" 母 (Mother, 1920) and "Yi he ta" 伊和他 (She and he, 1920).

When Gu Jiegang complains in his preface to Barriers that the title of the collection inadequately represents its contents, he points to the

___

38. Mao Dun, "Du Ni Huanzhi" 讀《倪煥之》(On reading Ni Huanzhi), Wenxue zhoubao 8, no. 20 (12 May 1929); reprinted in Mao Dun, Mao Dun wenyi zalun ji, pp. 277–94, here p. 286.

stories that evoke a deep communion between characters. The title is appropriate, he writes, only to those few stories, such as the title story, "A Life," and "Yige pengyou" 一個朋友 (A friend, 1920), which take as their subject the social barriers that separate individuals. The distinction Gu marks here is a real one, but not, as he seems to suggest, of thematic consequence. Both kinds of stories share a common ethical preoccupation, of which they are the positive and negative formulation: the barriers of the title are precisely the psychological and social obstructions that inhibit consciousness of *tongqing*. The stories differ, however, in their strategic representation of this moral concern and in their management of the plot. In what might be called the sentimental stories the protagonist is permitted to achieve a lyric awareness of *tongqing*, which readers are invited to experience sympathetically. The redemptive value of the experience is then affirmed by the text discursively, rather than dramatized. For example, the story "Chun you" 春遊 (A spring outing, 1920), in which a married woman experiences an intense feeling of communion with both her husband and the natural surroundings while strolling by a lake one day, concludes: "Her life was as before, unaltered. But she stubbornly held on to her memory of that feeling, and in light of that feeling, you couldn't say that her life was unchanged."[39] The woman's epiphany is credited with powers of spiritual transformation that significantly remain closed off from narrative; at the level of the plot, "nothing has changed."

Much, however, changes, if to little effect, in stories of the other variety, which we might call melodramatic. The frequently anthologized "A Life," for example, takes the form of a brief biography, but its protagonist's life, a busy tale of mistreatment, flight, and widowhood, is denied the spiritual elevation that would lift it above melodrama. The animation of the plotting appears meaningless as long as the spiritual elevation of *tongqing* is denied. It is finally left to the narrator to proffer a sense of the protagonist's humanity, since she is herself denied consciousness of it. What was declared in the original title of the story, "Zhe ye shi yige ren" 這也是一個人 (This too is a human being),[40] is now communicated through a thin veil of irony in the animal references that are repeated throughout the story. "She" is

39. Ye Shaojun, "Chun you" 春遊 (A spring outing), in *Gemo*, pp. 6–9, here p. 9.
40. Shang Jinlin gives this as the original title for the story in his "Ye Shengtao nianpu," p. 261.

nothing more than a kind of chattel: to her family "she was an ox, not entitled to any opinions of her own; so now that they had no further use for her, they had better sell her off."[41] Dimly conscious only of her sorrow and able to express herself only through tears, she is less a positively defined character than an affective sponge, steeped in the authorial emotion of *tongqing*. Closure brings the narrator's regretful awareness of the "barriers" that deny individuals the spiritual elevation that would give meaning to their lives and invites readers to make up that lack—and indulge their own sense of moral superiority—by extending pity to the captive or blinded characters of the fiction. Taken together, the two kinds of stories in *Barriers* clearly assert the greater authenticity of the lyrical interludes that the protagonists of the sentimental stories enjoy over the exuberant plotting of the melodramas; it is as if Ye believed the events of a life are nothing but meaningless distractions from its psychological and spiritual realities.

On a deeper level, Ye Shaojun's resistance to narrative arises from apprehensions about the operation of time in the world, for time drives the purposeless activity depicted in the stories, activity that in turn generates social barriers. Invariably in Ye Shaojun's stories, the individual experiences time as a process of disillusionment, as a falling away from the consummate awareness of *tongqing* figured in the mutual attentions of mother and child. Perhaps the most suggestive of all the stories in Ye's first collection is "Ku cai" 苦菜 (Bitter greens, 1921), which concerns an attempt to counter the forces of disillusionment by cultivating a personal sense of growth and productivity. The story begins with the narrator's description of a plot of vacant land behind his house, which is used by "cheeky youngsters" as a playground. The narrator views their play as a "waste" of the land, so he has the plot fenced off to make a garden. His purpose in taking up gardening is not pragmatic, however, but spiritual: he harbors "a fervent, profound hope that this piece of empty land will be the spring of my new life."[42] Indeed, at first he feels empowered by the simple physical labor of sowing the stubbly soil. His perception of spiritual decay is replaced with a vital sense of the self's ripening: "I didn't feel time passing; no thought or emotion troubled me. I was transformed!

41. Ye Shaojun, "Yisheng" 一生, in *Gemo*, pp. 1–5, here p. 5. This story has been translated by Wenxue as "A Life," in Ye Shengtao, *How Mr. Pan Weathered the Storm*, pp. 13–17.
42. Ye Shaojun, "Ku cai" 苦菜 (Bitter greens), in *Gemo*, pp. 79–91, here p. 80.

Power [*li* 力] is I, I am power; the development of I-Power is true time" (84). But as he waits for the garden to grow, this vitality gives way to a growing feeling of impatience. In the end, his exaggerated idealism simply induces anxiety.

The mingling of hope and restlessness in the narrator's psychology is set in marked contrast to the attitude of the long-suffering gardener, Futang 福堂, whom the narrator enlists to help him. For Futang farming is a detested routine, whose "flavor" is bitter like the vegetables the narrator's gardening project predictably produces. Farming provides Futang with a living but no personal satisfaction; it can at best be endured. To the narrator's dismay, Futang shows no "pity" for the damaged or undeveloped plants and dreams only of freeing himself from dependence on the land (he dreams, perhaps, of the untrammeled merrymaking that the children once enjoyed but that the narrator has now banished from the garden). In a way typical of Ye Shaojun's early stories, Futang's misery provides the occasion for a wave of authorial *tongqing* followed by the formulation of a transferable moral: the narrator recognizes that he is no better than the gardener, that he has allowed his other endeavors—pedagogy and the "life of art"—to become routinized. The encounter here between classes, the intellectual bent on his spiritual development, the farmer on survival, is finally not allowed the critical illumination such confrontations elicited in Lu Xun's stories. In the airing of platitudes with which the story concludes, Futang's misery is assuaged by moral self-congratulation. But if the narrator's project of self-cultivation fails in part because he has violated his class role (by engaging in an inappropriate activity), at a deeper level it miscarries because the narrator has not understood the nature of time, which, as the parent of disillusionment, may be endured or transcended but never mastered.

By the time his second collection of stories, *Huozai* 火災 (Conflagration, 1923), was published, Ye had matured considerably in his art. Stylistically, the stories in *Conflagration* are written in a purer colloquial language, exhibiting fewer evidences of archaic vocabulary and grammatical compressions. There is a discernible movement away from the exploration of emotional states for their own sake toward more self-contained narratives. The plotting of the stories has become more complex and assured, and a new self-consciousness about narrators and their role in the transmission of the story makes itself felt. Often the narrator takes on the persona of eavesdropper or father confessor: in such stories as "Xiaoxing" 曉行 (Morning walk, 1921), "Beiai de zhongzai" 悲哀的重載 (Tragic load, 1921), and "Lülu de banlü" 旅路的伴侶 (Traveling companion, 1921), the details of the story are overheard by the narrator or eagerly related to him by the protagonist during a chance encounter. The narratives thus disclosed are further material on which the authorial emotion of *tongqing* may be exercised, and the narrator's sympathetic response is duly recorded. But the narrator's role as outsider secures a personal distance from the events recounted, as a result of which his sympathetic response, however sincere, seems ineffectual. By providing an opportunity for the protagonist to air his complaints, the text for its duration draws him out of the stream of events into a timeless moral and affectional sphere of the narrator's making. But in the absence of any sustained relationship with the character, the narrator can offer neither to relieve his suffering in practical terms nor to provide long-term spiritual consolation. Closure, where the narrator and the protagonist are forced to part ways, brings only a resigned recognition of the inevitable return of the quotidian.

In these stories Ye Shaojun seems to have lost his earlier confidence in the power of *tongqing* to bring about real spiritual transformation and to have concurrently ceded a new authority to time and its effects. The process of erosion through which the characters' cherished ideals and ambitions are disabused takes on an ever-greater sense of inevitability. *Tongqing* increasingly seems to be operable only within the boundaries of the text itself; and once the reach of the narrator's pity is limited in this way, it inevitably becomes subject to a cathartic purging at closure. As a result, new questions arise concerning the efficacy of such values as pity and sincerity. In what follows, I will look briefly at two stories, the title story of *Conflagration* and "Yunyi" 雲翳 (Nebulae, 1921), that specifically address these questions and in a larger sense probe the role of writing itself in the self's struggle to win a correspondence between personal moral ideals and the exigencies of the time-bound external world.

At the opening of "Conflagration," the protagonist Yan Xin 言信, who was in fact modeled on an acquaintance of Ye Shaojun,[43] is pointedly associated with the primary virtues of sincerity and pity that

43. Yan Xin 言信 was modeled on the poet Xu Yunuo 徐玉諾. The events narrated in "Bitter Greens" were also based on an actual incident in Ye Shaojun's life, according to Shang Jinlin, "Fang Ye Sheng lao de di erge guxiang, Luzhi" 訪葉聖老的第二

Ye Shaojun everywhere preaches: his name means "speaks truth," and his first act in the story is to calm the narrator's restless infant with his sympathetic attention. He explains his success with the child in the following way: "We must attend to her wholeheartedly so that her little heart will be comforted completely, so that she will be cocooned in happiness. If we let our attention stray just a little, she feels it immediately and cries out for reassurance" (157). But Yan Xin's capacity for *tongqing*, however useful in pacifying the child, is ineffective in the adult world, which appears to have abandoned itself to the cynical pursuit of "excitement." Life in Yan Xin's hometown, which he describes to the narrator, is a clear example of this: besieged by warlords, who themselves seem motivated by a pure passion for adventure, the peasants have perversely grown to enjoy the bandit attacks as a diversion from the routines of village life. In context we understand that this psychological distemper is simply a variation of the child's restlessness, a debased expression of the natural human need for sympathy and attention. This need is the tinder for the conflagration that eventually consumes the town: "Yan Xin's prophecy was now realized; the fire in men's hearts had incited an actual conflagration" (162). Yan Xin himself has fallen victim to the general passion for stimulation; as he confesses to the narrator in a resigned and self-contemptuous tone, he has been so scarred by events that he too has adopted the "mad" spirit of the other villagers.

The narrator, on hearing Yan Xin's confession, performs his only act in the story that has any effect on the plot: he proposes that Yan Xin compose an account of the conflagration in his village for the enlightenment of those on the outside. Yan Xin responds to the suggestion with enthusiasm: "Conflagration! That will be my sole project when I get back there! Never mind about the others, I will mail it directly to you chapter by chapter" (161). The narrator apparently thinks the writing project he has suggested will serve as a therapy for his friend, but Yan Xin, who is "powerfully stimulated" by the suggestion, clearly views it as simply another means of appealing for the attention of a sympathetic other. The narrator's writing contract thus plays directly on both Yan Xin's desire for *tongqing* and his craving

---

個故鄉角直 (On visiting Ye Shenglao's second hometown, Luzhi). See Chen Liao, *Ye Shengtao pingzhuan*, pp. 68–69. Page numbers given in the text for citations from "Huozai" and "Yunyi" refer to Ye Shaojun's collection *Huozai* (pp. 156–66 and pp. 64–74, respectively).

for stimulation. Significantly, for his part the narrator offers no more than the promise of a deferred sympathy in payment for Yan Xin's report. When, after a long period of waiting, he receives only an occasional letter from Yan Xin recounting his growing spiritual "numbness" and final surrender to malaria, the narrator's disappointment at the failure of the writing contract appears to override what concern he feels for his friend's ill health. His emotional investment in Yan Xin's account of the conflagration betrays a curiosity finally not distinguishable from the thrill seeking in which the villagers are engaged, but he is careful to risk exposing himself to the conflagration only indirectly. The narrative transaction thus allows the narrator to indulge in a show of *tongqing* without getting burnt. For Yan Xin, the urge to return home to the locus of a primal experience of *tongqing* and examine the subsequent decay proves self-destructive; he is able to speak the truth but unable to write it. A number of questions are suspended at the conclusion of the story. If writing as a moral project is, as Ye defines it in his critical writings, "speaking truth" by penetrating beyond the world of narratable events to a "home" of primal emotions, what is pure writing if not the silencing of narrative? Is the act of narration—such as that the narrator himself accomplishes in relating Yan Xin's story—simply part of the mad search for stimulation that consumes the adult world?

In "Nebulae," as in "Conflagration," Ye Shaojun did not so much tell a story as document a disturbance in narrative production. The story opens with the protagonist Meng Qing's 孟青 pious reflections on husband and wife as "one body," in which he scornfully dismisses notions of individual freedom and privacy as the source of barriers between people. But Meng Qing, a writer of fiction, then ironically proceeds to compose a story that casts doubt on the sincerity of a conjugal relationship. In the story-within-the-story a character named Mr. Fu 附, writing a letter to his wife, begins to relate a dream in which he conversed about art with an ill-defined female presence in a highly romantic garden setting. In the dream he felt that "for the first time in his life he had entrusted his innermost feelings to a human companion" (71). But as he writes he grows fearful that the content of the dream will cause his wife to doubt his full affection for her, and in the end he lies, telling her she is the one he encountered in the dream. The bad faith involved in Mr. Fu's suppression of the true nature of his dream is then repeated by Meng Qing himself, who, having completed his story, has second thoughts about publishing it: will his own wife doubt him, mistaking what was produced from "observation of others" for a reflection of his own true feelings? Mr. Fu's dream is at the heart of a complex series of revelations and concealments. If the dream itself is a thought buried in the subconscious mind, this thought is first revealed in its subversive significance to Mr. Fu as he writes, then suppressed in the letter he writes to his wife; it is then exhumed in the story that Meng Qing composes about Mr. Fu, suppressed again when Meng Qing burns the story ("burying the story in ashes and in his heart" [74]), and finally brought to light a final time in the story as we read it. As a manifestation of the unconscious mind, the dream is understood to represent the spontaneous, unfalsifiable "heart" of the dreamer. Its message is less the temptation of sexual infidelity than the suggestion that full honesty is possible only with a shadow figure of one's subconscious. The implicit solipsism of this message undermines the eager protestations of total conjugal communion made both by Meng Qing at the opening of the story and by Mr. Fu, who has gone so far as to claim an equivalency between his writing and his subjective self: "These are not my words, not my writing, but the beat of my heart" (69). Both Mr. Fu and Meng Qing take writing to be the expression and affirmation of their powers of *tongqing*, but in the process of articulating their personal feelings, what they write is twisted into something directly contrary to their intentions. They are forced finally to falsify or destroy what they have written in order to secure conjugal harmony and preserve their ideological authority. Much is made in the story of the "boundless" sensation of listlessness against which Mr. Fu struggles as he begins to compose his letter; in context this listlessness may be understood as a natural psychological resistance to the revelatory, divisive power of writing. If writing inevitably works against an author's best intentions and, as it were, destroys the trusting relationship with its audience that it simultaneously purports to build, this struggle should result either in the abandonment of writing or in the repudiation of doctrines that demand impossible standards of personal honesty and fellow feeling. The story "Nebulae" does not make such a choice, however, but, as if operating in opposition to the best intentions of its author, manages concurrently to express a profound suspicion of writing and to demystify the communalizing value of *tongqing*.

The complicated narrative embeddings in "Nebulae" allow Ye

Shaojun to explore the changes a story kernel (here, the dream) undergoes as it becomes the property of successive narrators, each of whom
relates it from his own point of view. Mr. Fu tells his dream in the first
person of the romanticists; Meng Qing chooses the third person of
much realist fiction. Neither mode of telling the story, however, has
quite the effect we might expect: writing in the first person does not
ensure Mr. Fu's honesty, despite his insistence that he speaks directly
from the heart; nor does writing in the third person provide Meng
Qing with immunity from the events and emotions he recounts, for, as
he realizes, the reader may suspect that he has simply transferred his
own feelings onto his characters. Mr. Fu's account is not unadulter-
ated self-expression, for he cannot drive from his mind the likely reaction of his reader (in this case, his wife); nor is Meng Qing's account a
fully disinterested, objective report, for his very selection of materials
is conditioned by a private interest in the theme they illustrate. In
either mode of telling the story, both subjective and social (or mimetic)
motives are at work. The compositional problem explored in the story
thus converges with the ethical dilemma that everywhere haunted Ye
Shaojun: both in form and content Ye was wrestling with the problem
of how to reconcile subjectively derived ethical imperatives with an
intransigent social environment, that is, how to externalize the self
without falsifying it.

It is perhaps not coincidental that concurrent with the composition
of such works, which suggest that writing is itself a disillusioning
force, Ye for the first time began to write stories that display a true
mastery of conventional realist techniques. In such stories as "Fan" 飯
(Rice, 1921) from *Conflagration*, and in many of the stories from the
three collections that followed in the 1920s, *Xianxia* 綫下 (Under the
line, 1925), *Chengzhong* 城中 (In the city, 1926), and *Weiyan ji*
未厭集 (Without satiety, 1928), Ye was able to objectify his ethical
concerns in narratives that appeal minimally to an authorially affirmed
lyricism or didacticism. Realism comes to be understood not simply as
a convenient medium for the thematic treatment of the experience of
disillusionment but as the consummate formal expression of a disabused consciousness. Despite its purported representational fidelity,
realism seems to offer, not a closer correspondence of text to external
world, but a reinforced sense of the line that divides them. This formal
division is reflected thematically in the stories by an increasing polarization of society and the individual. The interest in psychological ex-

ploration many critics have observed in Ye's works[44] is matched by a new abstraction of the social world as a controlling force in individuals' lives. In such stories as "Gudu" 孤獨 (Alone, 1923), "Chunguang bushi ta de le" 春光不是她的了 (Not hers the spring light, 1924), and "Weipo" 微波 (Ripples, 1926), individual characters do not simply undergo disillusionment at the hands of a cruel society but are depicted as permanently haunted by private emotions of loneliness and bitterness that are its reified product. Alienation, however, is not the only result of the disjunction between the social sphere and the individual psyche. To operate in a treacherous and competitive social environment, the individual is forced to construct a variety of self-serving social personae. In several stories reminiscent of Lu Xun's satirical fiction, Ye Shaojun exposes the resulting hypocrisy, manifested in the behavior of pedagogues and other petty bourgeois intellectuals.

Many of these satirical stories are set in schools and thus foreshadow Ye's most expansive fictional effort, *Ni Huanzhi.* Ye Shaojun had a lifelong interest in education: unable to attend university because of his family's straitened financial circumstances, he began teaching at the age of eighteen. Of the many teaching assignments he undertook in the years that followed, the one that had the greatest influence on him was at a middle school in the town of Luzhi 甪直, located not far from his home city of Suzhou 蘇州; a school mate of Ye's named Wu Binruo 吳賓若 established an experimental school there in 1917 and invited Ye Shaojun to join the staff. Ye accepted the offer and worked there until 1921; he later took the Luzhi school as a model for the fictional school in *Ni Huanzhi.* Wu Binruo shared many of Ye Shaojun's pedagogical ideals and proved a sympathetic headmaster. Ye's theory of education, outlined in several articles in the late 1910s and 1920s, emphasized the need to combine "knowledge and action, training and life." Social progress, he argued, in fact depended on the nourishment of "healthy individuals" in the schools.[45] As we shall see, similar ideals governed his fictional alter ego Ni Huanzhi's attitude toward education.

Ye Shaojun wrote about his move to Luzhi that "because of my

44. See, for example, Yang Yi, "Lun Ye Shengtao duanpian xiaoshuo de yishu tese," pp. 207–13.
45. Ye Shaojun, "Xiaoxue jiaoyu de gaizao" 小學教育的改造 (Educational reform in primary schools), *Xinchao* 2, no. 2 (1 December 1919).

youth and ignorance, I had come to feel after three years of teaching that it was a dull, unfulfilling profession; only after arriving in Luzhi did I realize that there was much to like in it after all."[46] Ye insisted that his early frustration with teaching had been the fault not of his students but of his narrow-minded colleagues,[47] who lacked the idealism of the progressive educators at Luzhi and as a result became alienated both from their students and from society at large. The picture of the pedagogue that emerges from Ye's stories reflects these frustrations, but it is also informed by sympathy. Teachers had been the butt of satire in some traditional Chinese fiction (such as the eighteenth-century novel *Rulin waishi* 儒林外史 [The scholars]), but the teachers in Ye's fiction face problems unknown to their predecessors: in the new society they are no longer budding scholar-officials but professionals in the Western sense. The designation as professionals forces a new social marginality on them; everyone treats them with contempt, from the bureaucrats who are their employers to their students, who show an uncanny ability to see through their efforts to preserve self-esteem. Those few teachers who still harbor a measure of reformist zeal encounter daunting obstacles and eventually give up their reform efforts;[48] the great majority succumb to a crippling apathy and treat their profession either as a simple source of income or as a retreat from the hazards of more active professions, such as politics.

In "Rice" and "Pan xiansheng zai nan zhong" 潘先生在難中 (Mr. Pan in distress, 1924) the protagonists are given impossible educational assignments in areas plagued by famine and warlord squabbles. Both Teacher Wu 吳 of "Rice" and Mr. Pan struggle valiantly to fulfill their duties, but in the context of these emergencies it is all they can do to feed and protect their own families. Both men's comic dilemma results from their inability to be in two places at once: circumstances finally force them to choose one responsibility over the other. Teacher

46. Ye Shaojun, "Xin shi fenbiebukai de" 心是分別不開的 (The heart cannot be rent), in *Weiyanju xizuo*, pp. 152–60, here pp. 155–56. The years of teaching to which Ye refers here were between 1912 and 1915, when he taught in a primary school in Suzhou. From 1915 to 1917 Ye was unemployed and made his living in part from the stories he wrote for *Libailiu* and other journals.

47. See Chen Liao, *Ye Shengtao pingzhuan*, p. 19, for several passages from Ye's letters where he expresses his frustration with his fellow teachers.

48. See, for example, the protagonists of such Ye Shaojun stories as "Da banzi" 搭班子 (Signing on, 1926), in the collection *Chengzhong*, and "Kangzheng" 抗爭 (Struggle, 1926), in *Weiyan ji*.

Wu leaves his students alone for a while during the school day, for that is only time that rice is available at the market. To neglect his class in this way is to elect self-preservation over his public obligation, and the students clearly recognize the significance of his action: "Teacher," they mutter, "is a lot richer than we are; when we've rotted, he'll still have a full, fat belly."[49] Wu's self-interest is further underscored at closure, when, after a series of humiliations, he takes consolation in the materiality of his pay: "After all, on the table was a shiny silver dollar. In spite of himself he took it in hand. It left a cold, hard sensation in his palm" (51). Teacher Wu's profession has been drained of its social rationale; it becomes for him simply a means to procure the rice that ensures his family's survival.

The teacher-protagonist of "Mr. Pan in Distress" is similarly torn between his responsibility to his family, whom he takes as refugees to Shanghai during a warlord attack, and his duty to his school. Faithfully following orders from the Bureau of Education, he returns alone to his endangered village and there drafts a circular encouraging continued attendance at the school:

> War and fighting might be worrisome, he wrote, but the education of young people was a necessity like food and clothing. Now that the summer holidays were over, school would start as usual. In the time of the great war in Europe, the notice went on, a net was spread in the air over the schools to catch bombs and allow classes to continue uninterrupted. This kind of heroism should not go unrivaled.[50]

Mr. Pan's comically exaggerated fealty is, of course, belied by his behavior, both in ensuring his own family's survival and in conniving to accumulate Red Cross banners and badges, which he uses as amulets in the belief that they will afford himself and his school some magical protection from the impending attack. Like "Rice," Mr. Pan's story ends with an image that underlines its protagonist's self-betrayal: after the invading warlord has been defeated, Mr. Pan is asked to prepare jingoistic posters applauding the virtue and benevolence of the general who defended the town. The crowd marvels at the sincerity of his

---

49. Ye Shaojun, "Fan" 飯 (Rice), in *Huozai*, p. 50. "Rice" has been translated by Frank Kelly, in Joseph S. M. Lau, C. T. Hsia, and Leo Ou-fan Lee, *Modern Chinese Stories and Novellas*, pp. 90–94.
50. Ye Shaojun, "Pan xiansheng zai nan zhong" 潘先生在難中 (Mr. Pan in distress), in *Xianxia*, pp. 195–221, here p. 210. For a full translation of this story, see Ye Shengtao, *How Mr. Pan Weathered the storm*, pp. 36–62.

calligraphy, but as he writes, Mr. Pan's consciousness is consumed with images of the destruction he narrowly escaped. In a world where expediency requires the suppression of the self's true concerns, sincerity becomes little more than a marketable faculty, in whose very demonstration the word's true content is lost. As a calligrapher to the powerful, Mr. Pan is reduced, as was Teacher Wu in "Rice," to the pure instrumentality of the professional.

As a refuge for beleaguered intellectuals, education is used by Ye's teacher-protagonists not simply to ensure survival but to excuse their withdrawal from the political activity engulfing the larger society. But political engagement is itself fraught with spiritual risks, as is illustrated in "Qiaoshang" 橋上 (On the bridge, 1923), one of the few stories Ye wrote depicting a motivated political act. In the story a young terrorist named Zu Qing 組青 plans and carries out the murder of a wealthy landlord. He undertakes this murder not for pragmatic purposes but as an act of communication: he wants both to demonstrate that he is not an idle bystander to social injustice and to "awaken" the "pitiable" masses with a violent symbolic act. The killing serves, in fact, as a substitute for writing: Zu Qing decides not to leave an explanation of it because the murder was "just like reading a book or writing a letter; if you felt like doing it, you went and did it."[51] As narrated, however, the murder is a profoundly absurd performance, possessed of a surreal ordinariness: "In a crazy, rapid movement his right arm shot out of the window as though he were picking off the most convenient target on an ordinary bird hunt. There was a sturdy *ping* sound" (79). Zu Qing's madness is rooted in an inability to differentiate the protected realm of the imagination (which is also the domain of literature and schematic ideology) from the real world, where acts have violent, irrevocable consequences.

The imaginative and operative worlds are brought into eerie proximity in "On the Bridge"; the danger of transgressing the border between the two worlds is more typically given comic treatment in Ye Shaojun's stories. In "Yibao dongxi" 一包東西 (The package, 1926) a schoolteacher is followed as he passes through a checkpoint while carrying what he believes is a package of incriminating propaganda handouts. The handouts as he sees them in his mind's eye illustrate the

51. Ye Shaojun, "Qiaoshang" 橋上 (On the bridge), in *Xianxia*, pp. 57–79, here p. 73.

violence that he fears will be his own fate: "The square package appeared to be a thick pile of bound papers, on which he felt sure was printed the picture of a grotesque corpse lying in a thick pool of blood, one of those recently fallen to the enemy. Doubtless under the picture was printed the stark warning 'A martyr to the people! Another enemy atrocity!'[52] In the panic of his flight from the checkpoint, he reexamines his unwillingness to become involved in a political movement he believes to be just, rationalizing his personal fear as loyalty to his profession ("It's not much of an ambition, but I'd like to make something of that school and see what becomes of those students" [61]). The story closes with an ironical reversal: the pamphlets prove to be nothing more threatening than announcements of an old woman's funeral. This discovery forces the schoolteacher to confront his cowardice: facing a mirror, he experiences as shame the profound disjunction between his private moral imagination and his social function and averts his own gaze. The only possible remedy for the schizophrenia that results from this disjunction is to engage in the repugnant and hazardous realm of arbitrary violence that is radical politics. To remain disengaged is to redirect that violence onto the self or, worse, to transfer its effect to the next generation through the unthinking practice of traditional pedagogy.

All of the concerns that we have observed in Ye's stories about educators surface in one way or another in his longest work, *Ni Huanzhi*, a novel that was commissioned by Ye's editor friend Zhou Yutong 周予同 in late 1927 for serial publication in *Jiaoyu zazhi* 教育雜誌 (Journal of education). Ye began writing the novel in January 1928, produced a chapter "about every seven or eight days," and was finished with the work by November of the same year.[53] Despite its publication in an educational journal, Ye intended his novel both as a general portrait of the changes Chinese society had undergone since

52. Ye Shaojun, "Yibao dongxi" 一包東西 (The package), in *Weiyan ji*, pp. 57–68, here p. 60. This story has been translated by Wenxue in Ye Shengtao, *How Mr. Pan Weathered the Storm*, pp. 63–71.

53. Wu Taichang 吳泰昌, "Yi 'Wusi': Fang Ye lao" 憶"五四"—訪葉老 (Remembering May Fourth: an interview with Ye Shaojun), *Wenyi bao* 1979, no. 5 (March). *Ni Huanzhi* was first published serially under the title *Jiaoyu wenyi* 教育文藝 (The art of education) in *Jiaoyu zazhi* 教育雜誌 (Journal of education) (20, nos. 1–12). Kaiming shudian then published *Ni Huanzhi* in book form in 1929. Page numbers in the text refer to this edition. My translations of passages from *Ni Huanzhi* are adapted from A. C. Barnes's full translation entitled *Schoolmaster Ni Huan-chih*.

the 1911 revolution (and it was as such that Mao Dun praised it)[54] and as an autobiographical study of his own troubled process of maturation during that period. The novel recounts the efforts of Ye Shaojun's alter ego, Ni Huanzhi, to bring a new vitality to each of three arenas of his life, the pedagogical, the romantic, and the political, each time with unsatisfactory results. First, in his role as teacher Ni tries to institute a program of reform that consists, in effect, of applying Ye's favored ethical ideals of pity and sincerity to education: Ni contends that one must "serve the child" by "projecting oneself into the child's world" (5) and that a troubled child is to be brought around not by discipline but by rational appeals to its better nature, a technique the other teachers contemptuously call "conversion by sincerity" (73). What Ni most vociferously opposes is a view of education as textual indoctrination, as the mere transmission of cultural *doxa* to a new generation. When first encouraged to go into education by his headmaster (who wishes to protect him from "the treacherous waters of the army or of politics" [16]), he is disturbed by a perceived similarity between teaching and his first job working in a telegraph office. Education as he has experienced it is pure "sign memorizing" (57), and the instructor, nothing more than a mechanical transmitter of information. But by bringing his ethical ideals into play, Ni transforms his profession into a mission, whose goal is not to pass on some stable, text-bound knowledge to children but to instill in them an intangible sense of vitality, or "energy" (47). In the words of the motto he chooses for himself, he wants simply to "get the children to live!" (19). In practical terms, this means introducing such nonverbal activities into the school curriculum as music making, exercise, and gardening (53–54). But at a deeper level Ni's reform project denies the value of all content that traditionally the adult educator was expected to communicate to children. The teacher is given only the passive role of "creating an environment" in which the children may develop instinctively. But the result of Ni's application of this theory is a discomfiting inversion of roles. The children naturally possess an abundance of precisely those qualities that in theory their teachers wish to inculcate but feel that they themselves lack. Thus, while attempting to instill a sense of vitality in his students Ni is himself increasingly bothered by a

54. See Mao Dun, " Du *Ni Huanzhi*," in Mao Dun, *Mao Dun wenyi zalun ji*, p. 284.

vague "dispiritedness" that he believes is due to exaggerated "expecta-tions." The spiritual elevation he seeks is available only in the expec-tant contemplation of his ideals, whereas the application of his theories in the operable world brings only disappointment. It is, signif-icantly, through the literary rehearsal of his ideas (in his letters or in his reading of the theoretical paper on education that the sympathetic headmaster, Jiang Bingru 蔣冰如, has written) and through theoreti-cal discussions with "fellow idealists" like his fiancée that Ni Huanzhi achieves his greatest professional satisfaction.

Shared pedagogical interests are, in fact, the ground on which Ni Huanzhi and his fiancée, Jin Peizhang 金佩章, first meet, and Ni brings to their relationship the same idealism that characterizes his program of educational reform. If progressive education is designed to break down barriers (33), so too love is a "cohesive force" (157) that surmounts the "invisible barrier" between the sexes (49). Though the couple's early conversations are limited to a discussion of pedagogical matters, they are colored by an awkward adolescent eroticism: we are told that while sharing Jiang Bingru's paper on education with his fiancée, Huanzhi "frees himself from the inhibiting influence of the sex barrier" sufficiently to announce, "It is an extremely penetrating piece of writing!" (52). Yet however strongly he is overwhelmed by the power of love, which, "like innumerable tiny snakes," must force its way out of his heart (139), he cannot bring himself to speak directly of his feelings to Peizhang but chooses a substitute means of expression, the love letter. The correspondence that follows illuminates not only the tentative, explorative sexuality of young people during the May Fourth period but also the sexual encoding of the colloquial language that made it the expressive ground for the potency of both a new poli-tics and a new sexuality. Huanzhi makes clear that he has chosen to write his letters in the vernacular in order to narrow the gap between writing and speech ("I feel I can express myself more naturally in it, just as if I were speaking to you face to face" [141]) and to commu-nicate better the sense of virility he has found in contemplating their romance. Peizhang, though pleased that in reading his letters "she could almost hear his musical voice and envision the charming way he looked at her," nevertheless finds them "blunt, naked, and in some ways rather rude" (142). For her response she chooses the classical language, the formal means of leaving herself uncommitted, of keep-ing the correspondence open while expressing nothing more than a coy "How can you say such things!" (173). Yet their letters, whether colloquial or classical, serve a purpose not met by personal encounters: they open an arena in which the imagination can contemplate an emotional union that later events prove is unattainable in the real world. For as soon as Ni Huanzhi's romantic ideal is subjected to the mundane requirements of marriage, it is disabused: after their wedding he quickly grows weary of domestic chores and disgusted with Peizhang's narrowing preoccupation with home life. His avid imagination must look elsewhere for an incarnation of its ideals, and he begins fantasizing about a new woman, a "martial goddess" with "bobbed hair, a close-fitting cotton gown, and a face glowing with vitality," who, unlike Peizhang, prefers to write her letters in "simple, straightforward colloquial language" (223). In spite of Huanzhi's protest toward the end of his correspondence with Peizhang that he has become "fed up with all this verbiage" (157), the letters appear retrospectively to represent the full measure of his love. As always, Ni finds his true fulfillment in the onanistic arousal of intellectual or romantic voluntarism—in the dream rather than in practice, in literary reveries rather than in life.

Ni Huanzhi's engagement in the third major arena of his life, radical politics, if viewed solely from the perspective of his subjective engagement in it, shows the same blend of vitalism and idealism that characterized his pedagogical and romantic involvements. Early in life he distinguishes revolutionary activity from ordinary politics. The latter, he complains, is nothing more than a "boring" succession of warlord squabbles (33). Revolution, however, transcends the arena of politics as usual: it is above all a kind of pure energy, a "force" hidden in people's minds (215). If this truth is forgotten, revolution itself becomes subject to a terrible debasement, as is demonstrated in the novel by the opportunist Jiang Shibiao 蔣士鑣 ("Tiger Jiang"), who exploits radical ideology for his private benefit. In his own activities Ni is not entirely innocent of the seductions of power, but the authority he enjoys for a time is not a pragmatic domination of others but a spiritual influence he imagines his speechmaking exerts over the crowd. Unwilling to doff his pedagogical ambitions, he bills himself as an "educator for revolution" (211) whose goal is "to have the whole public come to us for instruction" (185). His rhetoric remains saturated with the same phantasmic idealism that rendered his educational program inoperable: in choosing the slogan "We are together!" he is simply preaching *tongqing* on a larger scale. But as we learned in our examination of the two kinds of stories in *Barriers*, the call for *tongqing* may simply hide a sense of its absence, and it is this sense that is forcefully expressed by a bare-chested worker who appears at one of Ni's rallies and skeptically inverts Ni's slogan: "The Chinese will never pull together! If they did, why, there'd be no stopping us!" Ni's slogan, which, as formulated, expresses only an illusory hope, becomes in its inverted form a realistic assessment of both China's buried potential and the continued existence of barriers preventing its realization. It is, as Ni later concedes to himself, a concise expression of the "essential point" (218). When Ni attempts to strike up a conversation with the bare-chested man, he is ignored: "The man stalked haughtily past, not in the least interested to find that someone else sympathized with him. Huanzhi felt reluctant to let him go and turned to rest an admiring glance on his retreating back in its sweat-stained blue jacket" (205). As his largely proletarian audience immediately realizes, the young intellectual's rhetorical assertion of unity does not conceal his difference from them. Rebuffed, Ni begins to doubt the "preaching manner" of his speeches, and just as he discovered in his teaching practice that children fare better without adult interference, he comes to recognize that the workers and peasants require no teaching, that they already possess the essential empowering source, the "motive force that is in life itself" (217).

If the pattern of Ni's disillusionment with radical politics is immediately recognizable from his experiences with pedagogy and romance, it is, however, only one aspect of the novel's representation of revolution. Even before Ni Huanzhi becomes actively involved in it, the revolution has had a significant, if not fully acknowledged, impact on his life. Each subjective metamorphosis Ni undergoes throughout the novel is pointedly correlated with a development in the period's political history: the rumor of the empire's restoration generates an early presentiment of the disillusionment to follow (135); the May Fourth movement encourages a new interest in affairs beyond the village (177); the May Thirtieth Incident convinces Ni to abandon teaching for urban political activity (203); and the abortive 1927 revolution brings on his final descent into hopelessness and death (264). One may in fact trace the influence of the revolution back to Ni's early schoolboy memories. In a flashback we are told that news of the 1911 revolution first inspired in the young Ni a restless contempt for traditional education as the mere transmission of dead texts and provoked an overwhelming desire to act: "A flag, a bomb, a gun—anything would do so long as he could grasp it firmly in his hand and charge forward with it" (13). Characteristically, Ni grasps none of the above; he grasps a pen and redirects his energy into the composition of poetry. But Ni's vitalism, however expressed, was clearly sparked by his early exposure to the revolution. Not finally reducible to Ni's subjective conjuring, the revolution is thus accorded a higher reality in the text than pedagogy and romance as a persistent, generative force in Ni's life. This force is, however, experienced as intrusive. The revolution operates against Ni's will, obligating his public commitment and, through the agency of disillusionment, drawing him away from classroom and family, as well as from the literary reveries that, as we have seen, were at the root of his pedagogical and romantic commitments.

With Ni's increasing disillusionment, this view of revolution as an external historical force begins to take precedence in the novel over Ni's subjective view, just as fire supplants water in the natural imagery consistently employed throughout the text. Water imagery has embellished the characterization not only of Ni's voluntary political commitment but also of his other enthusiasms as well: his educational program is described as "releasing the fountain" (125), and the confessional sessions he conducts with his students are frequently the occasion for what his colleagues call "goody-goody tears" (75), as is his correspondence with Peizhang (142). At the rallies he attends, which are invariably enveloped in a sudden downpour, tears well to his eyes (207) and his words are endued with a "vital power, like a hot spring boiling and gushing up in the middle of a quiet little stream" (227). But the revolution as a historical force, though hopefully compared to a great tidal wave in Ni Huanzhi's dream (240), is more frequently evoked through the destructive, purifying image of fire: Tiger Jiang's forces are "like a fire that has just burst into flame" (257), and Wang Leshan 王樂山, Ni's radical friend, who eventually persuades him to give up teaching for political work, compares revolutionary violence to a child's learning the danger of fire in the only practicable way, by playing with it (264). Where for Ni Huanzhi the two views of revolution prove as irreconcilable as the elements, it is Leshan who, by radically internalizing the revolution, manages to eradicate all superficial emotionalism from his subjectivity and make his heart "a glowing coal of fire" (317). In the crucial scene where Ni

Huanzhi concedes his friend's spiritual superiority, Leshan acknowledges his own likely pulverization by the "wheels of history" but stubbornly affirms his intention to continue "driving them forward with his own hands" (317). In a modern formulation of the quintessential Chinese ethical problem, Leshan distinguishes those who withdraw from history (who "stand aside and stare") from those who commit themselves to it; he proudly aligns himself with the latter but continues to nourish the ethical purity traditionally associated with withdrawal by refusing all benefits that might accrue from involvement, even the most elementary—his personal survival. He has elsewhere denied that "the final chapter [of the revolution] will soon be written" and acknowledged that "to write this work, one must give a security, and that security is one's head" (233–34). Leshan's willingness to accede to martyrdom elicits from Ni Huanzhi the following words of admiration with their surprising religious imagery:

> Having spent a moment in thought, he grasped Leshan's hand and said, gripping it tightly, "The Buddha said, 'If I don't go to hell, who will?' There's something in that, you know."
> "Perhaps the Buddha was a lifelong inhabitant of hell because he wanted to suffer the same retribution and the same fate as all living creatures!" was Leshan's unhesitating reply. (264)

At the very moment that Leshan affirms his total commitment to the revolution (as well as, it should be observed, to the most rigorous standard of *tongqing*), the text evokes the cultural image most closely associated with retreat from the temporal world. A curious collapsing of ethical alternatives results: the revolution in its insistent, intrusive function as history becomes identified with fate, and the most engaged course of action possible for such as Leshan and Ni Huanzhi entails the passive acceptance of its arbitrary violence. They must, as Leshan soon does, heed its call to self-immolation.

The terminus of a voluntary commitment to *tongqing* would appear to be submission to the determinism of the revolution. Through his martyrdom Leshan keeps intact the moral integrity that allows his identification with *tongqing*, but Ni's proud proffering of sympathy to the disadvantaged is finally supplanted by his own bathetic appeals for pity as he succumbs to typhoid fever and finally descends into the confused fantasies that conclude the novel. Georg Lukács has written about the nineteenth-century Western novel that it is primarily concerned with self-fashioning, with wresting a "glimpse of meaning" from the heterogeneous events that make up a life.[55] As a quasi-autobiographical novel written in imitation of Western fiction, *Ni Huanzhi* promises to provide just such a glimpse of meaning for its protagonist. But Ni Huanzhi is instead disfigured, invaded, and scattered at closure, and it is the revolution—perceived in its objective role as the inexorable march of history and time—that must be recognized as the primary force behind Ni's decline. At once hero and villain, the revolution grinds all sentimental idealism underfoot as it marches toward a utopian fulfillment, to be enjoyed only by those who have no need of the novelist's self-fashioning and who would scorn his pallid sympathies.

As an experiment with the Western novel form, *Ni Huanzhi* may thus be said to disabuse itself. Like Ni's love letters, the modern colloquial novel purports to be more vital than traditional fiction, a truer participant in the real world, by which is meant not simply the external physical world but the operative political arena with its power struggles. Yet the novel remains disconnected, trapped in a vicious circle in which subjective fantasies are repeatedly disappointed only to be reconstructed in altered terms. Like Lu Xun with his stories, Ye Shaojun finally resorts to distortions at the close of *Ni Huanzhi* (specifically, Peizhang's determination to go out and work for the good of society) to point to possible solutions in the extraliterary world, alternatives that by definition remain external to the narration.

We began our discussion of Ye Shaojun by noticing the process of maturation toward realism that many critics have discovered in his work. Ye's explication of his own work, given in his occasional prefaces and essays on composition, would seem to confirm this process of change. In 1936 he wrote:

> Whenever I encountered something I felt was wrong, I took up my pen and satirized it. . . . I always tried to limit the expression of my own views as much as possible. It wasn't that I coveted the title of realist, but I felt if I devoted too much space to my own viewpoint, I would overstep the boundaries of the satire.[56]

---

55. See Georg Lukács, *The Theory of the Novel*, especially pp. 77–83.
56. Ye Shaojun, "Suibian tantan wo de xie xiaoshuo" 隨便談談我的寫小說 (A casual discussion of my fiction), in Ye Shaojun, *Ye Shaojun xuanji*; reprinted in Ye Shaojun, *Ye Shengtao lun chuangzuo*, p. 119.

From this passage, it is evident that Ye had radically revised his opinions about fiction since the time in the early 1920s when he wrote *On the Literary Arts*. He is no longer preoccupied with the expressive power of fiction and its role in the individual's moral cultivation; he now gives priority instead to the social function of satire, by which he seems to be referring to the critique of social peccadilloes found in some of his works. Significantly, however, this new emphasis on critique is accompanied by a loss of confidence in fiction's social efficacy: "The satire to which I refer is no more than self-consolation; I don't really believe it has any influence on society. . . . If you want to make a real contribution, fiction is much less useful than oral storytelling, skits, and so forth."[57]

Few readers, I think, would agree with Ye's retrospective characterization of his fiction: satire seems only a minor strain in his work taken as a whole. *Ni Huanzhi*, as an autobiographical novel, makes clear that at least until the late 1920s Ye continued to be fascinated with the problems of the self and its expression. For at the heart of Ye's fictional project was not the intention simply to reflect or capture the external world but a desire to mediate his personal subjectivity with the exigencies of that world. As we have seen, the very notion of self that Ye Shaojun inherited from neo-Confucianism required that the individual labor to achieve a correspondence between his subjective being and the world through the process of ethical cultivation; in other words, the aim of such cultivation was the perfect alignment of the self as subjective "I" with the self understood as an externally delimited "he/she." For Ye a truly unproblematic sense of self could be achieved only if the absence of *tongqing* that troubled both his inner world and the objective social environment was somehow remedied. We noticed in Ye's earliest works a fondness for lyrical episodes—moments when the self freely exercises its powers of sincerity and pity—as well as a distaste for the mechanics of narrative, including such basic components of fiction as plot and point of view. As he matured in his art, Ye began experimenting with these components, using point of view to examine the limits of sincerity in fictional expression and using plot to explore the disillusioning effects of time on individual hopes and ideals. But with *Ni Huanzhi* a new equation is made between time/

57. "Suibian tantan wo de xie xiaoshuo," in Ye Shaojun, *Ye Shengtao lun chuang-zuo*, Ibid., p. 120.

narrative and the revolution. This equation is both hopeful, promising a final overturning of the barriers that divide the social world, and fearful, since in its absolute objectivity it marshals a call for the demise of the questing bourgeois self that Ye had sought to forge. And it is this bourgeois self—with its confident command over an objectively observed social environment—that the Western realist novel, in imitation of which *Ni Huanzhi* was written, explores and affirms. In *Ni Huanzhi*, Ye Shaojun posits such a notion of the self as he experiments with the novel form, but in the end he subjects both to a reflexive moral examination that proves profoundly subversive. Realist fiction, formerly entrusted with the self's creation and expression, is in the end left only the task of enacting its deconstruction, a narrative suicide.

C. T. Hsia has written of *Ni Huanzhi* that "despite its apparent honesty, the sympathetic bond between author and hero is too personally close to generate the kind of ironic objectivity which distinguishes Ye Shaojun's better short stories."[58] That is to say, Ye has failed in his intention to suppress his subjectivity in the interest of the "satire," making his work simply too raw to offer a completely satisfactory aesthetic experience. We may agree that Ye failed in *Ni Huanzhi* to demonstrate the formal ingenuity of Lu Xun at his best, and as a result his struggle with the novel form is everywhere apparent. But a sympathetic reading of *Ni Huanzhi* must recognize the novel's ambition, which distinguishes it from the narrow scope of the short stories Hsia praises, for Ye hoped with his novel to solve the problems of individual and national self-invention that preoccupied his generation. In the process he did much more than merely adapt his Western model to Chinese circumstances; he actively probed the resources of his borrowed form, discovering and exposing its inherent limitations. The realist novel proved, however, to be too cramped a vessel for his aspirations. Ye Shaojun's fictional enterprise, like Lu Xun's, led its author from an idealistic confidence in the moral power of fiction to effect change to a formal impasse that would seem to throw into doubt the very possibility of literary transitivity.

58. C. T. Hsia, *A History of Modern Chinese Fiction*, p. 65.

4

Mao Dun, Zhang Tianyi, and the
Social Impediments to Realism

MAO DUN: POLITICS OF THE DETAIL

Much as the dramatic political events of the 1920s impinged on the life of Ni Huanzhi, drawing him away from his teaching career, so too did they induce the young critic and editor Shen Yanbing 沈雁冰, who was later to take the pen name Mao Dun, to set aside his literary work and step into the fray of revolutionary politics. Born into a declining gentry family in Zhejiang in 1896, Shen attended Beijing University for two years, until his family's financial problems forced him to quit and seek employment. Through family connections, he procured a position at China's largest publishing house, the Commercial Press in Shanghai. In the years that followed, he proved one of the press's most prolific writers and editors and, as we have seen, played a central role in introducing Western literature into China. As busy as his editorial work kept him, however, Shen was very active in radical politics as well, becoming one of the first members of the Chinese Communist party after its founding in July 1921 and eventually rising to membership in the executive committee of the party's regional branch. Shen personally participated in the demonstrations of May 30, 1925, when several Chinese protesters were killed by police in the International Settlement in Shanghai. This event, the May Thirtieth Incident, and the series of strikes and protests that followed it had the effect of intensifying Shen's political commitment, and near the end of that year he resolved to "sever" all his "professional ties with literature" and devote himself fully to politics.[1] He accepted an appointment as chief of

1. Mao Dun, "Jiju jiuhua" 幾句舊話 (Remarks on the past), in Lu Xun et al., *Chuangzuo de jingyan*, pp. 49–58, here p. 49. Yu-shih Chen's *Realism and Allegory in the Early Fiction of Mao Tun* includes a translation of much of this essay on pages 28–30. As Chen observes (p. 27), Shen's employers at the Commercial Press, embarrassed by his political activities, had begun curtailing his editorial and writing responsibilities in the months preceding his decision to retire.

the Chinese Communist party's Propaganda Department in Shanghai and early the next year went to Canton to represent the leftist faction of the Shanghai branch of the Nationalist party at the Second National Assembly. (The Communist party, it will be remembered, had formed an alliance with the Nationalist party in 1923 on orders from the Comintern.) In Canton, Shen made the acquaintance of Wang Jingwei 王精衛, Mao Zedong, and other important revolutionary leaders. But Canton, he was later to write, "was in those days a huge furnace, an enormous whirlpool—a colossal contradiction."[2] After the Zhongsan Gunboat Incident of March 20, the Communist party lost control of the Propaganda Bureau, and Shen, suffering his first taste of political disillusionment, returned to Shanghai.

In spite of this setback, Shen continued his political work with unabated energy, spending his days at meetings and in organizational work (but devoting his evenings to research into Chinese mythology, an activity he apparently found therapeutic). Early in 1927 the left wing of the Nationalist party consolidated its power in Wuhan 武漢 at the height of the Northern Expedition, and Shen departed for that city to accept an assignment as instructor of politics at the Central Military and Political Academy. Shortly thereafter, he was transferred to an editorial position at the *Hankou minguo ribao* 漢口民國日報 (Hankou daily republic), which, as he describes it in his autobiography, was "nominally the institutional voice of the Hubei branch of the Nationalist party but was in fact operated by the Communist party."[3] In the next few months he committed himself totally to the volatile political situation in the city, writing, among other things, outspoken articles decrying Jiang Jieshi's treatment of leftists within the alliance. At the end of June, apparently sensing the impending catastrophe, he sent his wife back to Shanghai, resigned from the paper, and went underground. Then on July 16, the Nationalist government in Wuhan announced its expulsion of the Communist party and began a violent purge of communist sympathizers. "That colossal contradiction exploded again," Shen later wrote, and Wuhan, like Canton before it, became "an enormous whirlpool."[4] A few days later, the party sent him to Jiujiang 九江 to deliver a bank draft; when he arrived there, his

2. Mao Dun, "Jiju jiuhua," in Lu Xun et al., *Chuangzuo de jingyan*, p. 50.
3. Mao Dun, *Wo zouguo de daolu* 1:322.
4. Mao Dun, "Jiju jiuhua," in Lu Xun et al., *Chuangzuo de jingyan*, p. 54.

contacts instructed him to take the draft on to Nanchang 南昌, where the Communists were gathering their forces. He soon discovered, however, that the roads to Nanchang were blocked, forcing him to take temporary refuge at the mountain resort of Guling 牯嶺 (which lies between the cities of Jiujiang and Nanchang). There he fell ill with dysentery.[5] While recuperating, he heard of the failure of the Nanchang Uprising, the first independent battle of the newly formed Red Army. After the feverish activity of the previous two years, Shen ironically found himself immobilized at a beautiful mountain retreat as the revolution for which he had fought collapsed around him. Remembering an outline for a novel he had started to sketch while in Shanghai the previous year, he decided to renew his contact with literature "on a nonprofessional basis": "Since I had nothing to do, I let it occupy my mind."[6] Shortly thereafter he returned to Shanghai, where, living in hiding and in great despair over the outcome of the revolution, he wrote the first two of the three novellas that make up his first work of fiction, *Shi* 蝕 (Eclipse). It was with the publication of these two novellas that Shen first adopted the pen name Mao Dun, which means "contradiction." Shen's failure in politics and his resulting apprehension of the complex forces (or contradictions) that governed political reality had somehow liberated his literary imagination. As he was later to say in an interview, "I became an author because I was unsuccessful at practical revolutionary work."[7]

Shen's first creative works were thus born of political frustration, but they also represented to him an expression of his will to live. He later wrote:

> I experienced one of the most complex scenes of China's chaotic modern history; as a result I came to feel disillusioned with the contradictions of human life. Feeling profoundly depressed and alone—to say nothing of the external circumstances that constrained me—I determined to light a spark in this confused, grey life from the remnant of the life force that still remained in me. Therefore I began to write.[8]

5. When Shen wrote about these events in the late 1920s and 1930s, he always maintained that he went to Guling to recuperate from illness; this story he later admitted was a cover for his actual intentions, which were as I describe them here. See Marián Gálik, *Mao Tun and Literary Criticism*, p. 154 n. 74. His memoirs do indicate, however, that he fell sick after arriving in Guling. See *Wo zouguo de daolu*, vol. 1, p. 340.

6. Mao Dun, "Jiju jiuhua," in Lu Xun et al., *Chuangzuo de jingyan*, p. 54.

7. Susannah Bernard, "Zoufang Mao Dun" 走訪茅盾 (Interviewing Mao Dun), in *Xin wenxue shiliao* 1979, no. 3; reprinted in Li Xiu, *Mao Dun yanjiu zai guowai*, pp. 562–73, here p. 571.

Clearly Mao Dun wrote out of a desire to make sense of the calamity he had experienced and, if possible, to restore his faith in the future of the revolution. He thus drew directly on his experiences in Shanghai and Wuhan over the previous two years for the subject matter of the first two novellas in *Eclipse*. The models for the love-obsessed female protagonists in "Huanmie" 幻滅 (Disillusionment, 1927) were his wife's coworkers in the women's movement: the political crisis, he wrote, exposed the true nature of these "modern women," many of whom he had watched "lose control of themselves, become depressed, and go under."[9] The plot of "Dongyao" 動搖 (Vacillation, 1927) originated in reports that crossed his desk at the *Hankou Daily Republic* concerning the violence and political chaos that followed the "excessive" reform efforts of "opportunists" and "left extremists."[10] Despite his desire to "light a spark" of hope through the composition of these novellas, both presented a sobering view of the revolutionary movement of the previous few years; as a result they soon became the object of heated attacks by ideological watchdogs at the Creation and Sun societies. Sensitive to his opponents' criticisms and perhaps himself disturbed by the negative undercurrent of the works he had written, Mao Dun composed "Chuangzao" 創造 (Creation), his first short story, in February 1928. He later frequently pointed to "Creation" as his first truly positive work, as proof that he had finally overcome the despair engendered in him by the Wuhan "debacle."[11] But Mao Dun could muster the "optimism" of "Creation" only for a short time;

---

8. Mao Dun, "Cong Guling dao Dongjing" 從牯嶺到東京 (From Guling to Tokyo), *Xiaoshuo yuebao* 19, no. 10 (10 October 1928); reprinted in Tang Jinhai et al., *Mao Dun zhuanji* 1:331–45, here p. 331.

9. In his "Jiju jiuhua" (pp. 51–52), Mao Dun identified the three specific encounters with women revolutionaries that inspired "Disillusionment." As he describes them, each of these meetings is infused with a sense of sexual mystery. Take, for example, the first, which occurred in August 1926 as Mao Dun was leaving a political meeting during a torrential rainstorm:

> The person walking next to me was one of the women who had attracted my attention. During the meeting, she had talked a great deal, and her face was still flushed with excitement. As we walked, I suddenly felt a surge of "literary inspiration." Had it been possible, I would have grabbed a pen right there and begun to write in the rain.

10. Mao Dun, *Wo zouguo de daolu* 2:9.

11. As late as 1979, in the preface to the two-volume *Mao Dun duanpian xiaoshuo ji*, Mao Dun was still arguing the case of this short story to critics who held that the novel *Hong* 虹 (Rainbow) marked the change from pessimism to optimism in his work.

while writing the third novella in *Eclipse*, "Zhuiqiu" 追求 (Pursuit 1928), he "once again sank deeply into pessimism and disappointment"[12] and produced a frankly nihilistic work that only increased the fury of his critics. Shortly thereafter, he took the advice of friends to "breathe a bit of fresh air" and left for Japan. But his critics hounded him even there, so that he finally felt it necessary to rise to his own defense with the two familiar essays "From Guling to Tokyo" and "On Reading *Ni Huanzhi*."

These essays, particularly the latter, which presents a "general rebuttal" of the Creation and Sun societies' criticisms in the guise of a defense of Ye Shaojun's novel,[13] give us important clues to Mao Dun's perception of his own creative effort in relation to the work of other May Fourth authors. Mao Dun and Ye Shaojun were friends, colleagues at the Commercial Press, and founding members of the Association for Literary Studies. Ye was one of the few former associates with whom Mao Dun was in contact during his months of hiding in Shanghai, and it was to Ye Shaojun that Mao Dun first showed "Disillusionment" upon its completion.[14] (Ye, then serving as editor in chief of *Short Story Magazine*, eagerly persuaded Mao Dun to submit the novella for publication.) During the Revolutionary Literature debate, their names were frequently linked by members of the Creation and Sun societies, who accused them both of practicing "naturalism." As we have seen, neither author accepted this designation: Ye Shaojun refused to align himself with any literary doctrine, and Mao Dun had long abandoned his advocacy of the mode. But in "On Reading *Ni Huanzhi*," Mao Dun does affirm a shared sense of artistic purpose, however defined, with Ye Shaojun and uses his friend's novel to argue the case for his own fiction. At the same time, as a practicing critic, he is forced to acknowledge certain inadequacies in Ye's novel, and in so doing he enumerates the ideological and formal pitfalls into which

---

12. Mao Dun, *Wo zouguo de daolu* 2:14.
13. See Mao Dun, *Wo zouguo de daolu* 2:42: "At the time [of composing 'On Reading *Ni Huanzhi*'] the stir created by 'From Guling to Tokyo' was already starting to subside, and my new article was intended as a general rebuttal of the critical response to it. I intentionally used Ye Shengtao's *Ni Huanzhi* for the purpose of this general rebuttal."
14. Ye Shaojun was also partly responsible for the pen name Mao Dun. Shen originally signed his first novella, "Disillusionment," with the characters for the word *contradiction* (*maodun* 矛盾); Ye suggested that he add a grass radical to *mao* to make the character look more like a proper surname. See *Wo zouguo de daolu* 2:6.

practitioners of the novel in a revolutionary period risked stumbling—
pitfalls that he clearly hoped to avoid in his own work.

Mao Dun's appraisal of *Ni Huanzhi* focuses on the notion of a
fictional work's *shidaixing* 時代性, which we may translate as "his-
toricity." As Marián Gálik has pointed out, this word is in fact a translation of Hippolyte Taine's term *moment*.[15] In 1922, during the
period of his advocacy of naturalism, Mao Dun had come under the
influence of Taine's views of literature, which emphasized the power
of the historical epoch and the national "milieu" in which an author
lived to determine the nature of his literary output. By 1930, however,
Mao Dun no longer fully accepted the deterministic implications of
Taine's theories. Though borrowing the French critic's term, Mao
Dun insists that *shidaixing* is dependent not simply on the contempo-
raneity of the work's content nor on its ability to evoke an ephemeral
"spirit of the times" but also on the work's capacity to express the
reciprocal influence of the "times" on individuals and of human effort
on history. To possess *shidaixing*, a work must show "how collective
human effort hurries the realization of historical necessity." Reviewing
the limited number of fictional works produced by Chinese writers
since the May Fourth movement, Mao Dun observes that before *Ni
Huanzhi* only Lu Xun's works possessed a measure of *shidaixing*.
Other writers, restricting the content of their fiction to the angst of
bourgeois youth, had attempted only a "narrow, partial" picture of
their times and even then showed only a superficial knowledge of that
part of the social order they took as their subject. In *Ni Huanzhi*,
however, Ye Shaojun had attempted to encompass the full scope of
the modern period by following an individual's growth as he was
exposed to a diverse range of experiences and social circumstances.
Ni Huanzhi is thus not the product of an impromptu inspiration, as
were so many of the stories by other May Fourth fiction writers,
but of "penetrating observation, sober analysis, and meticulous
composition."[16] The novel's formal capaciousness, which allows it to
capture a sense of historical process, clearly interested Mao Dun, but
so did the novel's thematic treatment of the problem of *shidaixing*.
Though he neglects to draw the connection explicitly, Mao Dun's de-

15. See Gálik, *Mao Tun and Literary Criticism*, pp. 66–67.
16. Mao Dun, "Dun *Ni Huanzhi*" 讀《倪煥之》 (On reading *Ni Huanzhi*), *Wenxue
zhoubao* 8, no. 20 (12 May 1929); reprinted in Mao Dun, *Mao Dun wenyi zalun ji*, pp.
277–94, here p. 286.

finition of the term owes much to Wang Leshan's attempted reconciliation of voluntaristic human effort with a deterministic sense of historical progress (expressed in his wish to "drive the wheels of history with his own hands").

In spite of Ye Shaojun's laudable ambitions, however, Mao Dun finds that several crucial passages of *Ni Huanzhi* fail to demonstrate the true relationship of individual effort to history as Mao Dun understood it, and this failure results in the several structural flaws that mar the book. There is a discrepancy, for example, between the densely textured first half of the novel, which treats in close detail the narrow issue of Ni's educational reforms, and the more schematic second half, which skims too hastily over his involvement in significant historical events. Mao Dun also regrets that Ye chose to present the May Thirtieth Incident only through Ni Huanzhi's subjective response to it; he should have given a fuller account of the collective base underlying the radical political movement and then described the event "positively and directly." Ye's subjective depiction "causes a slackening in tone, very inappropriate to the tense circumstances of the time."[17] Finally, Mao Dun objects to the apparently "miraculous" change in Jin Peizhang's thinking at the end of the book, which he considers a gratuitous expression of faith in the future for which readers are unprepared. In each case Ye Shaojun was apparently unable to fully overcome the characteristic limitations of May Fourth fiction: specifically, Ye shows a failure of historical imagination by confining himself to the subjective concerns of the troubled bourgeois youth he takes as his protagonist and intellectual laziness in allowing his fiction to become a medium for the expression of personal whims and frustrations. As a result Ye never achieves a truly detached historical perspective.

Mao Dun hoped in his own work to go beyond a personal, and therefore partial, perspective on his epoch; he hoped to make his fiction speak with the full authority of *shidaixing*, that is, with the voice of history itself. To borrow Erich Auerbach's description of Stendhal's method, he wanted to embed his characters "in a total reality, political, social, economic, which is concrete and constantly evolving."[18] Nevertheless, the criticisms Mao Dun levies against Ye Shaojun could have been—and in fact were—applied to his own early

17. Ibid., p. 286.
18. Erich Auerbach, *Mimesis*, p. 463.

works, particularly the *Eclipse* trilogy. Although Mao Dun insisted that in at least the first two of his novellas he had simply given an objective description ("as accurate as possible") of the times and "kept his own feelings out,"[19] *Eclipse* has always been viewed as the most subjective of his writings.[20] The Creationist Qian Xingcun was to use the very terms of Mao Dun's critique of *Ni Huanzhi* to characterize "Disillusionment": "Structurally the book is divided into two parts. Chapters 1 through 8 concern [the protagonist's] life at school; chapters 9 through 14 concern her life in the revolution. . . . The material covered in the first part is concise and to the point, whereas the latter part is much looser and the material thin."[21] Qian further objected to the "indirect" method with which Mao Dun broaches important historical events: they become a mere backdrop for the characters' personal lives rather than the center of the story itself. Mao Dun was himself to concede the subjective concerns that motivated the composition of "Pursuit": "I acknowledge that the keynote of extreme pessimism was my own, although the young characters' dissatisfactions, their despair, and their search for deliverance were objectively observed realities."[22] It is true that in the composition of *Eclipse*, Mao Dun had eschewed the autobiographical approach of Ye Shaojun in *Ni Huanzhi* and rigorously restricted himself to "writing about others"; in defense of his work he seems to say that if his own frustrations were discovered in the psychology of his compatriots as well, they could be identified as objective facts and were therefore acceptable for fictional representation. But Qian Xingcun and others were quick to recognize that Mao Dun's personal disillusionment was the true motivating force behind his composition of "Pursuit."

The compositional problems Mao Dun identifies in "On Reading *Ni Huanzhi*" had concerned him as a critic long before he began writing fiction. In essays from the early 1920s, such as "On Systemati-

19. Mao Dun, "Cong Guling dao Dongjing," in Tang Jinhai et al., *Mao Dun zhuanji* 1:333.
20. Yue Daiyun 樂黛雲 discusses the "subjectivity" of *Eclipse* in her article, "*Shi he Ziye* de bijiao fenxi" 《蝕》和《子夜》的比較分系 (A comparative analysis of *Eclipse* and *Midnight*), in Sun Zhongtian with Cha Guohua, *Mao Dun yanjiu ziliao* 2:182–204.
21. Qian Xingcun, "Mao Dun yu xianshi: du le *Ye qiangwei* yihou" 茅盾與現實—讀了《野薔薇》以後(Mao Dun and reality: after reading *Wild Roses*), *Xinliu yuebao* 4 (15 December 1929); reprinted in Fu Zhiying, *Mao Dun pingzhuan*, pp. 159–216, here p. 167.
22. Mao Dun, "Cong Guling dao Dongjing," in Tang Jinhai et al., *Mao Dun zhuanji* 1:332.

cally and Economically Introducing Western Literary Opinion" and "Naturalism and Modern Chinese Fiction,"[23] Mao Dun had confidently offered a prescription for overriding subjective impediments to aligning the self with historical process. He first urged writers to ground their works in careful observation of the real world and to avoid imitating other literary works. But he went on to advise that an author's observations be "arranged" or "organized" in a purposeful way. Without such arrangement, fictional works present disassembled pictures of the world that "read like account books." Descriptions of the account-book sort were, Mao Dun suggests, the common currency of the popular fiction of the late Qing and early Republican period, where they served only to arouse their readers' cravings for erotic stimulation or scandal—by encouraging, one assumes, a fetishization of the objects described. Only when fictional representation was structured to present a cohesive view of the world informed by strict scientific principles could fiction avoid sensationalism and achieve a comprehensive portrait of society. In examining the writings of such Western realists as Balzac and Zola, Mao Dun was impressed by their encyclopedic treatment of social phenomena: the inclusiveness of their vision was, he felt, an important concomitant of the "scientific" organization of detail. Mao Dun desired, in theory at least, that his novels would be formally capable of accommodating all aspects of Chinese society, from the grossest abstraction to the minutest detail. After Lu Xun's polished miniatures and the restricted scope of Ye Shaojun's "sincere" observations, this urge for comprehensiveness, and the fundamentally novelistic imagination that results from it (and that Mao Dun exhibits even in many of his short stories), must be recognized as something new in modern Chinese literature.[24]

23. Mao Dun's "Duiyu xitong de jingji de jieshao xiyang wenxue de yijian" 對於系統的經濟的介紹西洋文學底意見 (On systematically and economically introducing Western literary opinion) was first published in *Xuedeng* 學燈 (Study lamp) [supplement to *Shishi xinbao* 時事新報], 4 February 1920; "Ziranzhuyi yu Zhongguo xiandai xiaoshuo"自然主義與中國現代小說(Naturalism and modern Chinese fiction) was first published in *Xiaoshuo yuebao* 13, no. 7 (10 July 1922). Both are reprinted in Mao Dun, *Mao Dun wenyi zalun ji* 1:14–18 and 83–99, respectively.

24. In his article "Lun Mao Dun de xianshizhuyi wenxue guan" 論茅盾的現實主義文學觀 (On Mao Dun's realist literary vision), the critic Wang Zhongchen 王中忱 compares Lu Xun and Mao Dun in the following way: "Lu Xun liked to reveal the depth of the human spirit, while Mao Dun concentrated on showing the breadth of social and historical life. The real [*zhen* 真] in Mao Dun's realist literary vision was closely related to the whole [*quan* 全]" (*Wenxue pinglun* 1984, no. 1, pp. 79–90, here p. 81).

Yet in practice, by calling for the simultaneous exercise of two very different cognitive functions during composition, the one strictly empirical, the other ideological and analytical, Mao Dun's prescription of observation and analysis provided a perplexing model for the would-be realist. In Mao Dun's own writing certain formal irregularities—particularly problems with length and closure—may be seen as vestiges of this struggle to remain faithful both to the integrity of realistic details and to the meaningful structural patterns into which those details were arranged. Though Mao Dun composed many of the period's most highly respected short stories, he frequently complained of his dissatisfaction with them. He wrote of the composition of his first collection of stories, *Ye qiangwei* 野薔薇 (Wild roses, 1929): "I was such a bungler I thought a short work of several thousand characters couldn't accommodate a complicated theme. Completing my first short story, 'Creation,' was more difficult than writing a longer work, and I felt I was simply not cut out to write short fiction."[25] As late as 1952 he reiterated this appraisal: "Strictly speaking, with the majority of my short stories I failed to create works that were at once concise and resonant with meaning. Many of my short stories did not succeed in giving voice to a 'slice of life.'"[26] Shorter works did not afford Mao Dun the leisure to draw out the complex, interrelated motivations and causes that could account fully for an event.[27]

Though Mao Dun never expressed such regrets about his novelistic output, a brief glance at the circumstances surrounding their composition reveals a similar problem with narrative closure. Almost all of Mao Dun's published novels represent scaled-down or fractured versions of the works he originally intended to write. *Eclipse* was to have

25. Mao Dun, "Wo de huigu" 我的回顧 (My reminiscences, 1932), in Tang Jinhai et al., *Mao Dun zhuanji* 1:354–57, here p. 356.

26. Mao Dun, "*Mao Dun xuanji* zi xu" 《茅盾選集》自序 (Author's preface to *Selected works of Mao Dun*), in Tang Jinhai et al., *Mao Dun zhuanji* 1:892–95, here p. 894.

27. Another reason for Mao Dun's discomfort with short forms was his distaste for the classical Chinese aesthetic, which was predicated on the virtues of conciseness and brevity. In his discussion of Soviet neorealism in "From Guling to Tokyo," he traces its origins to a paper shortage in postrevolutionary Russia that forced authors to compose in a "telegraphic" style, which then became fashionable. Telegraphic writing is inappropriate in China, he argues, both because linguistic compression is inevitably associated with the Chinese classical language and because the Chinese people and their popular culture are naturally verbose. See "Cong Guling dao Dongjing," in Tang Jinhai et al., *Mao Dun zhuanji* 1:343–44.

been a single narrative about a small group of characters going through different phases of the revolution, but "because I didn't have confidence in my creative power, I divided it into three novellas."[28] *Hong* 虹 (Rainbow, 1930) was to trace "an imprint of the great drama of China over the last ten years," but the author clearly tired of the subject, and the book as we have it covers its protagonist's story only through the first half of that period.[29] Even his lengthy portrayal of Shanghai in the early 1930s, *Ziye* 子夜 (Midnight, 1933), often praised as "panoramic" or "monumental," was originally to have treated both urban and rural China.[30] A later work, *Shuang ye hong si eryue hua* 霜葉紅似二月花 (Maple leaves as red as February flowers, 1943), was to have been the first part of a projected trilogy that the author "never found the time" to complete.[31] Mao Dun's difficulty in discovering proper boundaries for his fictional works, both long and short, and the resultant unfinished quality of so much of his writing, suggests that he repeatedly failed to discover a structural framework that would both envelop the particulars of his social observations and place those particulars in just proportion to one another.

This dilemma reveals itself in Mao Dun's fiction not only formally but thematically as well in the conflict between the ideal and the real, that is, betwen the clarity of structural pattern on the one hand and the refractoriness of an empirically observed social environment on the other. An interesting episode in "Pursuit" gives us some idea how this conflict made itself felt in the process of composition. In it the journalist Wang Zhongzhao 王仲昭, after his political efforts during the 1927 revolution come to naught, decides to limit his reformist zeal to the sphere of journalism. He is attracted to journalism because it is a "practical" profession where he can set aside the exaggerated idealism that governed his political life and deal objectively with the realities of life. After a battle with the editors of the newspaper where he is employed, he is allowed to establish a column, significantly entitled "Impressions," wherein he will record the results of his journalistic investigations. For the first of these columns he chooses the subject

---

28. Ibid., p. 333.
29. Mao Dun, "Ba" 跋 (Postscript), in *Hong*, p. 245.
30. Mao Dun "*Ziye* houji" 《子夜》後記 (Postscript to *Midnight*), in Tang Jinhai et al., *Mao Dun zhuanji* 1:827.
31. Mao Dun, "*Shuang ye hong si eryue hua* xin ban houji" 《霜葉紅似二月花》新板後記 (Postscript to the new edition of *Maple Leaves as Red as February Flowers*), in Tang Jinhai et al., *Mao Dun zhuanji* 1:908–11, here 908.

of Shanghai nightlife, which he wishes to treat not simply as an exposé but as an illustration of the spiritual confusion of Chinese society. Dutifully he accompanies his dissolute acquaintance Zhang Qiuliu 章秋柳 to several dance halls. But when he comes to write the column, he suffers from writer's block: his own impressions of the evening seem confused and elusive, and it is only the impassioned conversation of Zhang Qiuliu with its blend of erotic and political overtones that he remembers clearly enough to record. He quickly realizes that recording her conversation would only transmit her nihilistic ideology, and the result would be something quite different from the intended record of his own empirical observations. He asks himself: "Could it be that it was impossible even in a small matter like this to harmonize the ideal and the real? Could it be that the particular atmosphere he ordinarily associated with the dance halls was no more or less than his own hallucination?" (304).[32] What Wang Zhongzhao discovers here, and what we may assume Mao Dun himself had come to realize, is that the social realities that he would isolate, examine, and record do not have the property of simple material reality. The details in whose substantiality he had hoped to take refuge are themselves no more than the subjectively conjured phantasms of his imagination; to isolate and give them literary representation is inevitably to traffic in the system of ideas that supports them.

This episode may serve as a parable of the plight of both journalist and realist—of anyone who attempts a fundamentally representational form of writing. Wang Zhongzhao's journalistic efforts originate in an enforced retreat from political activity, where his actions were governed by received ideological assumptions; journalism will allow him, he hopes, to deal only with concrete and unambiguous realities. His approach to writing is first to delineate a field for research, a problem that he wishes to represent both to himself and his readership in its true light. The problems Wang includes on his list are the staples of journalism and realist fiction alike; they include kidnaping, robbery, rape, strikes, divorce, to all of which he gives the general classification of "social disorders." He then undertakes what he considers an objective investigation of his subject, but at the point of recording the results of that investigation, he discovers to his dismay that even his empirically observed details remain saturated with ideology. With this

32. Page references are to the 1981 Renmin wenxue chubanshe edition of *Shi*.

unwelcome reemergence of the ideological, Wang falls silent until less noble motivations—specifically, the thought of his paycheck and the desire to impress his girlfriend—compel him to produce an article that falls far short of his original intentions.

Like Wang Zhongzhao in his journalistic endeavors, Mao Dun undertook the composition of fiction as part of an intended retreat from ideology at a point of frustration with politics and with the resistance of history itself to conform to his ideals. Fiction offered a medium through which Mao Dun could explore the refractory quality of the real world, measuring it against the schematic ideology that had failed him. But as I have suggested above, Mao Dun believed that a balance of observation and interpretation was necessary to fictional composition, and he required a tool for analysis to complement his descriptive intentions. The pen name he chose when he published "Disillusionment" suggests that the notion of "contradiction" served this purpose for him. On one level the word simply gave expression to the profound sense of bafflement and indignation he felt after the setbacks of 1927. On another level, however, the term carried its own ideological connotations and, indirectly, a message of hope. With it, Mao Dun was clearly invoking the Marxist-Hegelian plotting of world history, whereby historical progress proceeds through the successive resolutions of such contradictions as he had observed in Chinese society. Each time Mao Dun employs the term *contradiction* in the *Eclipse* trilogy—and there are many such references—one senses that he is using it to reduce the complexities of the social environment to comprehensible or "typical" forces. The promise is held out that once these forces are understood, it should be possible to recognize the true direction in which history is moving and then point a way out of the present political (and psychological) impasse. By the logic of dialectics, the horrific collision of social forces in China must eventually give way to a harmonizing "synthesis." Through the notion of contradiction, then, Mao Dun attempts to communicate both a sense of the comprehensiveness of his social observations and an awareness of the dynamic process of historical change—the very factors by which he judged whether a work of fiction had achieved a true understanding of history, or *shidaixing*. But if we accept Mao Dun's rather bald invitation to read the novellas in *Eclipse* with the Hegelian dialectic in mind, we shall discover that the configuration of contradictions that make up his fictional world retain some distinctly non-Hegelian features and that they again and again fail to facilitate the hopeful resolutions they promise.

Mao Dun's early works are clearly constructed around certain binary oppositions. In none of his works are they more evident than in "Disillusionment," where Mao Dun's allegorical method of naming characters is only the first evidence of the novel's geometry of human relationships. The names of the two primary female characters, Hui 慧 (knowledge) and Jing 靜 (tranquillity) promptly identify them with the poles of experience and innocence, and this opposition is then echoed both through descriptions of the two characters (Hui is repeatedly described as an erotic, physical presence, whereas Jing is said to possess a spiritual beauty that is "indescribable") and through commentary (at one point, Jing thinks to herself, "The virgin's ideals and the young married woman's reality are always contradictory" [10]). Such an opposition is, of course, a familiar one in Western naturalism, where it is generally the occasion for the ritualistic seduction of the virgin by a representative of urban sophistication. In works of this kind, of which Émile Zola's *Une Vie* is typical, the transition from innocence to experience is accompanied by a psychological experience of disillusionment: once initiated, the former innocent belatedly recognizes the worthlessness of the values associated with sophistication. The title of Mao Dun's novella announces his indebtedness to works of this kind, and the plot of the first half of "Disillusionment" pursues a familiar course. The seduction scene, when it occurs, however, fails to achieve the expected sense of finality, in part because the opposition between innocence and experience, embodied in Jing and Hui, is from the beginning not beset with the usual tensions. In the same breath that the narrator establishes their opposition, he mentions the two women's similarity and interdependence: though "possessed of opposing characters," he says, "they share the same spoiled, proud temperament" (11–12). From the beginning they share as well a largely unruffled friendship, and Jing's attitude toward the experienced Hui is characterized less by fascination or envy than by a sense of personal identification and fellow feeling; she allows Hui to move into her tiny apartment because, she says, she feels "sympathy for the oppressed," that is, she recognizes that Hui's present hard-heartedness is in fact a kind of ressentiment, nourished by years of ill-treatment at the hands of men (11–12). Oddly, this negative capacity for sympathy—rather than any ambition or desire—is Jing's downfall. When the philanderer

Baosu 抱素, who has been flirting with both women but whose suit has recently been rejected by Hui, attempts then to seduce Jing, he expertly awakens her sympathy by comparing himself to a deflowered virgin, abandoned by his seducer Hui. That is, he plays precisely the victimized role that Jing has accorded Hui in her imagination (and also, of course, the role that Jing herself will be made to accept as the result of his stratagems). At this point, Jing has a sudden vision of pity as an undifferentiated recognition of the victimization of all humankind, as an all-embracing love. In the terms of the novel, Jing's submission is a demonstration of this love, a love whose object is less the hypocritical Baosu than that potential aspect of herself that Hui and Baosu both represent. Pity serves as the emotional lubrication by which a series of transferences becomes possible: through his ruse, Baosu identifies himself with Hui, while Jing, by allowing herself to be seduced, knowingly becomes Hui for a time.

The consummation of the seduction is suppressed, both textually and in Jing's psyche: she swoons, and remembers the event only as a "pleasant dream," although her later discovery of Baosu's hypocrisy brings on a temporary illness. In terms of narrative development, however, the episode does appear to free Jing to move to another stage of development (specifically, involvement in revolutionary politics) and clearly dispels what tension existed in the specific opposition of Hui and Jing as characters. But the dualism implicit in that relationship is not resolved but rather relocated in Jing's personal psychology. The text had earlier alerted us to the possibility of such a psychologization: "I'm not afraid of the outer world's lack of tranquillity [*jing*]; I only fear I can't calm my heart" (6). After the seduction scene, the vague feeling of vexation Jing had earlier felt becomes a clearly defined internal war between disappointment and hope. One side of her split psyche argues that "every hope results in disappointment, and every beautiful longing is ugly at heart," while the other encourages her: "Without hope, what is the meaning of life? . . . It is not disappointment that is painful but a life without hope or purpose!" (54). And indeed, the short time Jing spends in Wuhan, depicted in chapters 9 through 11 of the novella, is characterized by extreme fluctuations of emotional highs and lows. She is "moved to tears" at the assembly of revolutionary forces in chapter 9, but the day-to-day "sloganeering" of revolutionary work bores her. She is most troubled, however, by the hedonism that characterizes life among the revolutionaries in Wuhan:

her comrades seem trapped in cycles of "tension" and "exhaustion," i.e. between periods of feverish engagement in political and sexual activity and periods when they succumb to feelings of pessimism and despair. In this "contradictory" environment Jing grows ill and despondent, and what hope she still has for the revolution seems to ebb. Her women friends—identifying her once again with a passive, pitying role—recommend she take a job as a nurse at the mountain resort of Guling.

In the final section of the novella, a new dyadic opposition is explored in Jing's relationship with one of the soldiers under her care. In this new dichotomy, the soldier Qiang Meng 強猛 (whose name means something like "strength and ferocity" and whose style, Weili 惟力, means "by force alone") is associated with the doctrine of futurism, while Jing is equated with naturalism. Futurism, an important element of the Soviet avant-garde in the 1910s and 1920s, fascinated Mao Dun, who wrote several essays on the subject. While admiring its "fearlessness" and "dynamism," he was wary of its purely "destructive" spirit.[33] He believed futurism had developed as a radical antidote to Russian nihilism and that it was inappropriate for China; in particular, he criticized the tendency to spurn current realities in the interests of an idealized future. Qiang Meng was modeled after a young author named Gu Zhongqi 顧仲起, who had submitted stories to *Short Story Magazine* in the early 1920s and who later enlisted as a soldier. When Mao Dun encountered him in Wuhan in 1927, Gu confided his fascination with battle for its own sake and shocked Mao Dun with his repeated patronage of prostitutes. Mao Dun clearly saw in Gu Zhongqi another variety of disillusioned youth, one who had abandoned his idealism for an unending "pursuit of stimulation."[34] The character Qiang Meng in "Disillusionment" describes his fascination with combat to Jing: he calls the battlefield the "best setting for futurism" because it is a site of pure destruction. He fights "not to win or lose" but because of the "concentration of experience" that war provides: "Life on the battlefield is life at its liveliest and most volatile; it is also life at its most artistic" (83). Futurism, of course, is less an

33. Mao Dun, "Weilaipai wenxue de xianshi" 未來派文學的現勢 (The current development of futurist literature), *Xiaoshuo yuebao* 13, no. 10 (10 October 1922). See the discussion of futurism and Mao Dun in Yu-shih Chen, *Realism and Allegory*, pp. 72–74.

34. See Mao Dun, *Wo zouguo de daolu* 2:4–6.

ideology than an aesthetic doctrine, and Mao Dun clearly intended Qiang Meng to be understood not as an activist but as an artist of revolution: he approaches the revolution as pure experience and is completely disinterested in its social rationale.

Jing again plays the quiescent element of the pair. Her naturalism is a passive doctrine of resignation, but it too is the consequence of disillusionment (both with her earlier experiences with Baosu and with her political activities). Once again, Jing's feeling of pity for the wounded male allows and determines the relationship. And once again, no real conflict develops from the opposition between the two characters: during the course of their relationship we come to understand that his futurism and her naturalism are in fact mutually defining and interdependent creeds. As she puts it, "His futurism was nothing but a countercheck to an extreme form of tragic pessimism" (84). As futurist and naturalist, Qiang and Jing are halves who become whole only by recognizing the inevitability of their opposition. Without that recognition they are "wounded," Qiang in the heart (his "left breast"), Jing in the will. Their brief commingling results in a relationship based not on a dynamic synthesis of their opposing views of the world but rather on a recognition of their views' inevitable coexistence and alternation. Significantly, however, their relationship is played out in an environment removed from the ordinary affairs of the world and is soon dissolved when Qiang Meng is called back to the war. Before he leaves, Qiang consoles Jing by saying that he has disavowed futurism: "Didn't you tell me that futurism admires only force but neglects to ask whether the use of force is just? You've persuaded me!" (96–97). But even after this we are told that "Jing's powers of reason and Qiang's emotions struggled on in the dark" (97), and the future holds only a weak promise of success (or even survival) for the two lovers. At the close of "Disillusionment," Jing is left once again in the company of her women friends, feeling as if she has been awakened out of a "great dream."

Both of the romantic encounters that constitute the narrative kernel of the novella have thus been reduced in Jing's imagination to dreams. The contradictions that the text explores through these relationships have not led to any productive resolution nor even to any lasting consequences at the level of plot. Mao Dun acknowledges as much in his discussion of "Disillusionment" in the essay "From Guling to Tokyo," where he says the novella explores precisely the alternation of "unending seeking and unending disillusionment" in the protagonist's psychology.[35] Jing's hopes are inevitably dashed by the mechanisms of the plot, but just as inevitably her disappointments generate new hopes. Though superficially offering a linear plot line, the novel is constructed around a series of alternating polarities, variously defined as innocence and experience, hope and disappointment, naturalism and futurism. Instead of placing these polarities in dynamic opposition, Mao Dun has preferred to set them in temporal conjunction and explore their interdependence as mutually defining conceptual spheres. Mao Dun's contradictions thus come to be understood less as conflicts inhering in the real world—or even in the social order given representation in the text—than as conflicting perspectives on an ever-elusive reality. Such oppositions resist pragmatic resolution; one can at best momentarily rob them of their agonistic quality through the subjective exercise of pity.

Mao Dun's handling of contradictions thus fails to generate a dynamic sense of historical progression and would even seem, from this description, to have more in common with traditional Chinese attitudes toward dyadic oppositions (as in the familiar opposition of yin and yang) than with the Marxist-Hegelian dialectic Mao Dun espoused. But the recurring alternation between binary poles in "Disillusionment" does not provide the philosophical consolation of the yin-yang dualism; instead one discovers in the characters' psychological response to the contradictions a distinctly modern sense of alienation and anxiety. All the commotion of the novella's plot comes to seem, in C. T. Hsia's words, a "caricature of purposeful action,"[36] and in the end the reader's attention is directed away from outer realities to Jing's psychological fluctuations.[37] In nearly all of Mao Dun's early novels there occur scenes where primary characters are suddenly overwhelmed by their disordered, chaotic perceptions of the external world—moments in which the social contradictions sketched in the external world are violently resituated in the subjectivity of the protagonist. Jing in "Disillusionment," Fang Luolan 方羅蘭 in "Vacillation,"

---

35. Mao Dun, "Cong Guling dao Dongjing," in Tang Jinhai et al., *Mao Dun zhuanji* 1:336.
36. C. T. Hsia, *A History of Modern Chinese Fiction*, p. 143.
37. Jaroslev Průšek has also observed this movement from objective description to psychological exploration, which results in a weakening of the line of action in Mao Dun's fiction. See "Mao Tun and Yü Ta-fu," in his *The Lyrical and the Epic*.

Wang Zhongzhao in "Pursuit," and Wu Sunfu 吳蓀甫 in *Midnight* all experience such moments. In each case we may observe a fundamentally triangular structure in which the protagonist stands apart from the poles of a traditional dyadic opposition as an alienated third party. Perry Link has analyzed such triangular plots in the period's popular romantic fiction, which often features a male character who finds himself unable to choose between an old-fashioned woman and a modern one: in the opposition of the two women Link sees figured the conservative and radical cultural alternatives facing China in the twentieth century.[38] But the triangle was not only a romantic motif in China during the 1920s but characterized the political environment as well: it was the three-sided alliance of the Nationalist party, the Chinese communist party, and the Comintern that many radicals held responsible for the failure of the "great revolution" of 1927. Yu-shih Chen argues that many of the triangular personal relationships in *Eclipse* are in fact allegorical representations of this political reality.[39] But whether or not we choose to read the trilogy as a straightforward political allegory, it is evident that Mao Dun is playing with the figure of the triangle at both the romantic and political levels throughout *Eclipse*. We saw evidence of this already in the relationship of Baosu, Jing, and Hui in "Disillusionment," although there the male is not granted a significant interior life but serves largely to facilitate muta-

38. See Perry Link, *Mandarin Ducks and Butterflies*, especially pp. 196–235.
39. See Yu-shih Chen, *Realism and Allegory*, chapters 3 through 5. Chen's argument seems to me persuasive only in part. She is surely correct, for example, to interpret the meeting described in chapter 5 of "Disillusionment," where a group of students discuss and eventually condemn a triangular love affair, as an allegorical representation of the Communist party's debate over its alliance with the Nationalist party. But if the entire trilogy is intended, as she suggests, as an extended allegory of the "collective experience of the Chinese Communist movement" (with certain characters representing specific contingents within the party—Hui, the collaborationist faction; Jing, the faction believing in self-determination, and so forth), this judgment at the very least undercuts her high evaluation of the literary merit of the trilogy. For as a schematic allegory, even with the help of Yu-shih Chen's key, *Eclipse* seems murky and inconsistent. I believe that Mao Dun may have flirted with such allegorizing in parts of "Disillusionment" but that the trilogy best reveals its strengths when read as a work of psychological realism. We need not view the incidents in the novel as simply anecdotal, however. Realism always traffics in types, and Mao Dun clearly intends his characters to represent the general trends and attitudes that characterized Chinese society during the "great revolution." Mao Dun may even have intended us to equate these trends and attitudes to some extent with the policies of specific parties or factions (for example, the cynicism Hui embodies may indeed have characterized a certain faction of the Communist party). But the characters are not simply emblematic of those parties and factions; that is, they do not stand in for them in an overarching political allegory.

tions in the much more powerfully articulated dyadic relationship of Jing and Hui. In "Vacillation," the second novella of the *Eclipse* trilogy, however, triangularity is brought to center stage.

At the most superficial level "Vacillation" concerns a love triangle, involving the protagonist, Fang Luolan; his wife, Meili 梅麗; and the political activist Sun Wuyang 孫舞陽. Although Fang still loves his passive, tradition-bound wife, he becomes increasingly fascinated with the sexually liberated Sun Wuyang, who, like Hui in "Disillusionment," has made a conscious decision that "no man will be loved by me, only toyed with" (214). But Mao Dun was not content to simply reproduce in "Vacillation" a love triangle like those in popular fiction. Although the two women clearly represent tradition and modernity to Fang, each plays a more complicated role in the novel than that opposition would suggest. When Fang's desire for her becomes evident, Sun Wuyang argues the case for Fang's marriage, discouraging him from any thought of divorce. She frankly admits that although she frequently acts on her "instinctive drive" for sexual expression, she is unable to return another's love: "My sexual drive cannot bind me to anyone. . . . I am used to my freedom; I can no longer be anyone's wife" (214–15). When she proceeds, however, to offer her body to him "for a few minutes of satisfaction," she seems less a champion of individual freedom than a slave to her promiscuous instincts. Her proposition leaves Fang bewildered and unable to respond. On the other hand, Meili proves unexpectedly self-possessed and forceful when she finally recognizes her husband's true feelings for Sun. Requesting a divorce, she tells him, "The education I received was not modern, of course, but it did teach me not to play the fool" (206). Fang Luolan is as "bewildered" by this assertion as he is by Sun Wuyang's behavior, and he adamantly refuses the divorce. As the novella proceeds, Fang becomes increasingly trapped in a romantic double bind: the more he is rebuffed by one woman, the more powerfully he feels drawn—"unknowingly," as the narrator points out—to the other for the "solace" she will provide. He has fallen into what the protagonist of another of Mao Dun's early novels calls the "pit of triangularity."[40] Faced with an abundance of options (none of which, however, represents a really tenable choice), his apparent "freedom to choose" simply induces paralysis. Triangularity, by introducing a

40. Mao Dun, *Hong*, p. 228.

third, free element, undermines the fixed and mutually reaffirming identity of such alternating dyadic poles as those we observed in "Disillusionment."

Fang's inability to choose between the two women is symptomatic, of course, of the vacillation of the novella's title and of a general lack of self-knowledge. The latter manifests itself with more serious social consequences in Fang's waffling political behavior when, as the local Nationalist party representative, he is called upon to resolve the two major political disputes depicted in the novella. Each dispute concerns the village's response to a threatened uprising (in the first case by disgruntled store employees, in the second by local peasants), and significantly each is characterized by a triangular division of political forces in the village. Though the alignment of interests differs slightly in the two cases, the underlying division of power in the village is among (1) the forces commanded by Hu Guoguang 胡國光, a local demagogue who, like Tiger Jiang in *Ni Huanzhi*, has appropriated revolutionary rhetoric for his own purposes, (2) the representatives of the radical wing of the party, including Sun Wuyang, and (3) the more moderate faction of Fang Luolan and his followers. In each dispute the result is the same: Hu Guoguang, through skillful political manipulation, succeeds in securing an alliance with the radicals over the ineffectual objections of Fang and his faction. In the first case Fang issues a counterproposal, which is quickly overridden; in the second case he fails completely to articulate a temperate response to the impending crisis. When in the first dispute the shopkeepers who had expected him to argue their case confront him, the extent of his impotence and confusion is brought home to him:

> When Fang Luolan observed how enraged they were, he felt uncomfortable. He mumbled a few perfunctory words, but he could offer no definite answer. When it came to these practical problems, what right did he have to give a definite answer? Of course, he should at least have his own opinion, and there was nothing to stop him from expressing it. But somehow he felt powerless even to determine what his opinion should be. (163)

In failing to act, Fang cedes his power to Hu Guoguang, and the outcome in both cases is a brutal purge. In the end Fang is forced to recognize the harmful consequences of his vacillation: during the riot that erupts at the end of the novella he has a nightmarish vision in which the eyes of the slain stare at him "as if awaiting a reply," and he hears a voice intoning, "You wanted freedom but got tyranny" (249). In his political life, as in his romantic relationships, freedom offers choices that may simply induce hesitation; in the space of that hesitation other, less scrupulous individuals rush in to seize control.

To this point, we have viewed the romantic and the political strands of the novella's plot as separate but parallel illustrations of the dangers of triangularity. But the two lines of plot development (and, more generally, the two spheres of human activity they treat) are repeatedly conjoined, often to ironical effect, as in the scene in chapter 6 where Sun Wuyang sings the "Internationale" while boldly flirting with the party leader, Lin Zichong 林子冲. In Hu Guoguang's political maneuverings power and sex are also commingled; his authority in the village is secured at least in part by arranging erotic favors for his rivals. Moreover, as the plot of "Vacillation" develops, one notices a progressive infiltration of erotic concerns into the political life of the village: whereas the first uprising described in the novella revolves around the conventional affairs of politics (wages, strikes, store closings), the second comes increasingly to center on the issue of *gongqi* 共妻, or "wife sharing." This term is a neologism derived from *gong-chan* 共產, or "property sharing," the compound that is used to translate the term *communism*. The "local hoodlums and evil gentry" (*tuhao lieshen* 土豪劣紳) first spread rumors that the revolution will bring not only *gongchan* but also *gongqi*; the peasants, however, quickly take up the idea, since in their traditionalist view women are, after all, nothing more than a kind of property. The fear that *gongqi* initially inspires is soon supplanted, even among the peasants, with fascination. Hu Guoguang and the radicals (whose theories of women's liberation seem to provide a rationale for *gongqi*) take up the cause; over the feeble objections of Fang Luolan they decree that concubines will be "reallocated" and set up a "Women's Care Center" to take care of former bondsmaids and nuns. The center soon degenerates, however, into an officially sponsored brothel, and in the final riot these newly "liberated" women suffer the brunt of the violence.

If eroticism plays an increasingly intrusive role in public discourse in "Vacillation," its encroachment into the individual psyche is even more insidious, as Fang Luolan's interior monologues repeatedly demonstrate. When we first meet Fang, he is indulging in an extravagant daydream in which he sees the figure of Sun Wuyang bedecked with sparkling stars and fireworks. Later, similar reveries overwhelm him at crucial moments, hindering his ability to concentrate on the political problems it is his responsibility to solve. He later recognizes that his preoccupation with Sun Wuyang is in a sense the cause of the village's troubles: his "strange romance" with her has caused him to neglect public affairs, "allowing Hu Guoguang, who we knew from the start to be unreliable, to monopolize the authority of the party" (220). What would seem to be harmless, private fantasies thus incur terrible, public consequences. Fang's erotic life and indeed his subjectivity as a character is revealed in the terms of the novel as an excess—of desires, of choices, of possibilities—that at first inspires in him a fleeting sense of freedom. In the end, however, the choices blur his perception of reality and cripple his performance as an actor in events of public significance. Such at least is the judgment of Li Ke 李克, the "rational man" whom the party sends toward the end of the novella to prescribe a solution for the chaotic situation in the village. Li diagnoses the village's problem as "a lack of clear understanding," which has left the party representatives "uncertain whether to use force or to be lax" (238). In his memoirs Mao Dun writes that Li Ke is the only positive character in "Vacillation" but admits that he is a one-dimensional foil.[41] He possesses a comprehensive, clarified vision of Chinese society—but significantly he arrives too late to prevent catastrophe. Significantly, too, he is portrayed as devoid of psychology, whereas Mao Dun's fictional instincts are elsewhere drawn to the complexity and opacity of characters mired in psychological contradictions. As fascinating as such characters may be to Mao Dun, their psychological and erotic preoccupations are always perceived as a descent into irrationality, as a blurring of the complete and perfectly lucid view of history that Li Ke represents.

The excess of choices that troubled Fang's private world creates in the broader social world a new potential for hypocrisy and for promiscuous interchanges, and it is this danger that is explored in the character of Hu Guoguang. In sharp contrast to Fang, Hu welcomes the new environment and acts decisively to profit from it: as introduced at the beginning of the novel, he is "full of plans," "an old fox of long standing" who is adept at adjusting his schemes as the circumstances and the times demand. A skillful rhetorician, he readily adopts what-

41. Mao Dun, *Wo zouguo de daolu* 2:9.

ever ideological stance serves his private advantage. He was the first in the village to cut off his pigtail, the sign of China's submission to the Manchus, and now recognizing the imminent arrival of the revolutionaries, he promptly decides to join ranks with them. Even his personal name is subject to alteration: when he joins the revolutionary cause, he changes it from the feudal Guofu 國輔 (minister of the nation) to the modern Guoguang (light of the nation). His facility with the language again and again prompts unsuspecting individuals to seek his help: Hu's timid cousin Wang Rongchang 王榮昌 cedes his position in the Shopkeepers' Union to Hu, and Lu Muyou 陸慕游, a member of the union's standing committee, asks Hu to ghostwrite his speeches. Each time Hu uses the occasion to advance his own cause. Gradually appropriating others' powers of speech, he slowly infects much of public discourse in the village with his particular brand of linguistic instrumentalism. The dangers of the breach that such instrumentalism opens between public reality and public discourse is aptly reflected in the campaign to conflate *gongchan* and *gongqi* in the public mind. What was originally a misunderstanding of the party's intentions takes on increasing reality as more and more people accept it, and it eventually incites public violence—a tangible consequence.

Unlike Hu Guoguang, Fang Luolan continues to believe that political rhetoric should be more than an instrument of the individual's will to power, that it should in fact offer an objective and verifiable explanation of human relations. He finds himself, however, unable to discriminate among the diverse ideologies and creeds of the villagers, just as he is unable to choose between the charms of Sun Wuyang and his wife. Confronted with an excess of choices, he retains his nostalgic conviction that among these alternatives there must be a right one, if only he knew how to identify it. Fang is thus unable to achieve a binding linguistic representation of the world, yet at the same time he remains unwilling to embrace the arbitrariness of human relations in a society where name and reality do not necessarily correspond. Whereas Hu Guoguang is willing to assume the hypocrisy endemic to a world dominated by triangular relationships, Fang wishes to remain true to his word.

In the final novella in the *Eclipse* trilogy, "Pursuit," Mao Dun goes on to explore individual responses to a promiscuous social order in which political rhetoric has been effectively discredited. All of the novella's primary characters were, like Mao Dun himself, participants in the failed 1927 revolution and are said to suffer from the disease of the times (*shidaibing* 時代病), by which is meant not simply a disorder common to the era but a fundamental disturbance of the individual's relation to history itself. The young protagonists of "Pursuit" once imagined that through their political efforts they were acting in conjunction with the forces of history to create a new world, but after the movement's failure they must decide, each individually, either to restrict the scope of their reformist efforts or to embrace the world in its fallen state. They must, in effect, resign themselves to a lesser role in historical process. All three of the major alternatives to politics explored in the novel—pedagogy, journalism, and an eroticized aestheticism—are undertaken out of resignation to a world where truly original, productive work (such as the characters imagined their political efforts to be) is impossible; all three involve transmission rather than true creativity. Zhang Manqing 張曼青, having given up on his own generation's capacity to alter the world through a decisive political stroke, has grown suspicious of all group activity, which he believes subject to manipulation by unscrupulous individuals. He decides to pursue a modest career as an educator, transmitting his ideals to the next generation. But in practice he is constrained both by a conservative school administration and by a lack of materials ("It stands to reason that the best source for modern history should be newspapers, but Chinese newspapers have no reliable historical value" [355]). Furthermore, like Ni Huanzhi, he even doubts the possibility of guiding students in any direction other than the one they choose for themselves: "The young should follow their own historical path; no one can entice them down an alternative road!" (276). Since he lacks confidence both in the material he is to transmit through his teaching and in the value of its transmission for his students, in the end his pedagogical efforts are paralyzed. He observes ironically: "In our student days, I always thought that in the future our brothers would be happier than we, but today our successors have begun to envy our era its freedom. Life is just that perverse and contradictory!" (421).

The journalist Wang Zhongzhao shares Zhang Manqing's belief that his generation has courted disillusionment with its exaggerated idealism. He too decides to resign himself to reality and pursue a more modest ambition through his career in journalism. But as I have shown above, he too has problems finding material for his articles; the facts he finds seem invariably to dissolve as he arranges them for composition. He soon comes to wonder if his profession is not simply the transmission of rumors (288). In both cases, limited efforts to contribute to social progress come perversely to retard it, and the educator and the journalist feel themselves more and more out of step with history and ever more deeply trapped in disillusionment. Zhang Manqing and Wang Zhongzhao share more than their retreat from politics, however: both have redirected a measure of their former idealism onto their romantic life. Both choose fiancées whom they describe as feminine ideals, and both eagerly anticipate the refuge from public life that marriage will provide. But these dreams too are destined for disappointment: once Zhang Manqing has married, his wife proves as "shallow, mean, and petty" as his friend Zhang Qiuliu had predicted; and Wang Zhongzhao's romantic ideals are shattered even before he reaches the altar by his fiancée's disfigurement in an accident.

The futility of such efforts to redirect or contain a frustrated idealism is perceived most clearly by the nihilists Shi Xun 史循 and Zhang Qiuliu, whose voices are for this reason the most forceful in the novella. Shi Xun dismisses all the characters' ambitions, including his own fantasies of suicide, as nothing more than manifestations of "doubt" (283) and philosophically reduces all of life to alternating cycles of activity and quiescence. Qiuliu correctly prophesies Manqing's and Zhongzhao's professional and romantic failures, and as the events of the novel reinforce her bitterness, she comes increasingly to attribute everything to fortune. Wang Zhongzhao observes late in the novel that "she has raised a white flag in the face of fortune" (422). She herself remarks that "fortune toys with people" (394), and by herself toying with the affections of men she hopes to appropriate some of its power. She rationalizes her behavior, saying, "It's all right to deceive people as long as you don't hurt them" (337). But in fact the freedom she enjoys is, like Hu Guoguang's, predicated on hypocrisy, and the plot of the novella demonstrates that her cynicism carries dangers (toward herself as well as toward others) that she fails at first to recognize.

Zhang Qiuliu's flirtatiousness places her, like Hui and Sun Wuyang, in the category of experienced women. But she shows as well a profound capacity for pity that is reminiscent of the innocent Jing. This comes to the fore primarily in her relationship with the syphilitic Shi Xun, whom she nurses in the hospital when others have abandoned him. She makes it her cause to "remake" him, to resuscitate his will to live. But this project, despite its origins in her feelings of compassion, proves as misguided as Wang Zhongzhao's and Zhang Manqing's careerism: the night of lovemaking she enjoys with Shi Xun only hastens his death and introduces the spirochete into her own body. Syphilis proves more powerful than Qiuliu's mission of mercy; her pity has no power to counter its effect but simply provides a vector for its transmission. Venereal disease serves as the novella's most powerful metaphor for the contagious efficacy of disillusionment. Once Qiuliu is infected, the contagion reveals the full strength of its destructive power, for she is, at least metaphorically, at the center of all the characters' remaining hopes. Each of the men finds himself fascinated with her, and the women whom Manqing and Zhongzhao have chosen as ideal mates resemble her so closely that even their lovers confuse their identities (356, 360). The concluding event of the novel—the arrival of a telegram announcing the disfigurement of Zhongzhao's fiancée—marks the defacement of the text's last emblem of wholeness and seems to represent the collaboration of fate itself in Qiuliu's destructive flirtatiousness. In the final scene of the novella Zhongzhao is left holding in one hand a photo of his fiancée's smiling face and in the other the telegram announcing its disfigurement. This "last blow of fate" (430) puts an end to Zhongzhao's fond hope that he could ever, even through the practice of the strictest pragmatism, exert power over the Real.

Of the characters in "Pursuit," Zhang Qiuliu and Shi Xun exhibit most clearly the symptoms of *shidaibing*. They proudly deny the controlling power of time in their lives; during their night of lovemaking "they forgot the past and no longer worried about the future." But syphilis, the somatic equivalent of their spiritual malaise, by establishing an unwelcome connection between their past sexual behavior and present physical condition, serves as a powerful reminder of temporal continuity: as Qiuliu imagines it, "the tail of the black shadow of the past insisted on projecting itself onto the body of the present" (400). By refusing to recognize the power of history, the two remain bound to a view of the world that is just as fractured and partial as that professed by Manqing and Zhongzhao.

A similar inability to comprehend the whole of historical and social necessity afflicts the protagonist of Mao Dun's lengthiest and most famous novel, *Midnight*. Wu Sunfu, a powerful industrialist and a nationalist who hopes to win back the Chinese economy from foreign control by building up a strong national industry, appears to be in a much better position to command his social environment than the failed revolutionaries of "Pursuit." But his desire to rebuild his home village of Shuangqiao 雙橋 into a model town with "a forest of tall chimneys belching black smoke, a fleet of merchantmen breasting the waves, and a column of buses speeding through the countryside" (128)[42] is, in the terms of the novel, a pipe dream based on a naive misunderstanding of the true historical role of Chinese capitalism. Wu Sunfu's blindness, if not his dream, is shared by all the major characters, even the urban revolutionaries, who have allowed their energies to be depleted by promiscuous sexual behavior and empty sloganeering. The true nature of Chinese society is presented as a riddle, whose solution the characters seek in vain. For answers they look to various texts, all of which are denigrated by the novel: a storm rains through an open window to destory the feudal *Taishang ganying pian* 太上感應篇 (Supreme book of rewards and punishments); a child urinates on a copy of the *Sanminzhuyi* 三民主義 (The three principles), the bible of the Nationalist party; one of the factory girls uses a communist pamphlet to line the basket she carries while selling peanuts on the street. The riddle of Chinese society may be answered, the novel suggests, only by the text of *Midnight* itself. In the first chapter the "femme fatale" Liu Yuying 劉玉英, a character who in many ways resembles Zhang Qiuliu, asks the economics professor Li Yuting 李玉亭, "What sort of society are we living in?" He suggests that the drawing room next door, in which sit many of the novel's cast of characters, is "Chinese society in miniature" (25).

But we recall that *Midnight* presents a significantly scaled-down version of the novel Mao Dun had intended to write. In his memoirs Mao Dun gives a detailed summary of his original plan for the novel. He writes that his thinking at the time he began composition in 1930 was heavily influenced by a contemporary debate over the nature of Chinese society. As Mao Dun characterizes it, the debate was dominated by three schools of opinion: (1) the revolutionary faction, which held that China under Jiang Jieshi remained a semifeudal, semicolonial society and called for a revolution led by the proletariat, (2) the Trotskyites, who maintained that China was already "traveling the capitalist road" and that Chinese capitalists should take the lead in expelling

42. Mao Dun, *Ziye*. Page numbers refer to the 1975 Hong Kong reprint published by Nanguo chubanshe. My translations are adapted from the near-complete English rendition by Hsu Meng-hsiang and A. C. Barnes.

colonialism and feudalism from China, and (3) advocates of "national capitalism," who wished to see the suppression of both communism and colonialism in China, followed by the establishment of an independent capitalist society on the model of Western Europe and the United States. Mao Dun writes that *Midnight* was specifically intended as a rebuttal to the Trotskyites and the national capitalists: "China was not traveling the capitalist road; but under the exploitation of colonial and feudal powers, allied with the bureaucrat-compradore class, China was sinking deeper into a semicolonial, semifeudal condition."[43] In a more general sense, Mao Dun hoped to paint a contrasting picture of the "white city," where the colonial and feudal powers lorded over the urban proletariat, and the "red country," where peasants were beginning to assert themselves with the support of the Communist party.

As Mao Dun worked on the novel, however, he recognized that its scope was simply too broad and began deleting the sections that were to treat the rural peasantry. As the text now stands, only chapter 4 is set in the countryside, and its focus is on the rural gentry; the peasants appear only as an undifferentiated, vengeful crowd. Their effective absence means that the novel can only claim to present the society of Shanghai—not all of Chinese society—in miniature. Curiously, too, the people Mao Dun identifies as the ultimate villains of modern Chinese history, the Western imperialists, who had made Shanghai the largest foreign concession in the country, are present only as a vague threat at the borders of the narrative. *Midnight* thus fails to give representation to the two crucial forces determining the historical course of China in the 1930s—that is, to the forces that Mao Dun must have recognized as the fundamental poles of the historical dialectic. As a result the Shanghai of the novel is cut off from the true dynamics of the historical moment. Belonging neither to the old world (feudal China) nor to the new (revolutionary rural China), the city is a contained, dead place where all activity is stillborn and unproductive. The events of the novel are little more than pseudo events: the central conflict of the plot, the strike in Wu Sunfu's silk factory, leads of necessity to a stalemate. Wu Sunfu, a national capitalist trying desperately to stem the tide of the imperialist economic

43. Mao Dun, *Wo zouguo de daolu* 2:92.

takeover, is not the true enemy of the workers, nor are they, members of China's tiny urban proletariat, the true standard-bearers of revolutionary change in China.

But if from the ultimate perspective of history Shanghai is unproductive, it is anything but inactive. On the contrary, it is the locus of a maximum concentration of energy. The opening paragraph of *Midnight* describes a huge neon sign that looms over the city, proclaiming in English "LIGHT, HEAT, POWER." The city's economic energy comes, however, not from productive labor (the actual sources of production—the factories and farms—are in total disarray), but rather from the pure fluidity of funds within the city. The one thing Shanghai has no shortage of is money. In the "speculation fever" (39) that has contaminated the city, money is the sole object of nearly everyone's pursuit, yet as one character says, "There is plenty of cash in Shanghai; nobody can say money's tight" (42). Economic life in the city does not simply entail the accrual of funds. The nature of money is to be exchanged, and the pleasure of possessing it resides precisely in its potential transmission. The pursuit of wealth inevitably draws the seeker into the market, and in the overheated economic environment of Shanghai, one can maintain riches only by venturing them.

The same metaphors—of fever and reckless transmission—that characterize Shanghai's economic life are applied in the novel to the sexual pursuits of its citizens. Old Mr. Wu, the family patriarch who comes from the country to visit Shanghai in the first chapter, is overwhelmed by the erotic environment of the city. The city streets appear to him like a spinning "kaleidoscope" of color and sound (9), and his family's drawing room, to which he is brought, seems to be "filled with countless swelling bosoms, bosoms that bobbed and quivered and danced around him" (14). The old man quickly expires of what the doctor pronounces to be "overexcitement," a death that clearly symbolizes the demise of the old China. But the young people who come to the city (of whom Wu Sunfu's sister, Huifang 蕙芳, is emblematic) soon take on the addiction to stimulation that characterizes the city's older, more hardened denizens. Were it to stop, they would be left "in the grip of a terrible despondency" (489). The young romantic Zhang Susu 張素素 seems to have caught this spirit when she describes—with an eager delight—the climactic "upheaval" she foresees, an earthquake that will leave "the whole universe in chaos" (24). More typically, characters try to take pragmatic advantage of the crescendo of desire in the city. In becoming mistress to the speculator Zhao Botao 趙伯韜 and later to Wu Sunfu himself, Liu Yuying, for example, is calculatedly taking advantage of the fact that "whereas men used money, women used themselves as capital" (317). As with money, the value of sexuality lies in its expenditure. But in the Shanghai of the novel, desire acted upon is not exhausted but amplified. The result is an inflation of eroticism that exactly parallels the city's economic inflation.

Wu Sunfu suffers a process of character erosion similar to that we observed with Fang Luolan in "Vacillation." His noble ambition to revive China's economy is gradually subverted by the twin temptations of Shanghai's speculation fever and its free-floating eroticism. The two contend within his brain, each interfering with the function of the other. Frustrated with business, he alleviates his stress by raping an innocent maid; but when trying to concentrate on professional matters, he falls prey to disjointed erotic fantasies: "No matter how he tried, he just could not concentrate, especially when the memory of Liu Yuying's inviting smile, her lovely voice, and her limpid eyes kept hammering away at his brain and distracting him as he tried to wrestle with his business problems" (355). As politics was infected by sex in "Vacillation," so the financial world—and the psyches of its captains—is contaminated in *Midnight*.

Although Wu Sunfu is unable to integrate the erotic and economic spheres of his life, the novel brings the two together cogently in the woman of his daydreams, Liu Yuying. In a scene early in the novel, when she is still playing the role of Zhao Botao's mistress, Liu Yuying overhears Zhao discussing his plans to manipulate the market. Realizing the importance of this information, she goes to sell her "secret retail" at the stock market, which is described as an erotic battlefield, "suffocating, and reeking with sweat" (317). Her possession of this secret, whose revelation would render the frenzied activity she observes around her meaningless, gives her a distinctly sexual pleasure:

> When Liu Yuying looked down and saw that her dress of pale blue gauze was soaked with sweat and that her nipples showed through as two round, rosy blurs, she could not help smiling. How comical it all was, she thought. . . . All these men here were fighting in the dark and she alone knew what was going on: what an immense joke it all was!
> (318)

But only the potential revelation of the secret makes it powerful, and to prolong her enjoyment, she proceeds to conduct what can only be called a flirtation with the speculator Feng Yunqing 馮雲卿: she coyly hints at what she knows yet stops short of revealing it. But Feng, who has ironically despatched his own daughter on a mission to detect just the information Liu Yuying is offering him, proves too obtuse to recognize her hints. Knowing that her information can always find a buyer, Liu Yuying is not fazed, and she takes her secret next to Wu Sunfu, who responds with the appropriate mixture of erotic and financial curiosity.

Liu Yuying's secret, so eagerly sought by the speculators in the novel, is the sort of enigma that frequently serves as a plot motivator in realist fiction. It offers one explanation for the feverish activity in Shanghai, that is, the specific mode of manipulation used by the powerful speculator Zhao Botao to control the market. But this secret is very different in kind from that which, we recall, the novel as a whole purports to harbor: the answer to the riddle of Chinese society itself. The first secret is particularistic and partial and is taken possession of with a sense of erotic fascination, almost as though it had temporarily intruded itself physically into the knower's body. It acquires value only through a ritual of concealment and revelation; upon transmission its value is spent and only a new secret may replace it. Mao Dun's sought-for truth is, on the other hand, comprehensive, manifest, and communal. It is knowledge that is not possessed by the individual or the individual text but contains and structures the entire social order, indeed, all of history. The madness of the capitalistic social order depicted in *Midnight* is its fetishization of the transmissible object, which occludes a broader vision of the interdependence of all objects in the natural world. But secrets and details, the currency of the realist novel, appear themselves to be subject to the rules of the transmission of objects in capitalist society. The novel, in its possession of details, temporarily elevates the described object above the other materials of a disassembled world, and this elevation threatens to de-center the larger, analytical structure of the fictional world.

Mao Dun labored, through both the scale and the artifice of his fiction, to reconcile the detail to the structure and the individual to history. His "ornate, literary" style,[44] which caused several early cri-

44. C. T. Hsia, *A History of Modern Chinese Fiction*, p. 165.

tics to complain that his works moved too slowly and bogged down in description,[45] is in part a reflection of this labor. It is as though he hoped to integrate the detail into the larger structure by explicitly drawing out its relations to all other elements of the represented world in a series of ever-broadening concentric spheres. But his problems with length and closure suggest that the sought-for exterior sphere that would encase the world of the fiction as a meaningful whole and place all its parts in just proportion remained an elusive goal. Finally, the realist novel must take its place within the capitalist drift, a necessity Mao Dun recognized and resisted. At the end of *Midnight*, when Wu Sunfu decides in a fit of hysterics to leave for Guling "to have a look at this Red Army that everybody's so afraid of" (549), the text itself seems to recognize the tenuous historical moment on the eve of revolution that permits its appearance. Unable to fully equate realist fiction with history, Mao Dun appears to court the extinction of the very mode of fiction he had so effectively promulgated.

ZHANG TIANYI:
FICTION AS SOCIAL PERFORMANCE

The fiction of Zhang Tianyi, recognized by many critics as "the most brilliant short-story writer" China produced during the 1930s,[46] offers an interesting counterpoint to the fundamentally novelistic impulses that underlay Mao Dun's oeuvre. Although, as I shall show, the fictional output of the two authors must in the end be judged radically dissimilar in tone and structure, they shared a number of important presuppositions about literature. Not the least of these was a persistent theoretical commitment to realism: calls for truth and reality in fiction recur like a litany throughout Zhang's critical writings. In 1933, in a humorous account of his career entitled "A Tale of Writing," Zhang told how, upon learning that the realist school was out of fashion, he tried writing more modish works in the style of the "School of Incomprehensibility." But the results were unsatisfactory:

45. See, for example, Han Shihang, "*Ziye* de yishu, sixiang ji renwu" 《子夜》的藝術、思想及人物 (The art, thought, and characters of *Midnight*) and Lin Hai 林海, "*Ziye* yu *Zhanzheng yu heping*" 《子夜》與《戰爭與和平》 (*Midnight* and *War and Peace*), both reprinted in Zhuang Zhongqing, *Mao Dun yanjiu lunji*.
46. C. T. Hsia, *A History of Modern Chinese Fiction*, p. 212.

Originally I had hoped to build an ivory tower, but ivory proved too expensive, so I had to make do with cow bones. But where was I to place this cow-bone tower? The city was filled with gunfire from the May Thirtieth and March Eighteenth atrocities, and the countryside was as always teeming with calamities, both man-made and heaven-sent. No matter where I looked, I still found myself in the real world.

Acknowledging failure, I had no choice but to step out of my cow-bone tower and try writing about real events in the real world.[47]

Like earlier realists, Zhang insisted that his literary product had an intimate connection with the external social environment. But as he frequently pointed out, his sense of realism conditioned not only the content of his stories but his style as well: "Since I was going to write about real events, I felt I had to use real language, language that would be understandable to everyone."[48]

As is clear from the passage about the cow-bone tower, Zhang Tianyi perceived the real world as an arena of conflict. And like Mao Dun, Zhang regularly employed dialectical thinking to make sense of its contradictions. His reliance on this method is already evident in a brief 1932 essay entitled "On the Lack of Vigor in Composition: Its Reasons and Its Cure," an article whose earnest tone contrasts sharply with the jocularity of "A Tale of Writing." Contemporary writers, he wrote, themselves embodied a poignant contradiction:

The majority are petty bourgeois intellectuals. The times have forced them to recognize that the class to which they belong has reached a dead end, so they strive to rid their writings of individualism and redefine themselves as part of the collective. On the one hand they have already abandoned (or partially abandoned) the individualistic lyricism of the old literature, as well as its focus on trivial personal affairs, but on the other hand they have not yet fully grasped the new consciousness. Their works as a result seem extremely impoverished.[49]

Zhang's solution for this problem recalls Mao Dun's argument about

---

47. Zhang Tianyi, "Chuangzuo de gushi" 創作的故事 (A tale of writing), in Lu Xun et al., *Chuangzuo de jingyan*; reprinted in *Zhang Tianyi wenxue pinglun ji*, pp. 303–8, here pp. 304–5.
48. Zhang Tianyi, "Chuangzuo de gushi," in Zhang Tianyi, *Zhang Tianyi wenxue pinglun ji*, p. 306.
49. Zhang Tianyi, "Chuangzuo bu zhen zhi yuanyin ji qi chulu" 創作不振之 原因及其出路 (On the lack of vigor in composition: its reasons and its cure), *Beidou* 2, no. 1 (20 January 1932); reprinted in Zhang Tianyi, *Zhang Tianyi wenxue pinglun ji*, pp. 5–6, here p. 5.

the dual need for analysis and observation. A work of literature, Zhang wrote, has a double source, the author's "thought" and the author's "life experience." Literature emerges from the fusion of these two, but each of these elements is itself to be understood dialectically. Ideologically, Zhang called for authors to submit to a kind of "theoretical cultivation" whose base was the "scientific dialectic." Only through "correctly and firmly grasping the dialectic" can authors overcome "the remnants of the old consciousness within themselves." Experientially, Zhang called for a new confrontation of the author's self with the collective: "All new writers should leave their windows and writing desks and enter the broad society of workers, peasants, and soldiers."[50]

Fiction writing, in this formula, entails an active purging of the self-involvement that, Zhang felt, marred earlier May Fourth literature. Like Mao Dun, Zhang Tianyi took as axiomatic a definition of the author as first and foremost an observer of others.[51] Both Mao Dun and Zhang spoke with contempt of authors who wrote only about the "trivial contingent affairs" (*shenbian suoshi* 身邊瑣事) of their private lives; they both resolutely divorced their own fiction from autobiography. This severance did not mean, of course, that they never took the people and events they encountered in their personal lives as material for their fiction: Mao Dun's *Eclipse* trilogy was based on the experiences of his acquaintances during the 1927 revolution, and Zhang Tianyi's many stories about school children are the unmistakable product of the years he spent as a teacher. But their fiction rarely presents the overt exploration or affirmation of the self that we find in the writings of Yu Dafu, Guo Moruo, or even Ye Shaojun.

The one exception to this rule in Zhang Tianyi's oeuvre is his first work of fiction to receive serious attention, "San tian ban de meng" 三天半的夢 (A three and a half day's dream, 1929).[52] As Zhang's only

---

50. Zhang Tianyi, "Chuangzuo bu zhen zhi yuanyin ji qi chulu," in Zhang Tianyi, *Zhang Tianyi wenxue pinglun ji*, p. 6.

51. See Zhang's discussion in "Tan renwu miaoxie" 談人物描寫 (On character description), in Zhang Tianyi, *Zhang Tianyi wenxue pinglun ji*, pp. 109–92, especially pp. 152–60.

52. In 1922 and 1923 Zhang Tianyi published a number of detective stories, which he was later to dismiss as juvenilia, in popular journals like *Libailiu* under the name Zhang Wujing 張無諍. A list of the titles of these works is available in Shen Chengkuan 沈承寬, "Zhang Tianyi zhuzuo xinian" 張天翼著作繫年 (Chronology of Zhang Tianyi's works), in Shen, Huang, and Wu, *Zhang Tianyi yanjiu ziliao*, pp. 502–3. "San tian ban de meng" 三天半的夢 (A three and a half day's dream) was first published in

story to refer overtly to his personal affairs, "A Three and a Half Day's Dream" may be interpreted as a metaphorical purging of the author's autobiographical impulses. In the story, through a series of letters to a friend, the narrator describes his departure from X (by which letter he designates the city in which he presently lives and works) to make a reluctant filial visit to Hangzhou 杭州, a place he hates precisely because, as his friend observes, "his home is there." He soon finds his parents' attentions and small talk cloying: "We talked about relatives and colleagues and friends in X, we talked about the weather and public figures in X, we talked about the buildings, . . . we discussed just about every trivial thing imaginable" (8). He is troubled by his parents' growing reliance on him for financial support and emotional coddling, as their new dependency seems to mark an inversion of the parent-child relationship as he understood it. Viewing his parents' self-limited lives, centered almost entirely on their son, he is consumed with guilt and a profound sense of pathos. He finally decides he is suffering from an irritated "nerve of contradiction" (*maodun shenjing* 矛盾神經) due to his divided loyalties—on the one hand to the "emotional prison" of family life, on the other to his sense of personal freedom. While in Hangzhou he fleetingly feels that his life in X "was nothing but a dream" (8), but upon returning to X, he instead consigns his visit home and the impression left by his "pitiable parents" to the unreal status of a dream (16). The story ends with his resolve to "buy back" his freedom.

The narrative situation in "A Three and a Half Day's Dream" parallels Zhang Tianyi's own life story.[53] Zhang was born in Nanjing, but during his childhood his family moved several times. His father, who was a teacher, finally settled the family in Hangzhou. In the mid-1920s Zhang studied for a brief time at an art school in Shanghai and then went north to attend Beijing University. He entered a science program there because at the time he "felt that there were so many irresolvable problems in the world (relating to life, the revolution, and love) that I could see no practical value in the literary arts." At heart, however,

---

Benliu 1, no. 10 (24 April 1929) and has been reprinted recently in Zhang Tianyi, *Zhang Tianyi wenji* 1:3–16. Page numbers given in the text here and in the discussion of other stories by Zhang Tianyi refer (unless otherwise specified) to *Zhang Tianyi wenji*.

53. The most detailed account of Zhang Tianyi's life is "Zhang Tianyi shengping yu wenxue huodong nianbiao" 張天翼生平與文學活動年表 (Chronology of Zhang Tianyi's life and literary activities), in Shen, Huang, and Wu, *Zhang Tianyi yanjiu ziliao*, pp. 8–46.

"my interests still lay with literature."[54] After only a year of study, Zhang grew tired of his science classes and dropped out of the university. During his stay in Beijing, however, he had been exposed not only to new literary trends but also to a variety of radical political ideas, including Marxism. In 1927 Zhang returned south to undertake a series of temporary jobs (as teacher, office worker, and journalist) and to begin writing in earnest. While living in Shanghai, he received the encouragement of Lu Xun and met other important figures of the New Literature movement. Lu Xun and Yu Dafu themselves encouraged Zhang to publish "A Three and a Half Day's Dream" in the journal *Benliu* 奔流 (Currents). By the early 1930s Zhang had become recognized as an important newcomer on the literary scene and was actively involved in the activities of both the Communist party and the League of Left-Wing Writers.[55]

In 1927 Zhang's father retired, leaving his family in poverty. Zhang's classmate Zhou Songdi 周頌棣 later wrote that one of the major reasons Zhang was so prolific during the early 1930s (publishing five novels and a dozen volumes of short stories between 1931 and 1937) was that he relied on the income from his books and articles to support his elderly parents.[56] Other friends have also recorded the close filial relationship between Zhang and his father.[57] "A Three and a Half Day's Dream" thus clearly tapped a central concern in Zhang's

54. Zhang Tianyi, "Zuojia zishu," p. 276.
55. Wu Zuxiang recalls that in the early 1930s Zhang "undertook whatever tasks he was capable of for the party" but does not specify what these tasks involved. See the interview with Wu Fuhui, "Wu Zuxiang tan Zhang Tianyi" 吳組緗談張天翼 (Wu Zuxiang discusses Zhang Tianyi), in Shen, Huang, and Wu, *Zhang Tianyi yanjiu ziliao*, pp. 73–84, here p. 80. Zhang Tianyi's activities for the League of Left-Wing Writers included serving on the Mass Literature Committee and on the editorial boards of such magazines as *Beidou* and *Shizi jietou*. In 1932 Zhang was given the responsibility of organizing the Nanjing branch of the league.
56. Zhou Songdi 周頌棣, "Wo he Tianyi xiangchu de rizi" 我和天翼相處的日子 (The days I spent with Tianyi), in Shen, Huang, and Wu, *Zhang Tianyi yanjiu ziliao*, pp. 61–72, here p. 70.
57. Cao Ming 草明 visited Hangzhou with Zhang Tianyi in 1935. He later wrote about that trip:

> The feelings between [Zhang] and his father were quite deep. The old man thoroughly loved his son. In the letters he sent Tianyi, he would always write some humorous phrase at the end, like "As many as the bamboo shoots after a spring rain" or "As many as the threads of rain during a fall shower," and would never repeat himself. . . . [Tianyi] explained, "He means his kisses are as abundant as bamboo shoots after a spring rain." "Zhang Tianyi he *Xianshi wenxue* ji qita" 張天翼和《現實文學》及其他 (Zhang Tianyi and *Realist Literature*, etc.), in Shen, Huang, and Wu, *Zhang Tianyi yanjiu ziliao*, pp. 91–94, here p. 93.

personal life at the time he wrote it. Nevertheless, in the context of Zhang's literary development, it is the story's unique—and finally dismissive—treatment of such autobiographical details that is remarkable. The contingent affairs of one's personal life, the conclusion suggests, may in the context of one's family life possess a compelling sense of reality, but this is an illusion: it is finally one's independent work in the larger society that aligns the self with the Real. "A Three and a Half Day's Dream" thus constitutes a definitive evacuation of the personal preoccupations from which such authors as Ye Shaojun labored for years to disengage themselves. The impatience the narrator of the story feels with his family's inconsequential gossip mirrors Zhang's irritation with the triviality of much contemporary writing, and the narrator's final pledge hints at Zhang's own resolve to produce a fiction unfettered by overt self-reference.

Zhang Tianyi's reception as an important newcomer on the literary scene in the early 1930s was occasioned not simply by his avoidance of autobiography, however, but also by his disparaging attitude toward the vacillations of young bourgeois intellectuals. In 1931 Feng Naichao 馮乃超 praised Zhang Tianyi for breaking away from old forms (including such isms as sentimentalism, individualism, idealism, and romanticism) and for moving in the direction of the "new realism." In particular, he lauded Zhang's use of a highly accessible vernacular and his willingness to write about a broad range of social types. Although many of Zhang's stories continued to have intellectual protagonists, Feng was pleased to note that Zhang did not focus exclusively on "characters who suffer disappointment in love or who become alienated and decide to resign from society." Feng Naichao was a former member of the Creation Society, and one senses that his praise for Zhang Tianyi was intended in part as indirect criticism of such older realists as Mao Dun and Ye Shaojun. (Mao Dun was frequently criticized even by his supporters for the difficulty of his language and at the time Feng Naichao wrote was still primarily known as the author of *Eclipse*.) Even as Feng praised Zhang Tianyi's accomplishments, he expressed some reservations about the realism he practiced: Zhang, he wrote, is developing into the kind of author the times require, but at present he still suffers from the "fellow traveler's attitude of detached objectivity."[58]

Feng Naichao's observation notwithstanding, many of Zhang's early stories do feature disappointed lovers and disaffected intellectuals; it is less Zhang's choice of subject matter than his treatment of these figures that distinguishes him from earlier writers. Where previously the spiritual infirmities of such characters were explored with a measure of authorial sympathy, in Zhang's works they are generally the target of an uninhibited mockery. Zhang's intellectual characters do not vacillate out of pure intellectual frustration; more often than not they recognize that political engagement offers a way out of their private contradictions, but they lack the courage or resolution to alter their behavior. The protagonist of "Zhuchangzi de beiai" 豬腸子的悲哀 (The sorrows of Pig Guts, 1931),[59] a famous author who recognizes that he and his literary product have become obsolete, is one such character. His account of his predicament reads very much like Zhang's analysis of the contemporary author's situation in "On the Lack of Vigor in Composition":

> The times are simply too powerful—so powerful that I no longer dare write. If I am asked to write about fine wine and women or to compose a tribute to decadence or to relate a few trivialities from my present life, I can do so without any trouble in a way that will entice readers. But the times do not permit such compositions; they force me to write something new. Unfortunately my life, my consciousness, my education, in short, everything about me, is still of the old style. (226)

As Pig Guts later acknowledges, he is unable to "resolve the contradictions" of his life, having grown too accustomed to the pleasures of his old "life-style," which revolves largely around drinking and socializing at dance halls and cafes.

Pig Guts several times invokes the times (*shidai*) and contradictions (*maodun*), notions that I suggested above were of serious concern to Mao Dun. But in Zhang's stories they are less substantive ideas than fashionable slogans, whose repetition serves ironically to screen the characters from changing social realities. The protagonist of "Jing Ye xiansheng" 荆野先生 (Mr. Jing Ye, 1930),[60] another effete intellectual who suffers from May Fourth vacillations, is typical:

58. Feng Naichao 馮乃超 [Li Yishui 李易水], "Xinren Zhang Tianyi de zuopin" 新人張天翼的作品 (The works of newcomer Zhang Tianyi), *Beidou* 1, no. 1 (20 September 1931); reprinted in Shen, Huang, and Wu, *Zhang Tianyi yanjiu ziliao*, pp. 230–36, here p. 231.

59. Zhang Tianyi, "Zhuchangzi de beiai" 豬腸子的悲哀 (The sorrows of Pig Guts), *Beidou* 1, no. 4 (20 December 1931); reprinted in Zhang Tianyi, *Zhang Tianyi wenji* 1:222–34.

60. Zhang Tianyi, "Jing Ye xiansheng" 荆野先生 (Mr. Jing Ye), first pub-

The pain he suffered was undoubtedly of a very modern kind... but he was hard put to say precisely what caused it. You might say it was the pain of vacillation. But that didn't express it exactly. For although he felt a measure of real discomfort, what he called his decadence did not really arise from his thinking anything in particular. It was more a matter of his fearing that life was becoming too drab and ordinary, of his craving a bit of stimulation.... But—if we may employ the conjunction here one more time—in the end he didn't have a clue to what motivated his own behavior. (39–40)

The narration here satirically underlines the self-canceling nature of Jing Ye's vacillations by calling attention to the repeated use of the adversative *but* in his interior monologue. Unlike the vacillations of intellectuals in Lu Xun's stories or in Mao Dun's *Eclipse*, Jing Ye's anxiety is less a frustrated response to historical exigencies than it is a complement to the character's romantic self-image. Jing Ye's friend Lao Hui 老惠 employs a bilingual pun to collapse the notions of *shidai* and *maodun*: "Everybody thinks he is 'of the times'... but in the modern world there is only contradiction [*maodun*]; in my opinion the English word *modern* should be translated as *maodun*" (45).

To expose the shallowness of Jing Ye's vacillation, Zhang has him confront a radical alter ego in the person of an acquaintance named Ge Ping 戈平. In a dream Ge Ping appears to Jing Ye and gives the following interpretation of his vacillations: "Of course [what you suffer] is the general pain of modern times, but this pain will not simply stretch on forever; a day will come when we will enter a new epoch, which will put an end to the present pain" (41). Ge Ping proposes that instead of seeking the essence of the times (*zhao shidai de zhongxin* 找時代的中心), Jing Ye should work to trade the present epoch for a new one (*huan yige shidai* 換一個時代). Jing Ye is troubled by this dream, and later, after suffering false imprisonment and witnessing Ge Ping's execution, he undergoes a change of heart. He resolves to exchange the vacuity (*kongxu* 空虛) of his present life in Beijing for a new life of engagement, of fullness (*chongshi* 充實), in southern China. In a surprising formal move, however, the story declines to relate the consequences of Jing Ye's resolution. Half a year later his friends in Beijing gather to discuss the incompatible reports they have

lished under the title "Cong kongxu dao chongshi" 從空虛到充實 (From vacuity to fullness) in *Mengya yuekan* 1, no. 2 (1 February 1930); reprinted with the present title in Zhang Tianyi, *Zhang Tianyi wenji* 1:35–73.

heard of Jing Ye's new life: some say that he has reverted to a life of decadence, some that he continues to struggle to rehabilitate himself, and others that he has taken a wife and become a successful business-man. Although these reports are "contradictory to the point of absurdity," Lao Hui contends that "they are all possible" (46). The friends depart, feeling puzzled.

This ending reflects in part Zhang's uncertainty about the prospects of reform for such intellectuals as Jing Ye, but more importantly it subverts readers' expectations of fictional closure. It makes Jing Ye's character an assemblage of possibilities rather than an integrated per-sonality, thus destroying the consistency of characterization that read-ers expect from realist fiction. But Zhang Tianyi is less interested in producing a static portrait of intellectuals like Jing Ye than in explor-ing moral choices. The story's open-ended conclusion functions as a defamiliarization technique, disallowing a simple cathartic response to the story and forcing readers to take a moral stand, both for Jing Ye and for themselves. In approaching his characters in this way, Zhang rejects the reflectionism of conventional realism—which entails pas-sively delineating the representative characteristics of individuals and social groupings—for a more activist fiction that explores the poten-tial for change. The conclusion is, in short, Zhang Tianyi's formal means of choosing Ge Ping's path over Jing Ye's.

Defamiliarization techniques abound in Zhang Tianyi's early ficton, especially in his first two novels, *Guitu riji* 鬼土日記 (A diary of hell, 1931) and *Chilun* 齒輪 (Cogwheel, 1932).[61] These works have received little critical attention, but the latter is of particular relevance to our discussion here because it offers, among other things, an ex-tended parody of the realist novel. While superficially burlesquing Turgenev, *Cogwheel* covertly targets the early works of Mao Dun. This choice of target may seem surprising, given the similarities be-tween the two authors that I have detailed above, but in fact Zhang Tianyi intensely disliked certain features of the older writer's art, in particular his elaborate scenic descriptions and his bent for psycholog-ical exploration. In an article on literary popularization published the same year as *Cogwheel*, Zhang made a series of prescriptions for

61. Zhang Tianyi first published *Chilun* in 1932 under the pen name Tie Chihan 鐵池翰. In 1938 Daxia shudian in Shanghai reprinted the novel, changing the title (without the author's permission) to *Shidai de tiaodong* 時代的跳動 (Pulse of the times). Page numbers here refer to this later edition.

fiction writing that seem designed to point out the shortcomings of the realism Mao Dun practiced: he advised that fictional scenes be developed rapidly, that characters be revealed through action rather than psychological description, and that descriptions of objects and scenery be kept as brief as possible.[62]

The text of Cogwheel makes these same points through a series of satirical asides. At various points the narrator baldly announces the text's resistance to metaphor ("Some people said his mouth was a bit like...well, we won't try to find a comparison but just say straight out that his lips seemed a bit thin" [22]), to physical description ("To describe a person, there's no need to get wordy and go into all these details; I'm just trying to tell you her shoulders were a bit crooked" [23]), to disquisitions on psychology ("If you must have some psychological description here, the author can tell you" [37]), and to the treatment of romantic themes ("I really can't tell love stories—I start stuttering. If the reader likes love stories, I've heard Turgenev has written all kinds of them—you might try borrowing one of his to read" [269]). Other devices common to realist fiction are employed, but self-consciously: a flashback, for example, is announced first with a quotation from Turgenev ("Pardon me, beloved reader, but let me guide you back several years") and then with a blunt heading in bold letters ("ADDITIONAL NARRATION") that makes an absurdity of Turgenev's delicacy (49–50). Most radically, the ending of the novel, like that of "Mr. Jing Ye," intentionally frustrates readers' curiosity about the outcome of the plot. In the final chapter Zhang stages an interview in which the narrator tries to wrest from two of the novel's characters the information he needs to wrap up their story; they refuse to cooperate and walk off remarking, "If you don't mind, we have things to do; in times like these, how can you keep chattering on about such trivia?" (271). This ending amounts, of course, to an assault on the readers, who, it is implied, should themselves be attending to better things. Such a parody of the formal conventions of realist fiction allows Zhang to achieve a double purpose: while continuing to employ the suspect conventions to structure and pattern his story he at the same time calls them into question.

62. Zhang Tianyi, "Wenxue dazhonghua wenti zhengwen" 文學大眾化 問題徵文 (Reply on the problem of literary popularization), *Beidou* 2, nos. 3–4 (20 July 1932); collected in Zhang Tianyi, *Zhang Tianyi wenxue pinglun ji*, pp. 7–10, here p. 9. These same points are elaborated upon in his "Chuangzuo de gushi."

The plot of *Cogwheel,* which concerns the radical education of a naive country girl at the hands of a group of self-styled revolutionaries, also makes specific parodic reference to Mao Dun's "Disillusionment." The girl resembles Jing, and her name, Huixian 慧先, which means "before knowledge," clearly refers to the character Hui in Mao Dun's novella. Her education, like Jing's, is at once political and sexual. In such psychological description as the narrator allows himself, politics and sex are ironically entwined to thoroughly deflate the political idealism the group preaches. Observing the older girls at a rally, for example, Huixian thinks:

> She used to envy those girls; she felt she couldn't measure up to them. They felt free to love the country (indeed, they had loved a number of countries more than once, mostly in May), and they could sing foreign songs and wear high heels. But today, at long last she felt she was a match for them: here she was at a rally loving her country, and she was perfectly capable of wearing high heels too if she chose to. (38)

In the end political rallies become confused with theatrical performances, and the characters' behavior itself comes to seem purely performative, detached from any ideological moorings. The young people use the rallies as occasions for sexual cruising, fussing more over their personal appearance than over the content of their slogans ("While shouting, he combed his hair with his fingers" [81]). When bored with political rallies, they rush off to the theater, but the major rally that occurs near the end of the book is itself little more than a vaudeville show, whose bill of fare includes speeches, songs, dances, and even a skit prepared by Huixian's friends, entitled "Action News" and touted with the slogan "Art can save the country" (214–15). In the penultimate chapter the characters' fatuous conversations—about such fashionable topics as contradictions and the meaning of life—are set against stark headlines announcing the Japanese invasion of Shanghai. Eventually, as though to restore some sobriety to the novel's treatment of this important historical event, the narration abandons its characters and resorts to a straightforward journalistic account, interrupted by the cries, not of fashionable revolutionaries, but of the anonymous masses reacting with heroic indignation (251–60).

Cogwheel is a hothouse in which one finds growing all the elements of Zhang Tianyi's fiction: parodic exaggeration, which finds its freest expression in the farcical novels *A Diary of Hell* and *Yangjingbin qixia*

洋涇浜奇俠 (Strange knight of Shanghai, 1936); an inventive, if somewhat flippant, narrative persona used most effectively in his children's works; the earnest moralism that dominates his proletarian, or mass, fiction; and the satirical examination of social manners characteristic of the bulk of his fictional output. At the time of *Cogwheel's* publication critics failed to recognize its parodic intent; they soberly noted its inconsistencies of tone and pronounced it a failure. An anonymous reviewer in *Les contemporaines* complained that Zhang presented the Japanese invasion only in "broad outline" and failed to give a true sense of how "the masses" responded to that event.[63] Mao Dun himself wrote a review of *Cogwheel* in which he acknowledged its unusual style but pronounced its jocular tone out of keeping with its subject matter. He chided the author for the work's loose structure and its failure to provide a serious analysis of the "consciousness" of its characters. He concluded: "Maybe the author intended the whole book to be humorous . . . but paying too much attention to formal innovations or to making people laugh while ignoring content is finally not the proper way for an author to develop his talents."[64]

Mao Dun was not the only author to be offended by the humor of Zhang Tianyi's fiction. Even some of those who had been the first to recognize his talent objected to the wilder manifestations of Zhang's parodic spirit. Lu Xun wrote in a letter to Zhang that his fiction was often "too jocular,"[65] and Qu Qiubai, in a review of *A Diary of Hell*, complained that his writing was too schematic and self-indulgent.[66] Wang Shuming 王淑明 observed that owing to Zhang's comic bent, his fiction was robbed of seriousness and constituted not a true realism but only the shadow, or "relief," of realism.[67] But all of these criti-

63. "Shuping: *Chilun*" 書評《齒輪》(Book review: *Cogwheel*), *Xiandai* 2, no. 3 (February 1932), pp. 508–11.

64. See Mao Dun, "Jiu Yi Ba yihou de fan Ri wenxue—sanbu changpian xiaoshuo" "九一八"以後的反日文學—三部長篇小說 (Anti-Japanese literature after September Eighteenth—three novels), *Wenxue* 1, no. 2 (1 August 1933); reprinted in Shen, Huang, and Hu, *Zhang Tianyi yanjiu ziliao*, pp. 237–42.

65. Lu Xun, letter to Zhang Tianyi, 1 February 1933, in Lu Xun, *Lu Xun quanji* 12:143–44, here p. 144.

66. Qu Qiubai, "Hua gou ba" 畫狗罷 (Just painting dogs), *Beidou* 1, no. 1 (20 September 1931); reprinted in Shen, Huang, and Hu, *Zhang Tianyi yanjiu ziliao*, pp. 215–24, here p. 219.

67. Wang Shuming 王淑明, "*Yangjingbin qixia*" 《洋涇浜奇俠》(*Strange Knight of Shanghai*), *Xiandai* 5, no. 1 (1 May 1934); reprinted in Shen, Huang, and Hu, *Zhang Tianyi yanjiu ziliao*, pp. 246–50, here p. 250.

cisms assume the conventional realistic standards that the parodic passages in Zhang's works were designed to undercut. Zhang disdained the earnest artisanship that underlay those standards, as his rapid and somewhat carefree writing habits make clear: Zhou Songdi wrote that Zhang "would write every day for more than ten hours without stopping. He was frequently able to finish an eight-thousand-to-nine-thousand-character short story, and averaged more than two thousand characters a day."[68] Zhang viewed his stories not as polished and enduring works of art but as rapid-fire, topical communications; to him they were less objects for meditation than incentives to act. The stylistic and formal innovations he employed—the aborted closures, the comic-book expletives, the caricatures—were all designed to challenge the complacency of his audience and thus to prevent his stories from simply being "consumed" as examples of a bourgeois art form.

Perhaps the most insightful critical evaluation of Zhang Tianyi by one of his contemporaries is an essay written by Hu Feng in 1935, entitled simply "On Zhang Tianyi." Hu Feng praises Zhang Tianyi's fiction in many of the same terms used by Feng Naichao. Zhang, he writes, has overcome the individualism and sentimentality of earlier May Fourth fiction and succeeded in painting a fresh and convincing picture of the self-delusions and cruelties of China's petty bourgeoisie. Hu Feng goes on, however, in an analysis of Zhang Tianyi as a plain materialist (*supu de weiwuzhuyizhe* 素樸的唯物主義者), to make a telling criticism: in the treatment of his characters Zhang seems primarily concerned with their "social coloring, the designs they harbor in their relations with others."[69] This means that Zhang restricts his interests to his character's external behavior while avoiding extensive psychological exploration. As a result Zhang's characters lack nuance: they are often mere caricatures, drawn "only to prove a necessity."[70]

The necessity Hu Feng speaks of here is that of a reified social pattern. Eschewing both physical and psychological description, Zhang is forced to define character solely in terms of the individual's socially

68. Zhou Songdi, "Wo he Tianyi xiangchu de rizi," p. 69.
69. Hu Feng, "Zhang Tianyi lun" 張天翼論 (On Zhang Tianyi), *Wenxue jikan* 2, no. 3 (16 September 1935); reprinted in Shen, Huang, and Hu, *Zhang Tianyi yanjiu ziliao*, pp. 269–96, here p. 296.
70. Hu Feng, "Zhang Tianyi lun," in Shen, Huang, and Hu, *Zhang Tianyi yanjiu ziliao*, p. 279.

meaningful acts and intentions. Since characters are denied any internal reality divorced from such patterning, they are compelled, as it were, to simply play the role in which society has cast them. As a consequence, all behavior in Zhang's fictional world takes on a theatrical quality. Actions are dictated by a purely situational social logic. Characters struggle, not to remain true to internal psychological or ideological compulsions, but simply to maximize their control over whatever social circumstances present themselves.

In an essay he wrote on the subject of humor, Zhang Tianyi once wrote, "Isn't it true that we Chinese most love face?"[71] To succeed in their social manipulations, the characters in Zhang's world must present a consistent and understandable face to the world, and the construction of such social personas is the primary subject of Zhang Tianyi's fiction. Maintaining face is, of course, an essentially theatrical project, which relies for its success on the actor's awareness of his or her audience. Social behavior, as Zhang Tianyi presents it, is thus in its essence specular: individuals discover and define themselves by carefully monitoring the response others give to their actions. To convey this understanding of human behavior, Zhang frequently resorts to situational irony: typically, a character is confronted successively with two very different audiences; to maintain face with each group he or she must give two highly contradictory performances. Readers are left to evaluate the discrepancy between these two performances and answer for themselves the moral question posed by that discrepancy. "Dizhu" 砥柱 (The bulwark, 1936)[72] is perhaps the best known of Zhang's stories constructed on this model. Its protagonist, Huang Yian 黄宜庵, is first introduced to the reader as a protective, if rather sanctimonious, father. The story recounts a boat trip he takes with his daughter to visit her prospective groom, an important official who, Huang feels, will make an advantageous match. With an apparently excessive zeal, Huang rails against the immoral influences to which his daughter is exposed on the boat, including a bawdy conversation that wafts in from the neighboring compartment. His daughter, however, remains innocently uncomprehending of the conversation, and it soon

---

71. Zhang Tianyi, "Shenme shi youmo?" 什麼是幽默? (What is humor?), in Zhang Tianyi, *Zhang Tianyi wenxue pinglun ji*, pp. 24–27, here p. 25.
72. Zhang Tianyi, "Dizhu" 砥柱 (The bulwark), *Zuojia* 1, no. 2 (15 May 1936); reprinted in Zhang Tianyi, *Zhui*. A translation of "The Bulwark" by Nathan K. Mao is included in Lau, Hsia, and Lee, *Modern Chinese Stories and Novellas*, pp. 336–44.

becomes clear that not so much his daughter's innocence as the bulwark of his own morality is being assailed. While self-righteously intoning to his daughter that "a person shouldn't listen to things that aren't proper," he feels himself increasingly fascinated by the "irresistible" conversation next door. He finally goes to inquire, only to discover that one of the conversationalists is an acquaintance, President Xiao 蕭 of the Society for the Study of the Confucian Classics. When President Xiao flatters him on his own amorous conquests, Huang eagerly joins in the conversation he had abhorred. Given the purpose of the voyage, Huang's earlier moral outrage was clearly motivated more by a desire to protect his daughter's market value than by a true ethical concern. His contradictory behavior results from a desire to impress two very different audiences, first his daughter and the presumably proper official they are going to visit and second the lascivious conversationalists. He exists at the intersection of two distinct discourses, the one puritanical, the other pornographic. That this position is more than Huang's private contradiction and is in fact endemic in his social circle is confirmed by the character of President Xiao, who also straddles these discourses. The resultant social incongruity has particularly severe psychological consequences in Huang's case, however, as the narrator reveals in part through interior monologue but more tellingly through the description of Huang's many unpleasant mannerisms: he is described throughout as itching, sniffing, and drooling, as if the tension of compartmentalizing his various personas was constantly erupting in his physical being.

Crucial to the situational irony of "The Bulwark" is the story's setting: the passenger ship is the site of a convergence of social groupings that make it impossible for Huang to maintain a clear partitioning of social roles. In Zhang Tianyi's longer fiction the city plays a similar role. The constant collision of social spheres in the urban environment provides repeated opportunities for hypocritical behavior, as well as for its exposure. Fascinated by the challenge such encounters constitute for individuals as they struggle to maintain face, Zhang situated all of his later novels in the city, including the two that conform most closely to the realist model, *Yi nian* (A year, 1933) and *Zai chengshi li* (In the city, 1937).[73] The premise for both these novels is the same: an

---

73. Zhang Tianyi's *Yi nian* 一年 (A year) was first published in Shanghai in 1933. It has been reprinted by Nanhua shudian in Hong Kong under the title *Fuyun* 浮雲 (Floating clouds). Page numbers in the text refer to the latter edition. *Zai chengshi li* 在城市里

unsophisticated villager arrives in the city, where he is gradually introduced to a wide array of imposters and evildoers. In *A Year*, we follow the progress of an honest village tailor named Bai Muyi 白慕易 who comes to the city to improve his fortune. Bai is forced to take up one humiliating job after another, eventually becoming involved with a band of drug dealers. He reluctantly discovers that there is simply not enough room at the top of the social ladder; just to maintain one's position is enough of a struggle. In the words of one of his acquaintances, "You think you're exceptional and want to climb to the top, but there are too many like you; you'll get nowhere" (265). Bai also learns that the primary means of advancing in urban society is active discrimination against one's inferiors. But such social climbing is a labor that is never finished, since the criteria determining social distinctions are themselves arbitrary and shifting, and only their repeated dramatization affirms and reproduces them.

At the time of *A Year*'s publication in 1933, a critic complained, with some justification, that the story "could be cut off at any point or could go on for another hundred pages" without significantly altering its effect.[74] *In the City* is considerably more successful, largely because it is organized around a central plot conflict, a family feud over a plot of inherited land. Like *A Year*, *In the City* opens with the arrival of a character from the country, in this case a shifty opportunist named Ding Shousong 丁壽松, who descends on his urban relatives with the hope that they can provide him with a job. The major figure of the novel, however, is not Ding, but the man to whom he first turns for assistance, Tang Qikun 唐啟昆, the head of one branch of the family. The Tangs and the Dings are in-laws: Tang Qikun's older brother married a woman of the Ding family only to die shortly thereafter, leaving the Dings fearful that "Second Master" Qikun, whose greed and mismanagement has led the family to the brink of financial ruin, will sell off the family's land and heirlooms without sharing the profits.

(In the city) was first published serially in *Guowen zhoubao* 國聞周報 between 6 July 1936 and 31 May 1937 and then published in book form in 1937. Page numbers in the text refer to the complete reprinting in Zhang Tianyi, *Zhang Tianyi xiaoshuo xuan*, vol. 2, pp. 503–817.

74. Shen Wu 慎吾, "Guanyu Zhang Tianyi de xiaoshuo" 關於張天翼 的小說 (On Zhang Tianyi's fiction), *Wenxue zhoukan*, 文學周刊 (Literature weekly) [supplement to *Yishi bao* 益世報 (Tianjin)] 38 (26 August 1933); reprinted in Shen, Huang, and Wu, *Zhang Tianyi yanjiu ziliao*, p. 244.

Ding Shousong and Tang Qikun represent two modes of self-interest, the one wily and sycophantic, the other pompous and despotic. Much of the comic effect of the novel results from their apparently contrasting but finally complementary styles of self-deception and manipulation. One of their early meetings is described as follows:

> Tang Qikun looked the other over. Ding Shousong's eyes, one small, one large, seemed to be begging for mercy, and his back was hunched as though he were cowering under the weight of Tang's authority. With his usual insight into character, Tang felt that this Ding, despite his surname, was a reliable sort after all. He would probably do whatever he was told, and that might make him useful for a variety of errands—once, that is, Tang had him completely under his thumb.
> Tang's face suddenly took on a severe expression, as though, having accepted the role of master, he needed to exhibit his authority. (570)

A later encounter is described in similar terms:

> Looking at the wretched shape before him, Tang felt a rushing through his veins as though he had just injected a vial of glucose straight into his heart. He couldn't resist twisting his face into a furious expression and issuing a loud *harrumph* through his nose. Without saying a word, he fixed a powerful glare on Ding. He loved to watch people like this squirm.
> Ding gave a little cough and looked down with a mortified expression. Closing his left eye into a narrow slit, he peeped timidly at Second Master with his right eye.
> "What can I do for you, Second Master?"
> He knew he ought to say something more than that. He ought to ask how Second Master had slept last night or whether he had had too much to drink. But in this atmosphere even the best oiled of tongues would congeal, and Ding's mouth was stuck fast. (608)

Ding Shousong's groveling, however, proves just as affected as Tang's self-assurance: his servile manner is calculated to win Tang Qikun's patronage. His actual feelings when Tang first employs him are characterized as follows:

> Secretly he felt that Second Master should recognize his, Ding Shousong's, position. Everyone knew he had better opportunities than this and that his own family would help him out in a pinch. Lately these Tangs had been acting in a particularly high-handed fashion, and the

present proposal was something of an insult. Did they really expect him
to help promote a wastrel like Tang Qikun?
   But still, where there was a profit to be made, Ding could never just
walk away. (570)

The faces Tang and Ding present to each other, the one imperious,
the other deferential, are equally false. Tang Qikun's confident manner
conceals his growing desperation as the web of lies and pretense on
which his authority is based comes unraveled. Ding Shousong's servil-
ity, on the other hand, serves as a cover for his personal appetites. His
rather tenuous kinship ties with both branches of the family (the exact
nature of which are never spelled out) force both sides to grudgingly
admit him into their circle. These ties secure his loyalty to neither, and
he soon becomes a double agent, carrying information from one
branch of the family to the other; in the end he divulges to the Dings
Tang Qikun's plan to sell the family property, thus hastening Tang's
fall.
   When first enlisting Ding's services, Tang warns him several times
that "the city is not like the country" and instructs him not to run
loose (luan pao 亂跑) or to talk big (chuiniu 吹牛). Tang clearly fears
the social fluidity of the city, with its promiscuous association of individuals and free circulation of information. This was precisely the
aspect of the urban environment that Mao Dun stressed in his novels,
as we have seen. And in Zhang's novel, as in Midnight, money and its
pursuit come to represent the final reduction of social life to a principle
of indiscriminate exchange. The characters in In the City value "ready
cash" above all. Indeed, with the exception of the drunken rowdy
Ding Wenhou 丁文侯, all the Dings and Tangs eagerly embrace a plan
to trade the family's property in the country (a symbol of stability and
productivity) for cash, that is, for the immediate gratifications available on the urban market. Moreover, Zhang Tianyi, like Mao Dun,
sees his city-dwellers' avarice as the manifestation of a deeper alienation from time and history—a point that Zhang drives home through
repeated references to clocks and watches. The patriarch of the Tang
family, for example, keeps a collection of clocks, which ironically
serve only to blur the family's sense of time: though the clocks are all
set to different hours, the old man insists that they all tell the true time
(672). The clocks are valued by the family primarily as an investment,
as Ding Shousong soon recognizes; after his treachery is exposed and

Tang Qikun dismisses him, Ding goes to the study where the clocks
are kept to pilfer a few:

> The watches hanging on the wall were ticking noisily; they seemed to be
> competing to see which could go the fastest. One was ticking so enthu-
> siastically that it swung violently back and forth on its chain. Several
> alarm clocks stood by stiffly and haughtily as though awareness of their
> own loud chime made them contemptuous of the others. The desk
> clocks, however, seemed uninterested in this competition, absorbed as
> they were in their slow, rhythmic *tick, tock, tick, tock.* (795)

Ding Shousong is caught in the act and evicted from the Tang household, but the cacophonous sound of the Tangs' clocks echoes throughout the book.[75] At the novel's conclusion, Tang Qikun, wandering the
streets contemplating his ruin, ominously hears "the great clock by the
river strike twelve." Although the time struck here is noon, it carries
much the same sense of termination (and imminent rebirth) as the
stroke of midnight does in Mao Dun's novel. In both *In the City* and
Midnight such references connote an objective progression of time and
history to which the characters themselves remain blinded; we, as
readers, however, recognize that the march of events will inevitably
overtake the characters and in the process expose their petty ambitions
and squabbles as the mere flotsam of history.

These similarities to *Midnight* notwithstanding, Tang Qikun does
not attain the tragic stature of Wu Sunfu. He is, at least at the beginning of the novel, depicted as pure appetite, without the larger ideals
that motivate Wu Sunfu. Ironically, he only begins to elicit a measure
of sympathy when, late in the novel, we see him in the secret second
household he has established with a young woman named Yajie 亞姐.
Their adulterous union has produced a son who suffers from congeni-
tal syphilis (for which Tang, himself ill with the disease, believes himself responsible). Yajie and her son elicit from Tang Qikun the only
real moral awareness he shows in the novel:

> He heard her sniffling and rasping as though she had a cold. She was
> always whimpering about things and getting thinner and more haggard
> by the day. He couldn't bear looking at her anymore, for fear her piti-

---

75. Note also, in this connection, the scene (p. 753) in which the one successful
member of the family, the bureaucrat Ding Wenpei 丁文佩, smashes his watch while
gesticulating during an argument.

able, swollen face would confirm his feelings of guilt. He mumbled exasperatedly, "It's too much, I can't stand it!"

Suddenly feelings of regret and shame overwhelmed him. He longed to run to her side, utter some soothing words, and then move her and his son across the river, where she could live proudly in the city as his second wife. (698)

As Tang admits to himself, he has experienced a true familial happiness only with Yajie and her son. His desire to legitimize the relationship is perhaps the single good impulse he evinces in the novel. Unsurprisingly, however, he fails to act on it—not just because of the social embarrassment that would follow but also because making this second family public would destroy the pleasure he has found in it. In his legitimate family he is constantly forced to play a part, to assert his mastery by impersonating the gestures and mannerisms of the powerful; only in the private world of his adulterous family can he indulge his true feelings of powerlessness, regret, and shame. In the relationship's secrecy lies its ability to gratify his deeper emotions. This second family, however, is a luxury supportable only as long as Tang maintains his wealth and reputation in the outside society. When these are stripped from him at the end of the novel, he loses Yajie and his son as well. Just at the time he hears the news of his bankruptcy, he learns of the boy's death, an event that leaves him feeling "childless" despite his large legitimate family. Then in the final chapter, Tang Qikun learns that Yajie has herself run off with the man he hired to look after her. They have left only the ironical message "Thank you for serving as our matchmaker."

Zhang Tianyi's relentless focus on his characters' petty ambitions and on the superficial manifestations of social life can in longer works become repetitive and stifling; the touches of irony and psychological complexity that we have observed in his portrayal of Tang Qikun come as a welcome relief, although most readers would agree that they arrive too late in the novel. One senses that in works like *A Year* and *In the City*, Zhang has taken the criticisms of his earlier novels too much to heart and consciously suppressed his instincts for formal innovation in the interests of a conventionally realistic representation of Chinese society. Where Zhang allows his satirical and parodic instincts a freer reign, as in the inventive farce *Strange Knight of Shanghai* and in many of his short stories, he avoids the "plodding" quality that C. T. Hsia rightly complains mars *A Year* and *In the City*.[76] The short story, in particular, was well suited to Zhang's temperament and to the themes that preoccupied him as a writer; it allowed him to spotlight an isolated scene of social theater without belaboring its dramatization with the descriptive and interpretive passages that he found so tiresome in Turgenev's and Mao Dun's fiction. Zhang's spotlight commonly picks out a scene of considerable violence in which an empowered individual forces a victim to enact a ritual humiliation. Often these encounters are related through the eyes of the victim, generally a child or defenseless woman. From such a perspective the villain takes on a savage, comic-book quality; he or she comes to embody power in a threatening, almost abstract sense. In such stories Zhang confronts the reader with stark dramatizations—divorced from mitigating psychological or ideological rationales—of the exercise of power in Chinese society.

The leverage powerful individuals emloy to compel their victims' compliance in these stories is rarely a matter of simple brute force: often it is provided by the threat of a secret's exposure. The early story "Baofu" 報復 (Revenge, 1930),[77] for example, concerns a young woman who has broken off with her fiancé but then returns to request that he keep their sexual liaison a secret. He uses the occasion to get even by compelling her to participate in a final sexual act. If she complies, he tells her, he will not disclose the nature of their relationship. She "gratefully" agrees to this arrangement, thereby accommodating herself to a social order in which a total severance of name from reality is the rule, a society that is nourished on hypocrisy: the truth is suppressed to allow the continued performance of the very act that is to be kept secret. The bargain the couple makes is, of course, only possible in a society that condemns a woman's sexual indiscretion more severely than a man's. The same double standard informs the more sadistic encounter depicted in the story "Xiao" 笑 (Smile, 1934).[78] Its villain, the town bully Jiuye 九爺, forces an impoverished villager named Fa Xin Sao 發新嫂 to succumb to his sexual advances

---

76. *Strange Knight of Shanghai* is a parodic treatment of martial arts romances and is not directly relevant to our discussion here. For a description of the novel see C. T. Hsia, *A History of Modern Chinese Fiction*, pp. 231–35.

77. Zhang Tianyi, "Baofu" 報復 (Revenge), *Mengya yuekan* 1, no. 1 (1 January 1930); reprinted in Zhang Tianyi, *Zhang Tianyi wenji* 1:17–34.

78. Zhang Tianyi, "Xiao" 笑 (Smile), *Xiandai* 5, no. 4 (1 August 1934); reprinted in Zhang Tianyi, *Zhang Tianyi wenji* 2:108–25. A translation of "Smile" is included in Chi-chen Wang, *Contemporary Chinese Stories*, pp. 108–18.

and then gives her a useless foreign coin for her services. He is driven less by sexual need than by a desire to cuckold her husband, who has insulted him. Jiuye further mortifies Fa Xin Sao by insisting that she smile: "I'm not happy to see such a sour face. . . . Just give me a little smile!" (123). When she discovers the nature of the coin he has given her, she goes to a teahouse she knows he patronizes to insist he exchange it, but he taunts her: "How is it that I, Jiuye, should have given you a dollar? What kind of debt have I contracted? Tell me in front of everyone here, and I'll immediately give you another dollar in exchange" (122). That he has violated her is an open secret, but he knows that any public appeal for justice on her part would, in the eyes of the world, be tantamount to admitting she had prostituted herself. Fa Xin Sao clearly finds the enforced dramatization of her humiliation more agonizing than the rape itself.

In "Revenge" and "Smile" power is asserted nakedly, that is, without accompanying moral rationale. In both cases sex is not in itself the motivation for the male's violence but rather the means by which he avenges his bruised ego and asserts his authority. This authority arises, however, not just from his financial clout or physical strength but also from the sexual double standard; it is thus supported by the whole weight of a social order that sanctions, indeed mandates, certain kinds of hypocritical behavior. The bullying male may act the puppeteer in these ritual acts of aggression, but the social order with its conventions has provided the script.

Stories such as "Revenge" and "Smile" pit villains against victims in brutal power plays; ideology—the intellectual manipulation of the grounds for social conventions—has no place in the lives of these characters or in their stories. As we have already seen in our discussion of "Mr. Jing Ye" and "The Bulwark," however, Zhang Tianyi was frequently concerned with the nature and efficacy of ideological commitment. But his ideologically engaged characters, whether conservative defenders of conventional morality or self-styled reformers, typically discover, to their comic surprise, that their own behavior is working to undermine the belief system that they profess. Ideological explanations somehow never provide the fixed perspective on the social hierarchy that they are intended to provide. Ideology may serve a tactical purpose in a character's project of social ascent, but to the extent that beliefs are sincerely held, they serve only to hinder the climb. In "Yihang" 移行 (A hyphenated story, 1934), the protagonist,

Sanghua 桑華, sent by her revolutionary friends to wheedle funds for the cause from a wealthy industrialist, is herself enticed by the industrialist's opulent life-style and marries him. She becomes trapped in her own performance. In retrospect, of course, her revolutionary persona is itself revealed as purely theatrical. Ironically, she notes, "It was for the sake of the revolution that I got close to him!"[79] In "Huanying hui" 歡迎會 (Welcoming party, 1934)[80] the staff of a provincial school prepare a "part idealist, part futurist, part patriotic" play whose presentation is intended to publicize the school's political orthodoxy on the occasion of a bureaucrat's visit of inspection, but owing to a series of mishaps, the prompter gives the traitor's lines to the hero, and the play becomes part seditious, part anarchic. The teacher who wrote the play had hoped the inspector would recognize his literary genius and call him away to better things, but his social-climbing instinct ironically sets him on a path that leads to his imprisonment. In both stories, the superficiality of the protagonists' ideological convictions is uncovered in the actual performance of tasks dictated by that ideology.

Those who remain cynically immune to the self-deceptions of ideology and operate by a pure politics of performance fare better in Zhang Tianyi's world, although their actions are the object of chilling authorial disapproval. Such an individual is the title character of "Mr. Hua Wei,"[81] a story that was greeted upon its appearance at the height of the war with Japan as having precisely captured the nature of a certain kind of Chinese bureaucrat.[82] Mr. Hua Wei, whose surname means

79. Zhang Tianyi, "Yihang" 移行 (A hyphenated story), first published in his short-story collection *Yihang* (1934); reprinted in Zhang Tianyi, *Zhang Tianyi wenji* 2:145–79, here p. 149. A translation entitled "Mutation" is included in Edgar Snow, *Living China*, pp. 267–89.

80. Zhang Tianyi, "Huanying hui" 歡迎會 (Welcoming party), *Zuopin* 作品 (Composition), 1, no. 1 (June 1934); reprinted in Zhang Tianyi, *Zhang Tianyi wenji* 2:180–210.

81. Zhang Tianyi, "Hua Wei xiansheng" 華威先生 (Mr. Hua Wei), *Wenyi zhendi* 1, no. 1 (16 April 1938); reprinted in Zhang Tianyi, *Suxie sanpian*. This story has been widely anthologized; see, for example, Zhang Tianyi, *Zhang Tianyi xiaoshuo xuan* 2:493–501.

82. Wang Xichan 王西彥, in a somewhat exaggerated fashion, compares the influence of "Mr. Hua Wei" in its time to that of "The True Story of Ah Q." See "Dang 'Hua Wei xiansheng' fabiao de shihou" 當《華威先生》發表的時候 (When "Mr. Hua Wei" was published), in Shen, Huang, and Wu, *Zhang Tianyi yanjiu ziliao*, pp. 95–110, here p. 104. Zhang Tianyi later insisted that the story was intended as a specific attack on the Nationalist party and warned that the story should not be interpreted as a general portrayal of bureaucratic ineptitude. In fact, however, the story's topical political content is little insisted upon in the work itself, and the story's interest for contemporary readers remains its astute treatment of a particular kind of bureaucratic personality.

"China" and whose given name means "dignity" or "awe" but is a homophone for the character meaning "crisis," maintains his powerful position in the resistance movement simply by promoting the appearance of leadership. He does nothing but attend meetings, always arriving late and leaving early, proffering nothing more substantial than a call to step up resistance work and a reminder of the importance of preserving a "center of leadership"—by which phrase he clearly refers to himself. Mr. Hua Wei believes his dignity depends on two things: he must be informed of every local meeting related to the War of Resistance, and he must make at least a cursory appearance at each of them. Associates who fail either to report meetings or to invite his personal attendance risk accusations of treason or worse. As Mr. Hua Wei well understands, his power comes first from a panoptical awareness of all activity connected with the resistance and second from the constant reminder of his omniscience that his personal appearances constitute. He intuitively understands that his political position is determined not by substantive actions or ideas but solely by his appearance at these meetings. Such performative politics may be effective within the closed system of Chinese society in aligning relations of power so that they favor Mr. Hua Wei, but, as the text with its larger vision makes clear, they are not only ineffective in the face of such threats to the system's existence as the Japanese invasion but seriously undermine its powers of resistance as well. The national crisis announced by his name is at once the excuse for Mr. Hua Wei's activities and the result of the kind of self-aggrandizing leadership he represents.

In Zhang Tianyi's world all behavior, whether political or sexual, is thus reduced to an expression of the will to power. In a few exceptional stories even the arts are examined in this light. In "Xia ye meng" 夏夜夢 (A summer night's dream, 1936),[83] for example, an operatic apprenticeship becomes a sustained metaphor for a child's initiation into the violent performative arena of adult life. The story's protagonist is a young orphan named Yunfang 芸芳, who has been adopted by a "singing school," where she is given vocal training by day and made to perform each evening to earn her keep. Fear that she will be unable

---

83. Zhang Tianyi "Xia ye meng" 夏夜夢 (A summer night's dream) was first published in his collection *Tongxiangmen* in 1939. Page numbers given here refer to the translation by Sidney Shapiro in *Stories from the Thirties* 1:363–92.

to perform pervades her dreams: in one nightmare she finds herself on stage unable to utter a sound, to the amusement of the audience and the fury of her "Mama" at the orphanage, who beats her. Even in her waking hours she experiences no natural pleasure in singing; training makes her feel as if "things, tightly bound, were being dragged forcibly from her mouth." Her instructor, "Elder," a once-rich man who has squandered his inheritance on his passion for opera, has an explanation for her displeasure that reflects his personal dissatisfactions: "Singing's fun when you're an amateur, but when you turn professional, it disgusts you" (388). Yunfang is indeed being trained as a professional, who must for survival enact the nostalgic dreams of Elder's amateur past. As such, she is not expected to have personal feelings for the songs she sings or for the stories she enacts: upon observing her tearful response to a popular song, the matron of the orphanage admonishes her, "What are you bawling about, stupid! People will laugh at you. Movies aren't real!" (378). Nevertheless, the stories she performs, particularly those that concern the reuniting of loved ones, have become entangled with her personal dreams of her father's return; she is not sure whether the stories move her because she has heard them so often or because they "have some special connection with her fate" (370). One of the other girls at the school enviously interprets Yunfang's orphanhood as a kind of freedom: "Whatever you do, it's up to you; she's not your real mother anyhow" (379). But Yunfang herself feels differently: she keeps waiting for the vague memories of her infancy to be "reenacted" (380), for her relationships to take on a sense of reality. She enviously tells her friend, "You're much better off than we. . . . Your mother is your real mother, your kid brother is your real kid brother" (379). Her emotional life has become so inextricably bound up with the performance of others' fantasies that she can only wonder helplessly, "Why can't one pick one's dreams?" (376). Once her imagination has been contaminated with the drama she is compelled to perform, her spiritual imprisonment is as secure as her physical imprisonment by the school walls.

Another story composed the same year, "Yige ticai" 一個題材 (A subject matter, 1936),[84] suggests that Zhang Tianyi's own chosen pro-

---

84. Zhang Tianyi, "Yige ticai" 一個題材 (A subject matter), *Zhong xuesheng* 中學生 (Middle school student) 4 (April 1936); reprinted in Zhang Tianyi, *Chun feng*, and in *Zhongguo xiandai duanpian xiaoshuo xuan* 3:305–19. It is to this latter reprint that the page numbers given here refer.

fession, fiction writing, may contaminate those it touches in a similar way. The narrator in the story, a novelist called Master Han 翰 who has returned to his hometown during a period of artistic infertility, is visited by a distant relative, the illiterate but wily Auntie Qing Er 慶二. Marveling that Master Han has found a way to make money that "needs no capital," Auntie Qing Er has come to ask his assistance in selling a story of her own composition. Master Han strikes up an interesting narrative contract with her, suggesting she tell her life story—specifically, the details of her private life ("something not generally known"), whose revelation will give the story market value. He presses her into making a series of disclosures involving her activities collecting rent for the local landlord and her sexual misconduct. In the end, however, he finds her secrets insufficiently salacious: "I told her if I just wrote a piece about a married couple, no one would want it. I'd have to write about two women fighting over a man or about two men fighting over a woman or about some secret liaison. Only then could we wrap things up in a way that would satisfy people" (316). He finally persuades Auntie Qing Er to talk about her relationship with the landlord's son, "that affair of your youth that everyone talks about." Only when she has conceded he had "frequently raped" her is Master Han satisfied that they now have sufficient material for a story. But as Auntie Qing Er departs she suddenly turns to the narrator and whispers, "You mustn't let anyone know about what I've told you here today" (319).

Auntie Qing Er has been doubly violated, first by the landlord's son and then by Master Han, whose prying has humiliated her into retracting her story in the final line, thus enabling him to appropriate it and present it to us as his own. Auntie Qing Er was wrong about story writing; fiction does require a kind of capital—in the form of precisely such tales of personal violation as her own. But Auntie's illiteracy means that she can never directly deploy her capital on the literary market and that she must entrust her story to a representative of the literate class such as Master Han. His detective work—if not his prurient manner—may seem justified for its role in disclosing the underlying moral corruption of the landlord's son. But Master Han's project of ethical probing, to the extent that it is operative, succeeds only against the victim's will and in the wake of her personal mortification; it is an exclusively male dialogue conducted by directing blows at a female third party. As resourceful as Auntie is in dealing with social inferiors, her only means of establishing intercourse with her literate betters is by using either her physical body, subject to sexual exploitation, or the spoken word, itself subject, as the story dramatizes, to the exploitation of writing. In the same manner, all characters and objects given representation in fiction are, in the process of their translation into writing, subject to a kind of violation: their stories— their being—are taken in hand by an elevated third party (the author), who exploits their exclusion from writing to ensure that the literary product possesses the substantiality of the Real. They are inevitably and always found objects whose fictional presentation redounds to the authority of the finder. Just as the opera in "A Summer Night's Dream" both coerced Yunfang's performance and interfered in her own emotional life, so fiction not only elicits Auntie Qing Er's confessional performance but forces her to shape her life story into the sort of sensational material required for a short story.

As we have seen, both Mao Dun and Zhang Tianyi grounded their fictional projects in a refusal to engage in May Fourth introspection; both stubbornly turned their gaze away from the self toward society. This intention is evident in the content of their fiction (with its rejection of autobiography) and in their concern with the social efficacy of the new literature. Despite this common premise, however, and despite their shared understanding of society as an arena of conflict where historical contradictions play themselves out, the two authors produced fiction of markedly different styles and forms. Mao Dun, with his novelistic impulses, constantly labored to expand his narrative vision so that it would comprehend all of historical reality. Modeling his work on the great nineteenth-century Western realists, he sought to make his fictional world commensurate with society at large, to offer a descriptive portrait so complete that one could trace in it all the complex relations of cause and effect that determine historical progress. He attempted, that is, to repair the fragmentation of contemporary society through aesthetic means and thereby allow readers to glimpse—if only momentarily—the totality of the historical moment. Zhang Tianyi, on the other hand, actively fractured the surface of his fiction so that it would itself reflect the shattered social environment. He focused his attention less on the motivations of his characters than on the consequences of their actions; in particular, he was fascinated with the way in which all human behavior constitutes the enactment

—and finally the reinforcement—of fundamental social divisions. Zhang's emphasis on the externalities of social behavior is paralleled by the linguistic play that characterizes his work; whereas Mao Dun's highly literary style works to naturalize his narrative voice, lulling readers into a passive acceptance of his vision of the world, Zhang Tianyi's aggressive and often-facetious narrative personae repeatedly call attention to the linguistic surface of the text, shocking readers into recognizing an ingenerate relationship between the signifying practices the text parodies and the social practices it describes.

The highlighting of the text's performative quality in Zhang Tianyi's works—evident in his unusual stylistic and formal experiments and in his affinity for parody—reveals a high level of artistic self-consciousness and makes him, of all Chinese realists, seem closest in spirit to Western modernists. The Japanese critic Itō Keiichi 伊藤敬一, noticing his "bold experiments in fictional technique," has in fact questioned applying the label "realist" to Zhang Tianyi and stressed instead his indebtedness to a variety of "modernism," specifically, "neo-impressionism":

> Zhang Tianyi's point of departure was his disillusionment with reality and his desire to find a new means of expressing his despair. Humankind was, in his view, already stripped of hope and moral direction and no longer able to maintain a sense of spiritual wholeness. The old techniques of realism and romanticism were inadequate to communicate this kind of spiritual disintegration and self-alienation, so he turned to a more penetrating, impressionistic means of expression.[85]

Neo-impressionism did in fact exert an important influence over Chinese writers in the early 1930s (including such committed realists as Sha Ting 沙汀, whose works we will consider in the next chapter), but Zhang Tianyi would have been most distressed to hear his work identified with any variety of modernism. He remained stringently opposed to the formal or aesthetic transcendence to which modernism characteristically resorts,[86] and he specifically excluded from the field

85. See Itō Keiichi 伊藤敬一, "Zhang Tianyi de xiaoshuo he tonghua" 張天翼的小說和童話 (Zhang Tianyi's fiction and children's fiction), trans. Gao Peng 高鵬, in Shen, Huang, and Wu, *Zhang Tianyi yanjiu ziliao*, pp. 445–60, here pp. 448–49. Itō goes on to argue that Zhang Tianyi's formalistic, "modernist" tendencies find their freest expression in the children's fiction he wrote in the 1930s and continued to write after 1949.

86. Itō recognizes Zhang's eventual divergence from neo-impressionism in his article: "His point of departure was similar to that of the Japanese neo-impressionists, but

of representation the material whose exploration is the substantive heart of modernism, the subconscious and the surreal. In a 1939 article entitled "Art and Struggle" he wrote, "You are clearly standing there. You have your friends and your enemies. . . . Where is your ivory tower?"[87] Both author and work, he argues, are inextricably situated in an embattled social environment; in the end all literature must announce its allegiance in the larger social contest.

Here again Mao Dun and Zhang Tianyi meet on common ground: both writers, while giving full expression to their generation's feelings of disillusionment and despair, refused any means of consolation that did not recognize the fundamentally historical nature of their plight. Both denounced all recourse to aesthetic or psychological universals and insisted that their work was bound to a particular moment and to a particular milieu. Consolation was to be found only in the potential for change within Chinese society itself and in the capacity of fiction not simply to reflect the times in which they lived, but actively to propel the wheels of history. As realists, however, Mao Dun and Zhang Tianyi continued to insist that these progressive forces be discoverable within the world as they observed and described it, not forcibly imposed from an external ideological framework. They found themselves, in short, caught in an intermediate position, resisting both the determinism of a purely reflectionist aesthetic and the naive voluntarism of the ideologues. In the following chapter we will examine the various tactics employed by Chinese realists of the 1930s in their effort to stake out and defend this middle ground.

---

his later direction of inquiry was at complete odds with the situation in Japan. For example, writers like Yokomitsu Riichi [橫光利一] moved from impressionism to the pursuit of beauty, that is, to a kind of aestheticism that is the converse of proletarian literature" (Ibid., p. 449).

87. Zhang Tianyi, "Yishu yu douzheng" 藝術與鬥爭 (Art and struggle), first published serially in *Guancha ribao* 觀察日報 (Observer's daily), 2 March 1939 and 3 March 1939; reprinted in Zhang Tianyi, *Zhang Tianyi wenxue pinglun ji*, pp. 53–62, here p. 54.

5

Beyond Realism
The Eruption of the Crowd

As we have seen, realism was embraced during the May Fourth period as one element of the larger crusade to modernize China and regenerate its culture. But each of its major practitioners during the 1920s and 1930s was to discover that realism failed to wield the positive social influence it had promised. To escape its perceived determinism, Chinese writers sometimes resorted to deformations of the Western model (such as Lu Xun's distortions) or employed elaborate parodic or ironical contrivances to make the work its own self-criticism, in this way calling into question the limitations of the mode while expanding its expressive potential. Mao Dun's story "Creation," which, it will be recalled, he touted as the first of his works to overcome the pessimism that overwhelmed him after the failure of the 1927 revolution, offers a rich examination of this search for the source of practical—rather than purely literary or imaginary—change.

As its title announces, "Creation" is a reply to members of the Creation Society, who at the time of its composition were vigorously pursuing a campaign against "naturalists" like Mao Dun. On one level the story offers a critique of the Creationists' belief that revolution could simply be willed; on a deeper level, however, it probes in a highly personal way the general relationship of social critique to political praxis. In the story an intellectual named Junshi 君實 is forced to recognize his failure to deliberately mold his wife, Xianxian 嫻嫻, into an "ideal woman." He had wanted, as he confides to a friend "a woman who is completely modern, but not extreme, not dangerous,"[1] and had attempted to transform his wife into this creature of his imagination primarily by acquainting her with fashionable new books on culture and politics. But Junshi's ideals, based as they are on a fantasy

---

1. Mao Dun, "Chuangzao" 創造 (Creation), *Dongfang zazhi* 25, no. 8 (25 April 1928); reprinted in Mao Dun, *Mao Dun duanpian xiaoshuo ji* 1:3–29, here p. 14.

of modernity that disallows real change, have proven inflexible and confining, as we learn through a series of flashbacks. Xianxian lived up to Junshi's expectations of her only once: when they bathed together at a waterfall, she dressed only in her "vest" (a word whose sexual connotation is highlighted by its appearance in English in the text). The "liberation" Junshi desires for Xianxian is nothing more than an ornament for his personal delectation, and he is astonished to discover that the books he has given her to read have the effect not of increasing her devotion but of weakening her dependence on him. Stirred by the radical message in these books, she becomes actively involved in practical political work, and at the end of the story, in a scene reminiscent of *A Doll's House*, leaves, suggesting he catch up with her if he can. The story censures not the content or ideological value of Junshi's political ideals—he has available to him a correct understanding of the social order and its faults, if from no other source than his library of radical books—but rather the inertia and self-absorption that prevent him from making that knowledge operative in real life. He comes to believe that his "creation" of Xianxian was her "destruction" and in an extreme of solipsistic thinking decides that he has simply used her to accomplish a self-willed destruction of his own ideals. Finally, however, to avoid the pain of further self-analysis, he blames all on the "bewildering, contradictory society" in which he lives (25). Junshi's attempt to mold Xianxian is part of a convincing personal drama, but it is also intended as a metaphor for the project of nation building that engrossed Chinese intellectuals during the May Fourth movement. The thinking members of Junshi's class want, Mao Dun implies, a society that is entirely modern, yet not personally threatening; their ideas, however, have proven to have a life of their own and have led in directions they are unable to follow. For many, a once-burning idealism has gradually given way to a cynical pessimism, to a social critique that is better understood as the last refuge of their apathy and self-pity.

As presented by the story, the creation of a personality capable of active political involvement is a complicated process: it requires that one be nourished in critique (without Junshi's intervention, Xianxian would have remained the naive romantic she was when he first met her), and yet critique is not in itself sufficient to the task. The intellectual's critique must somehow be transplanted into the will of someone who possesses the natural vitality and activism the intellectual lacks. That person, in "Creation" and in Mao Dun's novel *Rainbow*, is a woman; in later stories by Mao Dun and in many stories modeled after them, the person is more typically a young male worker or peasant. In either case, the individuals who play the role are understood to possess a more intimate connection with the Real; though they may not exhibit the psychological complexity of the intellectual, they enjoy a superior material presence in the fiction both at the level of plotting and on the descriptive surface of the text. In the rather exceptional case of Mao Dun's heroines, the characters' materiality is assumed in the procreative power associated with their sexual beings (Mao Dun's women characters are invariably given elaborate physical descriptions, often focusing on their sexually provocative features, whereas male bodies are caricatured in a few brief strokes). In the more common case of lower-class protagonists, a close association with the land and the struggle for simple physical survival accords them an aura of generative vitality, which is frequently intensified by a dramatized initiation through hunger and poverty. More important, however, is the lower-class protagonists' identification with the "masses," a term which itself took on an ever-more-imposing aura in the 1930s, as we have seen in our discussion of the period's literary criticism. Indeed, worker or peasant characters come increasingly to serve as synecdochical substitutes for the crowd at large; they suffer in its name, and their virtues are the crystallization of its promise. The real protagonist of much of 1930s' fiction is no longer the individual struggling to achieve a critical perspective on a chaotic social environment, as it had typically been in the 1920s, but a special kind of crowd, abstractly conceived yet possessed of an overwhelming physical immediacy. The true drama of 1930s' fiction lies precisely here, in the adventure of May Fourth intellectuals willfully shaking themselves free of their disaffections and venturing out to meet—and to create—this new entity, the masses.

A review of crowd scenes in fiction from the 1920s will quickly demonstrate the historical novelty of this new method of representing the masses. We recall that in Lu Xun's stories the crowd represented brute ignorance and cruelty: in "The True Story of Ah Q" the crowd acts in unknowing conjunction with the oppressive forces of tradition to incite violence and cannibalistic behavior. The crowd instinct depicted in "The True Story of Ah Q," as well as in such works as "A Public Example," is dangerous because it is irrational and easily manipulated. Similarly, in Ye Shaojun's *Ni Huanzhi* crowds form around

the false revolutionary Tiger Jiang because the people "despite themselves" become "infected by the shouting."[2] Even such authorially endorsed revolutionary crowds as appear in 1920s' fiction are viewed
entirely from the perspective of the disaffected intellectual, who may
be temporarily stimulated by the noise and bustle of the crowd but
ends feeling profoundly alienated. It will be recalled that Ni Huanzhi,
although he is eventually disabused of the notion that he has anything
to offer the masses, involves himself for a time in revolutionary activities. After a stimulating rally, he delights in imagining himself "as a
fish, submerged in the sea that was them, immersed in their outlook on
life from head to tail; and they were also fish, swimming in friendly
shoals with him." Yet Ni Huanzhi's fantasy of merging with the
crowd somehow only serves to confirm the difference between him
and them, and his dream of the fish's happiness is immediately supplanted by a contrasting fancy, one that is both individualistic and
self-destructive: "He imagined himself as a bird in flight, with the som-
ber woods and the mist-blurred surface of the earth long lost to sight;
ahead in a bright cloudless sky was the sun in its age-old splendor
smiling a welcome to him, for his destination was none other than this
sun!" (219). Jing, in Mao Dun's novella "Disillusionment," similarly
enjoys a moment of encouragement when she attends a rally—she is
even moved to tears—but when the crowd is suddenly inundated by a
rainstorm, she leaves in discomfort; the event's most lasting influence
on her life is a bad head cold. In all these works the crowd remains an
intimidating other, at best to be envied and respected, at worst to be
feared.

In such works from the early 1930s as Zhang Tianyi's *Cogwheel*
and Mao Dun's *Midnight,* the crowd continues to be drawn from the
perspective of bourgeois intellectuals and fellow travelers, though the
inability of such characters to merge with the crowd is more frequently
the object of satirical treatment than of sympathetic psychological
examination. In chapter 9 of *Midnight,* for example, several of the
characters participate in a demonstration organized to commemorate
the fifth anniversary of the May Thirtieth Incident in Shanghai. They
come to the demonstration dressed in their best Western clothes and
stroll about looking for "fun and excitement." They move into the
crowd on the dares of friends, shout slogans to show off their nerve,

2. Ye Shaojun, *Ni Huanzhi,* p. 253.

and are generally stimulated by the potential for violence that they sense in the air. To the extent that they have any serious interest in the demonstration as a political event, the characters hope that by rekindling memories of the earlier strike with its unquestioned historical significance, they may reawaken a sense of connection to the true course of history, a sense that is elusive in the stagnant environment of Shanghai. But the demonstration finally proves to be nothing more than a memorial of the earlier event; the demonstrators, jostled about aimlessly by the police, lack motivation and focus. They "just weren't up to scratch," pronounces the poet Fan Bowen 范博文, having observed the activity from his "grandstand view" in a second-story restaurant.[3] The others criticize Fan Bowen's nonparticipation (he reminds one character of "Nero fiddling while Rome burned" [260]), but even those who do participate in the action on the street remain bystanders in an important sense. They watch the crowd like pornographers, half fascinated, half repulsed; though provided with a frisson, they preserve their emotional distance. The spiritual discharge that Elias Canetti suggests distinguishes the formation of a true crowd is never sparked;[4] the participants are never more than the sum of their parts.

In the early 1930s, in line with the "literary massification" campaign, several authors began writing stories that purported to give a voice to the true crowd, the Chinese masses. Ding Ling's "Water," which narrates the beginnings of a peasant uprising in the wake of a major flood, is the most famous. After its publication in the inaugural issue of Ding Ling's own magazine *Beidou* 北斗 (Big Dipper) in 1931, several critics credited Ding Ling with having invented a new form that overcame the individualism of May Fourth literature and took "the unfolding of collective action" as its theme.[5] Several other authors, including Zhang Tianyi, Ye Zi 葉紫, and Sha Ting, produced fiction cut largely to the same pattern in the years that followed. As a fictional motif, the crowds in 1930s' fiction, despite some variations, display highly regular characteristics. The crowds are first of all

3. Mao Dun, *Ziye*, p. 256.
4. Elias Canetti, *Crowds and Power*, p. 18.
5. See Feng Xuefeng 馮雪峯 "Guanyu xin de xiaoshuo de dansheng: ping Ding Ling de 'Shui'" 關於新的小說的誕生—評丁玲的《水》 (On the birth of a new fiction: on Ding Ling's "Water"), *Beidou* 2, no. 1 (20 January 1932), pp. 235–39. See also the discussion in Yi-tse Mei Feuerwerker, *Ding Ling's Fiction*, p. 68.

anonymous and undifferentiated: individual faces are sometimes sketched and individual voices heard, but characters find their identity only in the context of the crowd and its collective intentions. In the works of Lu Xun, Ye Shaojun, and Mao Dun, crowds had largely been viewed through the eyes of a single protagonist; they were part of the social background against which the psychology of the individual was measured. "Water" and stories like it do not provide a single perspective through which to focalize the reader's view of the crowd. The reader must identify directly with the crowd as an entity in itself, as one identifies with an individual character in other kinds of fiction.

The crowd as a protagonist, however, lacks the variety and uniqueness of the individual character, and its representation soon comes to rely on a limited set of techniques and motifs. The crowd is ever changing and constantly in motion, so without the introduction of a determinate perspective, taking a fixed view of it is difficult. Inevitably writers resort to certain predictable metaphors to evoke the transformations of the crowd, and all of these may be found with regularity in Chinese writings of the 1930s. Ye Zi, for example, employs all of the common metaphors within a few short pages in his story "Huo" 火 (Fire, 1933), including fire, water ("tide," "tempest," "torrent"), animal and insect packs ("frenzied tigers," "swarms"), and the wind.[6] Each of these natural metaphors conveys a sense of the crowd's restless movement, of its growth by expansion, and of its potential destructiveness. Ding Ling uses the water metaphor effectively: water—that is, the crowd of water that is a flood—both constitutes the disaster that forces people from their homes, thus creating the crowd of angry peasants, and instructs the crowd in the power of aggregation. Water and crowd are linked at two crucial moments in the text, first in unfriendly contiguity, then in metaphorical unity. In the first instance, dawn breaks on the sight of the "vast, turgid, yellow waters" that have buried villages and fields and also on the sight of the survivors, "pathetic humans" who "powerlessly, with withered skin and numbed stares," climb away from the water in all directions.[7] But by the end of the story the people have themselves amassed outside the town in such

6. Ye Zi 葉紫, "Huo" 火 (Fire), in Ye Zi, *Ye Zi xuanji*, pp. 47–70, here pp. 65–69. See Elias Canetti, *Crowds and Power*, for a discussion of metaphors used with crowds, especially pp. 87–108.

7. Ding Ling, "Shui" 水 (Water), in Ding Ling, *Ding Ling duanpian xiaoshuo xuan* 2:297–332, here p. 316.

numbers that the "half-naked young man" in a tree who encourages their rebellion can say, "Look about you; wherever there is a field, wherever there is land, we are there" (328). When they move on the town, they are "even fiercer than water" (332). The crowd has taken possession of the flood's power.

This power is kindled simply by the people's consciousness of increase: "Even in their suffering and starvation, they were together, a great crowd; they understood each other, there was an intimacy among them. . . . Their new power grew stronger with the increase of the crowd" (322). The crowd's assembly and the breakdown of ordinary social barriers that occurs in conjunction with it is explored more fully in stories written in imitation of "Water" by other authors. Zhang Tianyi's "Chouhen" 仇恨 (Enmity, 1932), for example, follows a ragged band of peasants as they flee from the devastations of war and drought across a desert landscape. Their identity as a group emerges above all from their sense of communal survival (they feel that "in all the world only they lived on").[8] In the course of the story they enlist into their group first a wounded conscript and then three soldiers, one of whom is also severely wounded. Both of the wounded strangers are near death, described as on the verge of physical erosion by the hostile environment. Their wounds, depicted in excruciating detail, are consumed by insects; one man painfully burrows into the dry earth "as if to plant his two arms there" (330). Both beg to be put out of their misery, but the ragtag tribe of survivors refuses to abandon them, despite earlier expressions of contempt for the soldier's trade. Here, as in "Water," an extreme trial of physical degradation and suffering serves to negate the ordinary social distinctions that separate individuals. When the tribe comes across the conscript, one of its members asks him, "Who are you?" but immediately feels that the question is out of place: in these extreme circumstances, the sheer fact of survival makes all conventional markers of identity irrelevant. Social discriminations are overridden by the simple use of the inclusive pronoun *we* (*zamen*), which announces the newcomer's acceptance into the crowd. One recognizes immediately the importance of this moment for the individual, who is otherwise literally threatened with extinction, but the moment is equally important for the crowd: in the

8. Zhang Tianyi, "Chouhen" 仇恨 (Enmity), in Zhang Tianyi, *Zhang Tianyi wenji* 1:311–34, here p. 315.

act of including the newcomer, the crowd reminds itself of its primary identity as an assembly of survivors and reaffirms its members' equality in the face of death. The crowd's survival is itself dependent upon the continuing accretion of new members, however tenuous a hold on life they may possess.

But the crowd cannot be defined exclusively by its internal dynamics; it has an external objective as well. In "Enmity" the tribe of survivors is motivated not only by their immediate needs for food and shelter but also by a primitive moral instinct that finds expression in the desire for vengeance evoked in the story's title. Their vengeance is at first directed against all military personnel. Once the group discovers the humanity of the soldiers they encounter, however, they are forced to rethink this: "It was awkward—on whom should they take out their anger?" (325). Though thereafter robbed of a clear-cut antagonist, their desire for vengeance persists, as evidenced by the story's final line: "Goddamn it, we've got to get our hands on some rifles" (334). Similarly, the uprising in "Water," although motivated on one level by immediate material needs (the desire for grain to prevent starvation), is also given an elaborate ethical pretext, articulated by the half-naked man in the tree and then ratified by a chorus of voices rising from the crowd. The owners of the granary they plan to raid, the man argues, have long exploited them, have in fact "cannibalized" their ancestors for many generations, so that storming the granaries will amount simply to retrieving what is rightfully theirs, "our own hearts' blood" (329, 331). The crowd's eruption into violence is thus justified on two fronts: it carries the authority of material necessity after the crowd's long toleration of starvation and injury, and it carries an ethical authority—a base in the peasants' "moral economy."[9] Significantly, the crowd's ethical motivation is never imposed from outside but emerges in its collective consciousness and finds expression in its disparate and anonymous voices. The crowd's discontent is in fact none other than the familiar social critique of the intellectuals, but that critique has now found a new origin and a new authority: it is no longer the property of the narrator or intellectual protagonist but is diffused democratically throughout the crowd.

This diffusion results in a theatricalization of the critical message:

9. See E. P. Thompson, "The Moral Economy of the English Crowd in the Eighteenth Century," *Past and Present*, no. 50 (1971), pp. 76–136.

the narrator steps aside and lets his characters speak for him. In fact, the theatrical nature of such scenes is often already evident in the behavior of the crowd itself. An anonymous character in Ye Shaojun's *Ni Huanzhi* cynically observes: "When you write a play or a novel, you have to put in all the various types of characters, like the hero and the heroine and the clown, the loyal minister and the public-spirited official, the villain and the fool. A revolution is probably much the same sort of thing, with the local bully and the evil landowner as indispensable characters in it."[10] Such revolutionary acts as the one that concludes Ye Zi's "Fire" appear to bear out this supposition: in the penultimate scene, when the abused masses overrun a local landlord's home, their true satisfaction comes less from the violence they inflict than from the opportunity to air their complaints—in a highly declamatory fashion—to the now-prostrate landlord. The crowd indignantly enumerates the secrets and corruption that have characterized his oppressive order; by raiding his house and his shrine they have opened up this once-forbidden ground to the truth and thereby undone the web of lies on which the existence of the old order depended. Wu Zuxiang went so far as to make the crowd's theatricality a recurrent motif in such stories as "Fan jia pu" 樊家鋪 (Fan family village) and "Yiqian babai dan" 一千八百擔 (Eighteen hundred piculs of rice); in the uprisings that conclude both these stories the peasants carry gongs and drums, wear devils' masks, and "shriek, jump, and whistle like demons."[11] At the end of "Eighteen Hundred Piculs of Rice" the peasants drag the district head to an abandoned stage, where the community had once prayed to the rain deity for relief from the drought, and use the site to act out the ritualized destruction of the old order and its superstitions.

As quickly became apparent, mass fiction, with its prevalence of stock metaphors and dramatic turns and with its poorly concealed instructional intentions, proved given to stereotype. Few of the more skillful authors who experimented with the genre wrote more than a few works of this kind. But the desire such works evince to give positive voice to the new communal instincts persisted, and veteran authors and newcomers to the literary scene in the mid-1930s faced

10. Ye Shaojun, *Ni Huanzhi*, p. 305.
11. Wu Zuxiang 吳組緗, "Yiqian babai dan" 一千八百擔 (Eighteen hundred piculs of rice), in Wu Zuxiang, *Wu Zuxiang xiaoshuo sanwen ji*, pp. 74–116, here p. 114.

continued moral and political pressure to give these instincts their due, even as they continued to experiment with more conventional realistic modes of description and plot development.

The careers and writings of Sha Ting and Ai Wu 艾蕪 are illustrative of the formal double bind that resulted from these conflicting imperatives. Former classmates from Sichuan who found themselves together in Shanghai in the early 1930s pursuing common literary ambitions, Sha Ting and Ai Wu jointly wrote Lu Xun in late 1931 asking for guidance. In their letter, which was printed the following January, together with Lu Xun's reply, in the journal *Shizi jietou* (Crossroads), they express dissatisfaction with the model of revolutionary literature then current: "We have read a few proletarian works, but we aren't willing to take fictitious characters and have them willy-nilly turn over a new leaf as revolutionaries; we prefer to truthfully carve out the likenesses of a few familiar models."[12] Lu Xun replied that works on any subject, as long as they were written from the perspective of the disadvantaged classes and (he added, with a rather characteristic qualification) as long as they were truly works of art, made a contribution to the present struggle. If the authors were themselves "militant proletarians," then their works would by definition have social value. But because of the authors' class status, works critical of their own class ran the risk of being "a family affair, like a brighter, more talented son's hatred for his unpromising brothers," and their works about the lower classes would be "cold glances from above," offering at best an empty pity. Neither was of any use in the present struggle. While Lu Xun encouraged his correspondents to keep writing, he urged them to renounce their class standing and "be at one" with the proletariat. With strength of purpose they would be able, he hoped, "to gradually overcome their own lives and consciousness and see a new road."

With this tepid encouragement, Sha Ting and Ai Wu continued to write, but neither author found a ready solution to the formal questions that had motivated their letter. Sha Ting's first volume of stories, *Falü wai de hangxian* 法律外的航綫 (Voyage beyond the law, 1932), was in fact criticized for exactly the formulism he and Ai Wu

12. Sha Ting 沙汀 and Ai Wu 艾蕪, "Guanyu xiaoshuo ticai de tongxin" 關於小說題材的通信 (An exchange of letters on subject matter in fiction), in Lu Xun, *Lu Xun quanji* 4:366–69, here p. 366.

had appeared to deplore in their letter to Lu Xun. Mao Dun praised the book, but privately expressed his disapproval of Sha Ting's "impressionistic" techniques and used his review of the book to launch a heated attack on the new formulism (which, however, he ascribes to only one of Sha Ting's stories). He wrote:

> This formula has in recent years become the rule of revolutionary literature, held sacred and beyond reproach. Self-styled revolutionary literati with no real experience of life use this formula to promote themselves, and young writers who do have a real experience of life, under the pressure of this formula, feel obligated to abandon what they know and fabricate or imitate what they don't. This is China's "new realism"![13]

Han Shihang likewise used Sha Ting to excoriate the new realism, but for slightly different reasons: Sha Ting's focus on disembodied "social phenomena" at the expense of individuals, he wrote, robbed his works of any power to go below the surface and achieve emotional depth.[14]

Sha Ting clearly took these criticisms to heart; after a return visit to Sichuan in 1935, where he later wrote that he "encountered life anew," he began to concentrate on character in his fiction.[15] In doing so, he joined Hu Feng and Mao Dun, both of whom advanced the opinion in the mid-1930s that an emphasis on character was the best means of achieving typicality in fiction without resorting to formulism. By privileging character over plot, authors could ensure that their fiction possessed a measure of felt life and was not simply the fleshing-out of abstract ideological schemes. Another quiet rallying call for realists in the 1930s was "local color": the monotonous, stereotyped view of the masses that had come to characterize much of leftist fiction could be avoided, they felt, by giving painstaking attention to the unique cultural and linguistic traits of peasant or village life in particular regions of China. The best of these writers are still read today largely as regionalists. Sha Ting's best-known works, for example, are

13. Mao Dun, "*Falü wai de hangxian* duhou gan" 《法律外的航綫》讀後感 (Feelings after reading *Voyage beyond the Law*), in Jin Kui, *Sha Ting yanjiu zhuanji*, pp. 161–65, here p. 163.

14. Han Shihang, "Wentan shang de xinren Sha Ting" 文壇上的新人沙汀 (Newcomer on the literary scene, Sha Ting), in Jin Kui, *Sha Ting yanjiu zhuanji*, pp. 201–7.

15. Huang Manjun 黃曼君, in his "Sha Ting 'Zuolian' shiqi dui xianshizhuyi de tansuo" 沙汀"左聯"時期對現實主義的探索 (Sha Ting's exploration of realism in the period of the League of Left-Wing Writers), quotes Sha Ting as saying, "I began to concentrate on character—an important change for me—after returning home in 1935 and encountering life anew" (Jin Kui, *Sha Ting yanjiu zhuanji*, pp. 138–57, here p. 155).

those written after 1935 that take Sichuan village life as their setting. Ai Wu is most famous for his depiction of the peasants of southwest China and Burma, where he traveled extensively in the 1920s. Other important new writers likewise wrote from their personal observation of peasant life, often in their home province: Anhui in the case of Wu Zuxiang, Manchuria in the case of Xiao Hong 蕭紅 and Duanmu Hongliang 端木蕻良.

But although these authors rejected the formulism associated with the new realism, the collectivizing instinct that informed it continued in many ways to influence the fiction that they wrote. The influence is evident even with the later fiction of Sha Ting, whose often pitiless satirical bent caused critics to dub him the purest of 1930s' realists, objective to the point of being "cold, unfeeling, unemotional."[16] Although in the fiction he wrote after 1935 Sha Ting rarely brought the crowd to center stage, he frequently evoked its presence as a necessary ethical foil to the corrupt or violent activities that the stories recount. "Daili xianzhang" 代理縣長 (Deputy magistrate of the county, 1936), for example, presents an inverted image of the situation in Ding Ling's "Water": both stories concern crowds that congregate to demand famine relief from government officials, but "Deputy Magistrate of the County" is drawn not from the crowd's perspective but from that of the corrupt county officials, who confiscate what little relief aid is available for their own purposes and then scheme to take further advantage of the situation by fining the peasants for trespassing. When this idea meets the crowd's understandable resistance, the unflappable deputy magistrate concocts a yet more ridiculous scheme, suggesting that the government sell the masses welfare tickets. Viewed in the context of the public disaster, of whose magnitude the ever-more-insistent crowds at the gate of the yamen serve as reminder, the otherwise mundane activities of the officials at the beleaguered yamen—the little comforts they pursue, so attentively described by the realist narrator, and their glib altercations—take on a monstrous quality. So too the avarice and fatuous posturing of the individuals

---

16. Chen Junzhi 陳君治, "Guanyu Sha Ting zuopin de kaocha" 關於沙汀 作品的考察 (Analysis of Sha Ting's works), in Jin Kui, *Sha Ting yanjiu zhuanji*, pp. 208–11, here p. 209. Tan Xingguo 譚興國 wrote of Sha Ting that he was "100 percent a realist" ("Lun Sha Ting chuangzuo de duchuangxing" 論沙汀創作的獨創性 [On the individuality of Sha Ting's writings], in Jin Kui, *Sha Ting yanjiu zhuanji*, pp. 158–60, here p. 158.

who people such works as Sha Ting's "Zai Qixiangju chaguan li" 在其香居茶館裏 (In the House of Fragrance teahouse, 1940) and his first novel, *Taojin ji* 淘金記 (The gold diggers, 1942), are measured against the enormity of the historical catastrophe that has engulfed the nation. But Sha Ting's characters maintain an almost perverse apathy toward public events, willfully refusing to draw the obvious connections between their personal stories and the larger historical narrative. As a result they become profoundly isolated from each other and in a sense from themselves: they prove unable to satisfy even their most limited private ambitions. The petty goals they pursue with such obsessiveness invariably draw them into mutual combat; but while his characters lock horns, Sha Ting the ironist quietly withdraws the object of their quest through some narrative twist, leaving them furiously squabbling over nothing. "In the House of Fragrance Teahouse" is perhaps the most accomplished example of such a narrative: just when the quarrel between Ward Chief Fang Zhiguo 方治國 and Loudmouth Xing 邢 over Fang's failure to prevent the conscription of Loudmouth's son breaks into fisticuffs, word comes that the boy has been dismissed from service because "he wasn't fit to fight for his country." The townsmen's impassioned quarrel is revealed as a mere tempest in a teahouse.[17]

In certain exceptional stories Sha Ting introduces the crowd not simply as an external force against which to judge the behavior of his characters but as a symbol of the yearning for commonality within the individual psyche. "Cili" 磁力 (Magnet, 1940), for example, concerns a young boy, Little Yuan 袁, who dreams of leaving his dreary village and his overprotective, nagging mother to make his way to "Yan'an, the cradle of the Chinese revolution." His dream of Yan'an is expressed in an image of the assembling crowd: he envisions "a boundless expanse of glistening snow with a stream of undaunted men and women plodding across it."[18] In the end Little Yuan leaves to "formally begin a long journey" of, we may assume, revolutionary adventure. In acting on his desire for immersion in the radical crowd, Little Yuan brings his most private desires into contact with the broader

17. Sha Ting, "Zai Qixiangju chaguan li" 在其香居茶館裏 (In the House of Fragrance teahouse), in Sha Ting, *Sha Ting duanpian xiaoshuo xuan*, pp. 98–114, here p. 114.

18. Sha Ting, "Cili" 磁力 (Magnet), in Sha Ting, *Sha Ting duanpian xiaoshuo xuan*, pp. 85–97, here p. 97.

historical reality in China and thereby frees himself from the petty constraints of his quotidian reality at home. His dream, which until his departure belongs solely in the imaginary realm, is finally granted a historical reality that the more conventionally realistic details of village life (whose description nevertheless constitutes the largest part of the work) are denied.

In another story offering a less tendentious rendering of the crowd instinct, "Yige qiutian wanshang" 一個秋天晚上 (An autumn evening, 1944), Sha Ting dramatizes an unexpected moment of fellow feeling between a prostitute and the squad leader who is assigned to guard her. The moment, though climactic, is understated and carefully situated in the context of a relationship built otherwise on self-interest. The squad leader releases the prostitute from the stocks (where she has been placed at the instigation of an official's jealous wife) with the intention of himself enjoying her favors. She, "true to her profession," eagerly agrees, but owing in part to his disappointment with her disheveled physical condition and in part to the coincidental intrusion of a bumbling guard, his ardor cools, and a somewhat coarse conversation replaces the intended sexual activity. While they converse, the woman's complaints about the succession of family disasters that led her to take up prostitution set the squad leader thinking about his own circumstances: "His family too had paid bribes more than once to keep him from being press-ganged into the army. . . . His father was in a poor state of health, his mother unable to stand the strain of much work, and now it was time to sow the wheat."[19] Through this small epiphany in which the distinctions between criminal and guard are momentarily overridden, Sha Ting discovers the nascent eruption of the crowd instinct. True to his manner, however, he is careful to give it expression in the most restrained and unsentimental way possible.

Such a moment of fellow feeling, in which social differences are temporarily obliterated in the recognition of shared adversity, may seem little different from the dramatized expressions of pity that such writers of the 1920s as Ye Shaojun made an important property of their fiction. But significantly, "An Autumn Evening" and works similar to it—particularly those by Ai Wu, who made a specialty of evoking such moments—dramatize not a privileged intellectual's conferral

19. Sha Ting, "Yige qiutian wanshang" 一個秋天晚上 (An autumn evening), in Sha Ting, *Sha Ting duanpian xiaoshuo xuan*, pp. 143–57, here p. 157.

of pity on the abused underdog but the fellow feeling awakened among members of the lower classes in the face of social oppression. Lu Xun had warned Ai Wu and Sha Ting in his letter that for bourgeois intellectuals writing about the lower classes, the expression of pity was "only a futile almsgiving."[20] Ai Wu, in his effort to remedy this perceived fault in May Fourth fiction, goes so far as to invert the direction of emotional almsgiving: in several of his early stories lower-class protagonists demonstrate compassion for representatives of the oppressor class and even for the narrator himself. Such redirected sympathy becomes necessary only after its recipient has been declassed, but Ai Wu had in fact made an effort to change his class standing long before Lu Xun advised him and Sha Ting to do so. The son of a Sichuan primary-school teacher, Ai Wu had in his youth hoped to attend Beijing University and take part in the progressive social movements brewing in the capital, but he was unable to gather the funds. Instead he determined to "go into the world and rely on my own hands and labor."[21] For the next few years he traveled around southwest China and Burma, taking on odd jobs for survival wages. When, in 1930, he was finally deported from Burma for political activity, he returned to Shanghai, where he began to write stories based on his experiences in the south.

The stories in Ai Wu's first volume, *Nanxing ji* 南行記 (A journey to the south, 1935) and the collections that followed it are reminiscent of Turgenev's *Sketches from a Hunter's Album*. They are loosely structured tales told by a largely unmediated authorial alter ego. But while Turgenev's aristocratic narrator has an essentially anthropological, if benevolent, interest in the peasants he describes, the narrator in Ai Wu's stories attempts a complete identification with his lower-class protagonists. In "Rensheng zhexue de yike" 人生哲學的一課 (A lesson in life, 1931), the first and most clearly autobiographical of the stories, the narrator undergoes an initiation into their world. A runaway arriving in Kunming 昆明 with his resources depleted, the narrator suffers a series of semicomical misadventures as he tries to find work and survive in this new environment. But perhaps his greatest trial is having to share his bed in a seedy inn, with a scabious peasant

20. Lu Xun, "Guanyu xiaoshuo ticai de tongxin," *Lu Xun quanji* 4:366–69, here p. 368.
21. Ai Wu, "Xu" 序 (Preface), in Ai Wu, *Ai Wu duanpian xiaoshuo xuan*, pp. 1–7, here p. 2.

the first night and with another beggared stranger the second. His experiences during the intervening day, however, have taught him to feel empathy for the second bedmate. Instead of being filled with disgust for the stranger's odor, "ordinarily enough to make one retch," he simply "savors his laborious travels, his painful toil, and his tragic disappointments."[22]

It is this initiation that qualifies the narrator of the later stories to speak of "we whom the world has abandoned" and thus to avoid the lofty glance against which Lu Xun was later to warn. But in fact this identification of narrator and protagonist remains problematic. In another, more accomplished story, "Shanxia zhong" 山峽中 (In the mountain gorge), the narrator takes up with a group of travelling thieves and even assists them in a heist. That evening, as they camp at a deserted temple by a gorge, the leader of the gang suddenly launches into a tirade about the book that the narrator has taken out to read:

> "What's that you're reading? What good's that nonsense in books? Worthless! Burn it, and it's not worth this stick of wood. Listen, and I'll teach you something. . . . Our learning's not written down on paper for those fools to read. . . . In a word, it's 'Fear nothing' and 'Lie.'. . . If you want to go along with us, what are you carrying those books for?"[23]

The narrator's literacy creates a gap so fundamental that even his sharing of the other men's physical suffering cannot bridge it. Like many of the stories in Ai Wu's early collections, "In the Mountain Gorge" ends with the separation of the narrator and the temporary companions who have made up the characters of his story. He wakes one morning to find them gone, but curiously they have left three silver dollars in his book. By this act the thieves prove their good nature and perhaps signal their toleration of the narrator's literary ambitions. But the act also points directly to the cause of his estrangement from them (the book), and the narrator is left in a melancholy mood: "Vague, dismal fancies rose in my heart like strands of mist" (40). Ai Wu's narrative alter ego has attempted to declass himself entirely, but his very possession of the medium that makes possible his fiction has defeated the attempt.

22. Ai Wu, "Rensheng zhexue de yike" 人生哲學的一課 (A lesson in life), in Ai Wu, *Nanxing ji*, pp. 6–23, here p. 22.
23. Ai Wu, "Shanxia zhong" 山峽中 (In the mountain gorge), in Ai Wu, *Nanxing ji*, pp. 24–40, here pp. 26–27.

In his later fiction Ai Wu avoided the use of such narrative alter egos, but he continued to explore the morality of class inversions in the context of the contemporary social upheaval. In "Haidao shang" 海島上 (On the island, 1936), three Chinese of different backgrounds returning from Southeast Asia find themselves quarantined by the British on an unidentified island within sight of the mainland. The self-effacing narrator paints a vivid picture of the other two, one a sickly, anxiety-ridden old man, who takes an excruciatingly sycophantic attitude toward his colonial oppressors, the other a brash and self-confident youth, who had once worked for the old man and has returned to China as a stowaway. The quarantine places them in temporary social parity, thus revealing the inequality of their natural gifts, giving the youth with his strength and health the advantage. Clearly relishing the situation, the youth forces the old man to enact an inversion of their former roles, redressing past wrongs through their satirical dramatization. But when the old man falls ill and must buy passage from the island to a hospital, the youth has second thoughts about his earlier theft of the old man's cash and secretly returns it. The quarantine, absurd both because it serves to keep the Chinese from their own land and because only the sick man escapes it, has fundamentally redrawn the relationship of the two men. The youth, who confides to the narrator that he has become "addicted" to theft as a way of undermining the arrogance of the wealthy, recognizes that in the new situation the act of theft no longer carries this meaning. He does not restore the money out of a superior quality of sympathy, however. In the elaborate metaphor by which he explains his act to the narrator, he denies that he felt any pity for a sick rat he once reluctantly killed; he just didn't like striking at an already-wounded creature. He acts instead out of a superior sensitivity to the nature of social oppression; he knows where to draw the lines of inclusion and exclusion in the distribution of social crowds. The old man, already chastened by his satirical dressing-down, now disabled by his illness and abused by his colonial masters, no longer deserves the young man's enmity.

The discovery of common interests among previously divided individuals that is dramatized in these stories by Sha Ting and Ai Wu significantly takes place in the inoperative domain of the individual psyche. The stories affirm the psychological reality of the crowd instinct and hold up a promise of an eventual change for the better, but they do not constitute the epic dramatization of change that Chinese theorists increasingly called for and that had been the raison d'être of such mass fiction as Ding Ling's "Water." The relationship between the subjective experience of the crowd instinct and pragmatic revolutionary action remained unarticulated, leading some writers in the late 1930s and early 1940s to introduce realist heroes into their works—lower-class figures whose ungainliness and ethical faults are elaborated to ensure their credibility but who nevertheless discover within themselves the courage to take a positive stand against the oppressive social order. Wu Zuxiang's story "Mouri" 某日 (A certain day, 1936) and his novel *Shan hong* 山洪 (Mountain torrent, 1941) are examples of such works. Indeed, Wu Zuxiang's tiny oeuvre, consisting of only two volumes of short stories and a single novel, exemplifies better than that of any other author, with the possible exception of Mao Dun, the variety of formal and tonal experiments made by Chinese realists in the 1920s and 1930s. His earliest stories, such as "Li jia de qianye" 離家的前夜 (The night before departure, 1930), are semiautobiographical sketches showing a personal sincerity and sensitivity reminiscent of Ye Shaojun's; "Guanguan de bupin" 官官的補品 (Young master's tonic, 1932) experiments with irony and satire to achieve effects similar to those in some of Lu Xun's best stories; and "Eighteen Hundred Piculs of Rice" and "Fan Family Village" offer closely observed descriptive studies of village life. The last two tales, Wu's longest and best-known stories, both dramatize the erosion of traditional familial relationships in the face of invasive political and social forces. In "Eighteen Hundred Piculs of Rice" representatives of the various branches of the powerful Song 宋 clan meet to discuss the allocation of their grain reserves after a drought; their conference soon deteriorates into a noisy squabble indicative of the profound divisions within the family that generations of corruption and self-interest have created. Caught in the grip of this internal feud, the clan members remain oblivious to the larger forces at work in the world outside—until, that is, the starving peasants break into the family compound at the conclusion of the story to seize the surplus rice. In "Fan Family Village" the more intimate circle of the nuclear family is disrupted and finally sundered by powerful external forces. In this highly dramatic three-part story—structured much like a well-made play—a village wife named Xianzi 線子 is subjected to increasing indignities as her village is beset by drought and civil war. The final blow comes when her husband, whose love is her only remaining source of stability, is arrested on a murder charge and an unctuous representative of the local yamen comes to demand a bribe. Xianzi turns for help to her mother, an acquisitive and superstitious old woman who has recently won a considerable sum of money at a lottery, but she is refused. In a fit of desperation, Xianzi murders her, only to learn in the final scene that a peasant revolt in town has already liberated her husband. As we observed earlier, the peasant crowds who rise up at the close of both these stories serve primarily as agents of a primitive ethical vengeance; their appearance signifies the destruction of the old order and situates the events recounted in the body of the story within a larger historical and ethical context.

Not until the composition of "A Certain Day" did Wu Zuxiang try to record an instance of constructive individual resistance to that order. This story too concerns a family's response to destructive external forces, but here the conclusion points to the eventual restoration of the family's dignity and integrity. In the story's climactic scene the protagonist, a young peasant named Da Mao 大毛, finds the strength to stand up to his father-in-law, a once-wealthy villager who has forced his blind and bad-tempered daughter on Da Mao because no one else would have her. Da Mao is encouraged in this scene by the presence of several other villagers, each of whom has his own grievance against the old man and willingly supports Da Mao when he takes his stand. This communal setting is only one of several factors that temper the reader's sense of Da Mao's heroism. His impotence and silent frustration in the face of a troubled home life has been meticulously described earlier in the story. And his opponent in the climactic scene is hardly formidable; the father-in-law, his body debilitated from years of opium smoking, alternates throughout between bouts of hysteria and moments of total enervation. Finally, the conclusion of the story leaves a sense of qualified hope: the rosy description of the farm ("The clouds had massed together and, suffused with sparkling and translucent colors, were shining with unusual freshness and beauty on the fields and huts")[24] suggests that something auspicious has transpired, but Da Mao's aunt continues to express reservations about the practical outcome of the squabble.

24. Wu Zuxiang, "Mouri" 某日 (A certain day), in Wu Zuxiang, *Wu Zuxiang xiaoshuo sanwen ji*, pp. 183–200, here p. 200.

Similarly, in his novel *Mountain Torrent*, Wu was careful to give a full exposition of the social and historical forces that created his heroic protagonist, a graceless, brooding peasant named Zhang Sanguan 張三官. The first half of the novel explores Zhang's complex emotional reaction to the sight of Chinese armies retreating across Anhui, the province in which his village lies, after the fall of Shanghai in 1937. Though Zhang Sanguan possesses an instinctive patriotism, he is not above considering ways of escaping the war and hardly seems heroic material. But at the conclusion of the first half of the book, he has a sudden vision of China in which he sees the crowd of refugees and soldiers moving through the countryside, hears their rhythmic singing "like the echoing of a great wind, like the sound of the river flooding in the spring," and has a quasi-transcendent experience:

> His chest suddenly felt fiery hot, as though something were pushing upward, relentlessly, blocking his throat. His heart was pounding, as though some hugely swollen thing were pressing on it. He stood erect, forgot his fears, forgot his worries, forgot his cousin and his mother, even forgot his own existence. He felt he had touched something real: this something was China.[25]

This is perhaps as powerful an expression of lyric immersion in the crowd as can be found in modern Chinese fiction. But as I have suggested above, such an experience remains inoperative, and Wu attempts to redress this perceived fault in the second half of the work, which narrates the arrival of several guerrilla workers to instruct the peasants in military techniques. But with the introduction of such mentor figures from the party, the once-spontaneous, vengeful crowd is redefined as an educable flock, to be organized and manipulated by forces that—however they may purport to speak in the name of the true crowd—cannot but take their position outside and above it. As the author was himself to concede, the style of *Mountain Torrent* becomes increasingly expository, and the second half of the novel fails to live up the promise of the first.[26] Wu Zuxiang apparently had no heart

---

25. Wu Zuxiang, *Shan hong* 山洪 (Mountain torrent). Xingqun chuban gongsi, 1946, pp. 90–91.
26. In his afterword to the 1982 edition Wu Zuxiang expressed his dissatisfaction with the novel, calling it "second-rate": "Because I lacked experience in combat, when I took up my pen to write, I felt as though I were walking in the dark" (Wu Zuxiang, *Shan hong*, 1982 edition, p. 210).

for the kind of didactic fiction that came increasingly to supplant critical realism in all its varieties after 1942.

In the decade preceding the Yan'an talks Chinese writers experimented tirelessly in an effort to mediate the conflicting demands of realism and political praxis. By the 1930s most saw that critical realism was not the simple tool for social regeneration its advocates had once believed it to be. In working with the mode, Chinese writers and critics had come increasingly to understand that realism did not naturally lend itself to the activism and populism that Chinese radicals felt the times demanded. Although they remained sympathetic to realism, the Chinese writers we have discussed here refused to accord their aesthetic instincts priority over their reformist aims and continued throughout their careers to introduce a measure of transitivity into their borrowed model. In so doing, they evinced what C. T. Hsia has called an "obsession with China"—an overriding preoccupation with the national crisis and with the role their own fiction should play in alleviating it.[27] In Hsia's view, this obsession has prevented much of modern Chinese literature from achieving the integrity of a truly personal and universal worldview. His terminology is pejorative, but it does succeed in suggesting the passionate determination with which Chinese writers pursued the goal of social efficacy in their literature, if not the richness and diversity of the fiction they produced. Although Chinese writers in the end failed to discover a completely satisfactory solution to what was at once an artistic and a social dilemma, the experimentation generated by their search for one has much to teach us not only about the Chinese revolution but about the presuppositions of realism itself.

The Western mimetic project, of which realism is just one expression, assumes a fundamental schism between word and reality, and the exploration of this divide is realism's hidden agenda. As Tzvetan Todorov has observed, perfect imitation is no longer imitation, but substitution.[28] And since a linguistic construct can never truly replace reality, the mimetic undertaking is destined to fail. Just as in linguistic theory words are both alienated from and bound to the objects they signify, so realist works are at once distinct from and dependent on the

27. C. T. Hsia, Appendix 1, "Obsession with China: The Moral Burden of Modern Chinese Literature," in *A History of Modern Chinese Literature*, pp. 533–54.
28. Tzvetan Todorov, *Theories of the Symbol*, pp. 112–14.

world they describe. So too is the critical mind of the author, as postulated by realism, both free of the social order and bound to it, both a part of the represented world and detached from it. Practitioners of realism appear to desire above all to bridge the gap that they complainingly assume between the critical intellect and the social order, but to do so would bring the immersion of critique and the extinction of the mode. With so much at stake, realism as practiced in the West generally contents itself with the reexamination and reaffirmation of that gap, offering readers an aesthetic consolation rather than a pragmatic instruction in life.

The cultural critique implicit in the very term *critical realism* assumes a polarization of the "I" of the observer and the society that is the object of the observer's analysis. Realism was adopted in China at a time when the nation's intellectuals were flirting with Western individualism in an effort to create a new national self. Early Chinese realists, despite their many points of disagreement with writers associated with such romanticist groups as the Creation Society, in fact assumed the newly fortified "I" of the romanticists, particularly in their self-assertive rejection of the traditional world order. But from the start realists recognized certain limitations to this new authorial ego—both in its relationship with the audience, the "you" to whom a fictional work is addressed, and in its power to benefit the disenfranchised "others," the "they" whom the new fiction had introduced for the first time into the field of fictional representation. Consciousness of these limitations inevitably weakened the hold of critical realism on the imaginations of Chinese authors. As the new literature met new historical challenges in the 1930s, these fundamental relationships of author, audience, and protagonist were gradually redefined. Where in the 1920s realists had largely addressed educated fellow travelers, by the end of the next decade the implied (if not the actual) readers of most realist fiction were instead members of the proletarian and peasant classes. And whereas realist fiction in the 1920s had taken as protagonist the oppressed or cannibalized social victim—the object of a humanistic pity—by the late 1930s the prescribed protagonist of much new fiction was the recently awakened realist hero. Perhaps most radically, the vengeful, persecutory crowds of 1920s' fiction, who had as often as not instilled feelings of terror in readers, were replaced by unified, purposeful political aggregations, that is, the masses. The new fiction aroused neither pity nor terror, making the experience of catharsis irrelevant. Moreover, mimesis itself began to lose its pertinence, for the new fiction was designed more to promulgate a new ideological vision of the world than to explore, as earlier works of realism had, the gap between a discredited worldview and the actual functioning of society.

The old realism came finally to seem powerless to repair the cultural schisms that opened everywhere in China after the fall of the traditional world order. In calling for mass fiction and socialist realism, Chinese writers acknowledged a new imperative: they began erasing the distinction between "I" and "they"—between the self and society—that had been an indispensable basis for the practice of critical realism, subsuming both in a collective "we." And with the formation of this new sense of the national crowd, or masses, critical realism was at last expelled from China as a trapping of colonialism. That expulsion has proven temporary, however, and the relevance of critical realism to the Chinese experience is not yet finished: indeed, the past few years have seen an erosion of Maoist collectivism, as well as a resurgence of interest in realism. Whatever direction Chinese literature is to take in the future, it is certain to involve a reexamination of critical realism.

Selected Bibliography

This bibliography incorporates all book-length works referred to in the notes, important articles that are not included in the such collectanea as *Zhongguo xin wenxue daxi*, as well as a few other general works on modern Chinese realism. The list of books and articles is followed by a list of the major journals consulted in the course of research. For more complete listings of the works of individual authors see the catalogue compiled by the staff of Beijing shi tushuguan 北京市圖書館 (Beijing municipal library), *Zhongguo xiandai zuojia zhu yi shumu* 中國現代作家著譯書目 (Catalogue of writings and translations by modern Chinese authors; Beijing: Shumu wenxian chubanshe, 1982).

BOOKS AND ARTICLES

Ai Wu 艾蕪. *Ai Wu duanpian xiaoshuo xuan* 艾蕪短篇小說選 (Selected short stories by Ai Wu). Beijing: Renmin wenxue chubanshe, 1978.

———. *Ai Wu wenji* 艾蕪文集 (Collected works of Ai Wu). 3 vols. to date. Chengdu: Sichuan renmin chubanshe, 1981–.

———. *Ai Wu zhongpian xiaoshuo xuan.* 艾蕪中篇小說選 (Selected novellas by Ai Wu). Tianjin: Tianjin renmin chubanshe, 1958.

———. *Ai Wu zhuanji* 艾蕪專集 (Writings by and about Ai Wu). Edited by the Chinese Department, Sichuan University. Chengdu: Sichuan daxue Zhongwen xi, 1979.

———. *Bajiao gu* 芭蕉谷 (Plantain valley). Shanghai: Shangwu yinshuguan, 1937.

———. *Haidao shang* 海島上 (On the island). Shanghai: Wenhua shenghuo chubanshe, 1939.

———. *Nanguo zhi ye* 南國之夜 (Nights in a southern land). Shanghai: Liangyou tushu yinshua gongsi, 1935.

———. *Nanxing ji* 南行記 (A journey to the south). Beijing: Renmin wenxue, 1980.

———. *Ye jing* 夜景 (Night views). Shanghai: Wenhua shenghuo chubanshe, 1936.

Aristotle. *The Poetics*. Translated by Friedrich Somsen. New York: Modern Library, 1954.

Auerbach, Erich. *Mimesis*. Translated by Willard R. Trask. Princeton: Princeton University Press, 1953.

Ban Gu 班固. *Han shu* 漢書 (History of the former Han dynasty). 12 vols. Beijing: Zhonghua shuju, 1962.

Barthes, Roland. *The Rustle of Language*. Translated by Richard Howard. New York: Hill and Wang, 1986.

Beasley W. G., and E. G. Pulleyblank, eds. *Historians of China and Japan*. London: Oxford University Press, 1961.

Becker, George J. *Documents of Modern Literary Realism*. Princeton: Princeton University Press, 1963.

Berninghausen, John, and Theodore D. Huters, eds. *Revolutionary Literature in China: An Anthology*. White Plains, N.Y.: M. E. Sharpe, 1976.

Brown, Carolyn. "The Paradigm of the Iron House: Shouting and Silence in Lu Xun's Short Stories." *Chinese Literature: Essays, Articles, Reviews* 6, nos. 1–2 (July 1984): 101–20.

Canetti, Elias. *Crowds and Power*. Middlesex, England: Penguin Books, 1981.

Chan, Wing-tsit. *A Source Book in Chinese Philosophy*. Princeton: Princeton University Press, 1963.

Chen Duxiu 陳獨秀. *Duxiu wencun* 獨秀文存 (Writings of Chen Duxiu). 4 vols. Shanghai: Shanghai yadong tushuguan, 1922.

Chen Liao 陳遼. *Ye Shengtao pingzhuan* 葉聖陶評傳 (A critical biography of Ye Shengtao). Tianjin: Baihua wenyi chubanshe, 1981.

Chen Mingshu 陳鳴樹. *Lu Xun xiaoshuo lungao* 魯迅小說論稿 (Draft discussion of Lu Xun's fiction). Shanghai: Shanghai wenyi chubanshe, 1981.

Chen Wanyi 陳萬益. *Jin Shengtan de wenxue piping kaoshu* 金聖嘆的文學批評考述 (The literary criticism of Jin Shengtan). Taipei: Taiwan National University, 1976.

Chen, Yu-shih. *Realism and Allegory in the Early Fiction of Mao Tun*. Bloomington: Indiana University Press, 1986.

Chow Tse-tsung. *The May Fourth Movement: Intellectual Revolution in Modern China*. Stanford: Stanford University Press, 1970.

Davis, Lennard J. *Factual Fictions: The Origins of the English Novel*. New York: Columbia University Press, 1983.

———. "A Social History of Fact and Fiction: Authorial Disavowal in the Early English Novel." In *Literature and Society*, edited by Edward Said, pp. 120–48. Baltimore: Johns Hopkins University Press, 1980.

de Bary, Wm. Theodore, ed. *The Unfolding of Neo-Confucianism*. New York: Columbia University Press, 1975.

Derrida, Jacques. *Of Grammatology*. Baltimore: Johns Hopkins University Press, 1974.

Ding Ling 丁玲. *Ding Ling duanpian xiaoshuo xuan* 丁玲短篇小說選 (Selected short stories by Ding Ling). 2 vols. Beijing: Renmin wenxue chubanshe, 1981.

Feigon, Lee. *Chen Duxiu: Founder of the Chinese Communist Party*. Princeton: Princeton University Press, 1983.

Feng Xuefeng 馮雪峯. *Lu Xun de wenxue daolu* 魯迅的文學道路 (Lu Xun's literary path). Changsha: Hunan renmin chubanshe, 1980.

Feuerwerker, Yi-tse Mei. *Ding Ling's Fiction*. Cambridge: Harvard University Press, 1982.

Fu Zhiying 伏志英, ed. *Mao Dun pingzhuan* 茅盾評傳 (Critical and biographical essays on Mao Dun). Shanghai: Xiandai shuju, 1931.

Gadamer, Hans-Georg. *Truth and Method*. New York: Crossroad Publishing Company, 1982.

Gálik, Marián. "Main Issues in the Discussion on 'National Forms' in Modern Chinese Literature." *Asian and African Studies* 10 (1974): 97–112.

———. *Mao Tun and Modern Chinese Literary Criticism*. Wiesbaden: Franz Steiner Verlag, 1969.

———. "Studies in Modern Chinese Literary Criticism." Part 3, "Ch'ien Hsing-ts'un and the Theory of Proletarian Realism"; Part 4, "The Proletarian Criticism of Kuo Mo-jo." *Asian and African Studies* 5 (1969): 49–70; 11 (1975): 145–60.

Geming wenxue lunzheng ziliao xuanbian "革命文學"論爭資料選編 (Selected materials from the Revolutionary Literature debate). 2 vols. Beijing: Renmin wenxue chubanshe, 1981.

Genette, Gérard and Tzvetan Todorov, eds. *Littérature et réalité*. Paris: Éditions du Seuil, 1982.

Girard, René. *Violence and the Sacred*. Baltimore: Johns Hopkins University Press, 1977.

Goldman, Merle. *Literary Dissent in Communist China*. New York: Atheneum, 1971.

————, ed. *Modern Chinese Literature in the May Fourth Era*. Cambridge: Harvard University Press, 1977.

Grieder, Jerome. *Hu Shih and the Chinese Renaissance: Liberalism in the Chinese Revolution, 1913–1937*. Cambridge: Harvard University Press, 1970.

Gunn, Edward. *The Unwelcome Muse*. New York: Columbia University Press, 1980.

Guo Moruo 郭沫若. *Chuangzao shinian* 創造十年 (Ten years of the Creation Society). Shanghai: Xiandai shuju, 1932.

————. *Guo Moruo shuxin ji* 郭沫若書信集 (Letters of Guo Moruo). Shanghai: Huadong shuju, 1937.

————. *Nüshen* 女神 (The goddesses). Beijing: Renmin wenxue chubanshe, 1958.

Han Shihang 韓侍桁. "Gaobie yu piping yu chuangzao" 告別與批評與創造 (Confession, criticism, and creation). *Beixin* 2, no. 22 (1 October 1928): 27–32.

Hanan, Patrick. "The Technique of Lu Hsün's Fiction." *Harvard Journal of Asiatic Studies*, no. 34 (1974): 53–96.

Hsia, C. T. *A History of Modern Chinese Fiction*. New Haven: Yale University Press, 1971.

————. *Twentieth-Century Chinese Stories*. New York: Columbia University Press, 1971.

————. "Yen Fu and Liang Ch'i-ch'ao as Advocates of New Fiction." In *Chinese Approaches to Literature from Confucius to Liang Ch'i-ch'ao*, edited by Adele Austin Rickett, pp. 221–57. Princeton: Princeton University Press, 1978.

Hsia, Tsi-an *The Gates of Darkness*. Seattle: Washington University Press, 1968.

Hu Feng 胡風. *Lun minzu xingshi wenti* 論民族形式問題 (On the problem of national forms). Shanghai: Haiyan chubanshe, 1947.

————. *Miyun qi fengxi xiaoji* 密雲期風習小紀 (Notes on customs in a foggy period). Hong Kong: Haiyan chubanshe, 1940.

————. *Pinglun ji* 評論集 (Collected criticism). 2 vols. Beijing: Renmin wenxue chubanshe, 1984.

————. *Wenyi bitan* 文藝筆談 (Literary essays). Shanghai: Shenghuo shudian, 1936. Reprint. Guilin: Guoguang chubanshe, 1943.

Hu Shi 胡適. *Hu Shi wencun* 胡適文存 (Collected works of Hu Shi). 4 vols. Shanghai: Yadong tushuguan, 1926.

Hung, Chang-tai. *Going to the People: Chinese Intellectuals and Folk Literature, 1918–1937*. Cambridge: Council on East Asian Studies, Harvard University, 1985.

Huters, Theodore D. "Blossoms in the Snow: Lu Xun and the Dilemma of Modern Chinese Literature." *Modern China* 10, no. 1 (January 1984): 49–77.

Isaacs, Harold R. *Straw Sandals: Chinese Short Stories, 1918–1933*. Cambridge: MIT Press, 1974.

Jauss, Hans Robert. *Aesthetic Experience and Literary Hermeneutics*. Minneapolis: University of Minnesota Press, 1982.

Jenner, W. J. F., ed. *Modern Chinese Stories*. Oxford: Oxford Paperbacks, 1970.

Jin Kui 金葵, ed. *Sha Ting yanjiu zhuanji* 沙汀研究專集 (Collected research on Sha Ting). Hangzhou: Zhejiang wenyi chubanshe, 1983.

Kane, Anthony James. "The League of Left-Wing Writers and Chinese Literary Policy." Ph.D. diss., University of Michigan, 1982.

Kristeva, Julia. *Powers of Horror*. New York: Columbia University Press, 1982.

———. *Le Texte du roman*. The Hague: Mouton, 1970.

Kubin, Wolfgang, and Rudolf G. Wagner, eds. *Essays in Modern Chinese Literature and Literary Criticism*. Bochum, West Ger.: Herausgeber Chinathemen, 1982.

Lan Hai 藍海. *Zhongguo kangzhan wenyi shi* 中國抗戰文藝史 (History of the literature and arts of the Chinese War of Resistance). Jinan: Shandong wenyi chubanshe, 1981.

Lau, Joseph S. M., C. T. Hsia, and Leo Ou-fan Lee, eds. *Modern Chinese Stories and Novellas, 1919–1949*. New York: Columbia University Press, 1981.

Lee, Leo Ou-fan, ed. *Lu Xun and His Legacy*. Berkeley: University of California Press, 1985.

———. *The Romantic Generation of Modern Chinese Writers*. Cambridge: Harvard East Asian Series, 1973.

———. *Voices from the Iron House: A Study of Lu Xun*. Bloomington and Indianapolis: Indiana University Press, 1987.

Lee Yee. *The New Realism: Writings from China after the Cultural Revolution.* New York: Hippocrene Books, 1983.

Legge, James, trans. *The Ch'un Ts'ew, with the Tso Chuen,* vol. 5 of *The Chinese Classics.* Hong Kong: Hong Kong University Press, 1960.

Levin, Harry. *The Gates of Horn.* New York: Oxford University Press, 1963.

Levine, George. *The Realistic Imagination: English Fiction from Frankenstein to Lady Chatterley.* Chicago: University of Chicago Press, 1981.

Li Helin 李何林, ed. *Jin ershi nian lai Zhongguo wenyi sichao lun, 1917–1937* 今二十年來中國文藝思潮論 (Trends in literary thought in China over the past twenty years, 1917–1937). Xi'an: Shanxi renmin chubanshe, 1981.

———. *Zhongguo wenyi lunzhan* 中國文藝論戰 (Chinese debates on literature and the arts). Shanghai: Shenghuo shudian, 1929.

Li Xiu 李岫, ed. *Mao Dun yanjiu zai guowai* 茅盾研究在國外 (Foreign research on Mao Dun). Changsha: Hunan renmin chubanshe, 1984.

Lin Yü-sheng. *The Crisis of Chinese Consciousness: Radical Antitraditionalism in the May Fourth Era.* Madison: University of Wisconsin Press, 1979.

Link, Perry. *Mandarin Ducks and Butterflies: Popular Fiction in Early Twentieth-Century Chinese Cities.* Berkeley: University of California Press, 1981.

Liu Hsieh (Liu Xie). *The Literary Mind and the Carving of Dragons.* Translated by Vincent Yu-chung Shih. Taipei: Chung Hwa Book Company, 1975.

Liu, James J. Y. *Chinese Theories of Literature.* Chicago: University of Chicago Press, 1975.

Lu Xun 魯迅. *Lu Xun quanji* 魯迅全集 (Complete works of Lu Xun). 16 vols. Beijing: Renmin wenxue chubanshe, 1981.

———. *Selected Works.* Translated by Yang Xianyi and Gladys Yang. 4 vols. Beijing: Foreign Languages Press, 1957.

Lu Xun et al. *Chuangzuo de jingyan* 創作的經驗 (The experience of writing). Shanghai: Tianma shudian, 1933.

Lukács, Georg. *Essays on Realism.* Edited by Rodney Livingstone. Cambridge: MIT Press, 1988.

———. *Realism in Our Time.* New York: Harper Torchbooks, 1964.

———. *The Theory of the Novel.* Cambridge: MIT Press, 1971.

Lyell, William A., Jr. *Lu Hsün's Vision of Reality*. Berkeley: University of California Press, 1976.

Ma Liangchun 馬良春 and Zhang Daming 張大明, eds. *Sanshi niandai zuoyi wenyi ziliao xuanbian* 三十年代左翼文藝資料選編 (Selected research materials on leftist literature and art of the 1930s). Chengdu: Sichuan renmin chubanshe, 1980.

Ma Tiji 馬蹄疾, ed. *Shuihu ziliao huibian* 水滸資料彙編 (Collected research materials on *Water Margin*). Beijing: Zhonghua shuju, 1980.

McDougall, Bonnie. *The Introduction of Western Literary Theories into Modern China, 1919–1925*. Tokyo: Centre for East Asian Cultural Studies, 1971.

Macherey, Pierre. *A Theory of Literary Production*. London: Routledge and Kegan Paul, 1978.

Maeno Naoaki 前野直彬. "Ming Qing shiqi liang zhong duili de xiaoshuo lun" 明清時期兩種對立的小說論 (Two opposing theories of fiction in the Ming-Qing period). Translated by Chen Xuzhong 陳熙中. *Gudai wenxue lilun yanjiu*, no. 5 (1981): 44–71.

Malmqvist, Göran, ed. *Modern Chinese Literature and Its Social Context*. Stockholm: Nobel Symposium, 1975.

Mao Dun 茅盾. *Hong* 虹 (Rainbow). Shanghai: Kaiming shudian, 1930. Reprint. Chengdu: Sichuan renmin chubanshe, 1981.

———. *Mao Dun duanpian xiaoshuo ji* 茅盾短篇小說集 (Collected short stories of Mao Dun). 2 vols. Beijing: Renmin wenxue chubanshe, 1980.

———. *Mao Dun lun chuangzuo* 茅盾論創作 (Mao Dun discusses composition). Shanghai: Shanghai wenyi chubanshe, 1980.

———. *Mao Dun wenyi zalun ji* 茅盾文藝雜論集 (A collection of Mao Dun's essays on literature and the arts). 2 vols. Shanghai: Shanghai wenyi chubanshe, 1981.

———. *Midnight*. Translated and slightly abridged by Hsu Meng-hsiang and A. C. Barnes. Hong Kong: C and W Publishing Company, 1976.

———. *Shi* 蝕 (Eclipse). Shanghai: Kaiming shudian, 1930. Reprint. Beijing: Renmin wenxue chubanshe, 1981.

———. *Wo zouguo de daolu* 我走過的道路 (Roads I have traveled). 2 vols. Beijing: Renmin wenxue chubanshe, 1981.

———. [Fang Bi 方壁, pseud.]. *Xiyang wenxue tonglun* 西洋文學通論 (Outline of Western literature). Shanghai, 1933.

———. *Ye qiangwei* 野薔薇 (Wild roses). Shanghai: Xin wenyi shudian, 1929.

———. *Ziye* 子夜 (Midnight). Shanghai: Kaiming shudian, 1933. Reprint. Hong Kong: Nanguo chubanshe, 1975.

Mao Zedong 毛澤東. *Zai Yan'an wenyi zuotanhui shang de jianghua* 在延安文藝座談會上的講話 (Talks at the Yan'an forum on literature and the arts). Beijing: Renmin chubanshe, 1972.

Maruyama Noboru 丸山昇. *Rojin—sono bungaku to kakumei* 魯迅—その文学と革命 (Lu Xun—his literature and revolution). Tokyo: Heibonsha, 1965.

———. *Rojin to kakumei bungaku* 魯迅と革命文学 (Lu Xun and revolutionary literature). Tokyo: Kinokuniya shoten, 1972.

Matsui Hiromi 松井博光. *Hakumei no bungaku: Chūgoku no riarizumu sakka Bōjun* 薄明の文学:中国のリアリズム作家茅盾 (Literature of twilight: the Chinese realist author Mao Dun). Tokyo: Toho shoten, 1979.

Ng, Mao-sang. *The Russian Hero in Modern Chinese Fiction*. Hong Kong: Chinese University Press; Albany, N.Y.: State University of New York Press, 1988.

Owen, Stephen. *Traditional Chinese Poetry and Poetics: Omen of the World*. Madison: University of Wisconsin Press, 1985.

Pickowicz, Paul. *Marxist Literary Thought in China: The Influence of Ch'ü Ch'iu-pai*. Berkeley: University of California Press, 1981.

Plaks, Andrew H., ed. *Chinese Narrative: Critical and Theoretical Essays*. Princeton: Princeton University Press, 1977.

Plato. *The Dialogues of Plato*. Translated by B. Jowett. Oxford: Clarendon Press, 1953.

Pollard, David E. *A Chinese Look at Literature: The Literary Values of Chou Tso-jen in Relation to the Tradition*. Berkeley: University of California Press, 1973.

Průšek, Jaroslev. *Chinese History and Literature*. Dordrecht, Holland: D. Reidel Publishing Co., 1970.

———. *The Lyrical and the Epic: Studies of Modern Chinese Literature*, edited by Leo Ou-fan Lee. Bloomington: Indiana University Press, 1980.

———, ed. *Studies in Modern Chinese Literature*. Berlin: Akademie-Verlag, 1964.

Qian Xingcun 錢杏村 [A Ying 阿英], ed. *Wan Qing wenxue congchao:*

xiaoshuo xiju yanjiu juan 晚清文學叢鈔:小說戲劇研究卷 (Compendium of late Qing literature: fiction and drama research). Beijing: Zhonghua shuju, 1960.

————. *Xiandai Zhongguo wenxue lun* 現代中國文學論 (On modern Chinese literature). Shanghai: Caihua shulin, 1933.

Qu Qiubai 瞿秋白. *Qu Qiubai wenji* 瞿秋白文集 (Collected works of Qu Qiubai). 5 vols. Beijing: Renmin wenxue chubanshe, 1986.

Ren Guangtian 任廣田. "Cong *Gemo* dao *Ni Huanzhi*—lun Ye Shengtao ershi niandai de chuangzuo sixiang" 從《隔膜》到《倪煥之》—論葉聖陶二十年代的創作思想 (From *Barriers* to *Ni Huanzhi*—on Ye Shengtao's theories of writing in the twenties). *Zhongguo xiandai wenxue yanjiu congkan*, no. 4 (1980): 209–25.

Roy, David Tod. *Kuo Mo-jo: The Early Years.* Cambridge: Harvard University Press, 1971.

Sartre, Jean-Paul. *Literature and Existentialism.* New York: Citadel Press, 1962.

Schwarcz, Vera. *The Chinese Enlightenment.* Berkeley: University of California Press, 1986.

Schwartz, Benjamin. *In Search of Wealth and Power: Yen Fu and the West.* Cambridge: Harvard University Press, Belknap Press, 1964.

Semanov, V. I. *Lu Hsün and His Predecessors.* Translated and edited by Charles I. Alber. White Plains, N.Y.: M. E. Sharpe, 1980.

Sha Ting 沙汀. *Sha Ting duanpian xiaoshuo xuan* 沙汀短篇小說選 (Selected short stories by Sha Ting). Beijing: Renmin wenxue chubanshe, 1978.

————. *Sha Ting wenji* 沙汀文集 (Collected works of Sha Ting). 4 vols. Chengdu: Sichuan renmin chubanshe, 1984.

————. *Taojin ji* 淘金記 (The gold diggers). Chongqing: Wenhua shenghuo chubanshe, 1943. Reprint. Beijing: Renmin wenxue chubanshe, 1980.

Shang Jinlin 商金林. "Ye Shengtao nianpu" 葉聖陶年譜 (A chronology of Ye Shengtao's life). 2 parts. *Xin wenxue shiliao.* 1981, no. 1: 253–67; 1981, no. 2: 258–67.

Shao Bozhou 邵伯周. *Mao Dun de wenxue daolu* 茅盾的文學道路 (Mao Dun's literary path). Wuhan: Changjiang wenyi chubanshe, 1955.

Shen Chengkuan 沈承寬, Huang Houxing 黃侯興, and Wu Fuhui 吳福輝, eds. *Zhang Tianyi yanjiu ziliao* 張天翼研究資料 (Research materials on Zhang Tianyi). Beijing: Zhongguo shehui kexue chubanshe, 1982.

Snow, Edgar, ed. *Living China: Modern Chinese Short Stories.* New York: John Day Press, 1937.

Stories from the Thirties. 2 vols. Beijing: Panda Books, 1982.

Su Guangwen 蘇光文. *Kangzhan wenxue gaiguan* 抗戰文學概觀 (Overview of War of Resistance literature). Chongqing: Xi'nan shifan daxue chubanshe, 1985.

————. *Kangzhan wenyi jicheng* 抗戰文藝紀程 (Chronology of literature and the arts during the War of Resistance). Chongqing: Xi'nan shifan daxue chubanshe, 1986.

Su Wen 蘇文, ed. *Wenyi ziyou lunbian ji* 文藝自由論辨集 (Collection of essays from the literary freedom debate). Shanghai: Shanghai shudian, 1933.

Sun Zhongtian 孫中田. *Lun Mao Dun de shenghuo yu chuangzuo* 論茅盾的生活與創作 (On Mao Dun's life and writings). Tianjin: Baihua wenyi chubanshe, 1980.

Sun Zhongtian with Cha Guohua 查國華, eds. *Mao Dun yanjiu ziliao* 茅盾研究資料 (Research materials on Mao Dun). 3 vols. Beijing: Zhongguo shehui kexue chubanshe, 1983.

Tagore, Amitendranath. *Literary Debates in Modern China: 1918–1937.* Tokyo: Centre for East Asian Cultural Studies, 1967.

Tang Jinhai 唐金海, Kong Haizhu 孔海珠, Zhou Chundong 周春東, and Li Yuzhen 李玉珍, eds. *Mao Dun zhuanji* 茅盾專集 (Collection of writings by and about Mao Dun). 4 vols. Fuzhou: Fujian renmin chubanshe, 1983.

Todorov, Tzvetan. *Theories of the Symbol.* Translated by Catherine Porter. Ithaca: Cornell University Press, 1982.

Touponce, William F. "Straw Dogs: A Deconstructive Reading of the Problem of Mimesis in James Liu's *Chinese Theories of Literature.*" *Tamkang Review*, no. 1 (Summer 1981): 359–90.

Wang, Chi-chen, trans. *Contemporary Chinese Stories.* New York: Columbia University Press, 1944.

Wang Yao 王瑤. *Zhongguo xin wenxue shigao* 中國新文學史稿 (Draft history of modern Chinese literature). 2 vols. Beijing: Kaiming shudian, 1951.

Wellek, René. *Concepts of Criticism.* New Haven: Yale University Press, 1963.

Wenxue yundong shiliao xuan 文學運動史料選 (Selected research materials on the literary movement). 7 vols. Shanghai: Shanghai jiaoyu chubanshe, 1979.

Wusi shiqi qikan jieshao 五四時期期刊介紹 (Introduction to the periodicals of the May Fourth period). 3 vols. Shenyang: Shenghuo, Du shu, Xin zhi sanlian shudian chubanshe, 1978.

Wusi yundong wenxuan 五四運動文選 (Selected documents of the May Fourth movement). Beijing: Shenghuo, Du shu, Xin zhi sanlian shudian chubanshe, 1979.

Wu Taichang 吳泰昌. "Yi 'Wusi': Fang Ye lao 憶"五四,"訪葉老 (Remembering May Fourth: an interview with Ye Shaojun). *Wenyi bao.* 1979, no. 5 (March).

Wu Zuxiang 吳組緗. *Fanyu ji* 飯餘集 (After-dinner pieces). Shanghai: Wenhua shenghuo chubanshe, 1935.

———. *Shan hong* 山洪 (Mountain torrent). Shanghai: Xingqun chuban gongsi, 1946. New edition. Beijing: Renmin wenxue chubanshe, 1982.

———. *Wu Zuxiang xiaoshuo sanwen ji* 吳組緗小說散文集. (Collected stories and essays of Wu Zuxiang). Beijing: Renmin wenxue chubanshe, 1954.

———. *Xiliu ji* 西柳集 (West willow). Shanghai: Shenghuo shudian, 1934.

Yan Jiayan 嚴家炎. *Lun xiandai xiaoshuo yu wenyi sixiang* 論現代小說與文藝思想 (On modern fiction and literary theory). Changsha: Hunan renmin chubanshe, 1987.

Yang Yi 楊義. "Lun Ye Shengtao duanpian xiaoshuo de yishu tese" 論葉聖陶短篇小說的藝術特色 (On the artistic characteristics of Ye Shengtao's short stories). *Zhongguo xiandai wenxue yanjiu congkan*, no. 2 (1980): 201–22.

Ye Shaojun 葉紹鈞 [Ye Shengtao 葉聖陶, pseud.] *Chengzhong* 城中 (In the city). Shanghai: Kaiming shudian, 1926.

———. *Gemo* 隔膜 (Barriers). Shanghai: Shangwu yinshuguan, 1922.

———. *How Mr. Pan Weathered the Storm.* Beijing: Panda Books, 1987.

———. *Huozai* 火災 (Conflagration). Shanghai: Shangwu yinshuguan, 1923.

———. *Ni Huanzhi* 倪煥之. Shanghai: Kaiming shudian, 1929.

———. (Yeh Sheng-tao) *Schoolmaster Ni Huan-chih.* Translated by A. C. Barnes. Beijing: Foreign Languages Press, 1958.

———. *Weiyan ji* 未厭集 (Without satiety). Shanghai: Shangwu yinshuguan, 1928.

———. *Weiyanju xizuo* 未厭居習做 (The notebooks of Without Satiety). Shanghai: Kaiming shudian, 1935.

————. *Xianxia* 綫下 (Under the line). Shanghai: Shangwu yinshuguan, 1925.

————. *Ye Shaojun xuanji* 葉紹鈞選集 (Selected works by Ye Shaojun). Shanghai: Wanxiang shuwu, 1936.

————. *Ye Shengtao lun chuangzuo* 葉聖陶論創作 (Ye Shengtao on composition). Shanghai: Shanghai wenyi chubanshe, 1982.

Ye Zi 葉紫. *Harvest*. Beijing: Foreign Languages Press, 1960.

————. *Ye Zi xuanji* 葉紫選集 (Selected works by Ye Zi). Beijing: Renmin wenxue chubanshe, 1978.

Ye Ziming 葉子銘. *Lun Mao Dun sishi nian de wenxue daolu* 論茅盾四十年的文學道路 (On Mao Dun's forty-year literary path). Shanghai: Shanghai wenyi chubanshe, 1959.

Zhang Haishan 張海珊. "'Zi bu yu guai, li, luan, shen' pingyi" "子不語怪、力、亂、神"評議 (Evaluation of "I don't discuss the fantastic, power, disorder, or spirits"). *Gudai wenxue lilun yanjiu*, no. 5 (1981): 80–90.

Zhang Ruoying 張若英. *Zhongguo xin wenxue yundong shi ziliao* 中國新文學運動史資料 (Research materials on the history of the Chinese new literature movement). Shanghai: Guangming shudian, 1934.

Zhang Tianyi 張天翼. *Chilun* 齒輪 (Cogwheel). Shanghai: Hufeng shuju, 1932.

————. *Chun feng* 春風 (Spring wind). Shanghai: Wenhua shenghuo chubanshe, 1936.

————. *Cong kongxu dao chongshi* 從空虛到充實 (From vacuity to fullness). Shanghai: Shanghai lianhe shudian, 1931.

————. *Fuyun* 浮雲 (Floating clouds). Hong Kong: Nanhua shudian, 1966. A later edition of *Yinian*.

————. *Guitu riji* 鬼土日記 (A diary of hell). Shanghai: Zhengwu shuju, 1931.

————. *Jiren ji* 畸人集 (The eccentric). Shanghai: Liangyou tushu yinshua gongsi, 1936.

————. *Shidai de tiaodong* 時代的跳動 (Pulse of the times). Shanghai: Daxia shudian, 1938. A later edition of *Chilun*.

————. *Suxie sanpian* 速寫三篇 (Three sketches). Chongqing: Wenhua shenghuo chubanshe, 1943.

————. *Tongxiangmen* 同鄉們 (Fellow villagers). Shanghai: Wenhua shenghuo chubanshe, 1939.

————. *Yangjingbin qixia* 洋涇浜奇俠 (Strange knight of Shanghai). Shanghai: Shanghai xin zhong shuju, 1936.

————. *Yi nian* 一年 (A year). Shanghai: Liangyou tushu yinshua gongsi, 1933.

————. *Yihang* 移行 (A hyphenated story). Shanghai: Liangyou tushu yinshua gongsi, 1934.

————. *Zai chengshi li* 在城市裏 (In the city). Shanghai: Liangyou tushu yinshua gongsi, 1937.

————. *Zhang Tianyi duanpian xiaoshuo xuanji* 張天翼短篇小說選集 (Selected short stories by Zhang Tianyi). 2 vols. Beijing: Wenhua yishu chubanshe, 1981.

————. *Zhang Tianyi lun chuangzuo* 張天翼論創作 (Zhang Tianyi on composition). Shanghai: Shanghai wenyi chubanshe, 1982.

————. *Zhang Tianyi xiaoshuo xuan* 張天翼小說選 (Selected fiction by Zhang Tianyi). 2 vols. Changsha: Hunan renmin wenxue chubanshe, 1981.

————. *Zhang Tianyi wenji* 張天翼文集 (Collected writings of Zhang Tianyi). 3 vols. to date. Shanghai: Shanghai wenyi chubanshe, 1983–.

————. *Zhang Tianyi wenxue pinglun ji* 張天翼文學評論集 (Collection of literary criticism by Zhang Tianyi). Beijing: Renmin wenxue chubanshe, 1984.

————. *Zhui* 追 (Pursuit). Shanghai: Kaiming shudian, 1936.

————. "Zuojia zishu: Zhang Tianyi" 作家自述：張天翼 (In the writer's own words: Zhang Tianyi). *Zhongguo xiandai wenxue yanjiu congkan*, no. 2 (1980): 276–80.

Zhao Jiabi 趙家璧, ed. *Zhongguo xin wenxue daxi* 中國新文學大系 (Compendium of modern Chinese literature). 10 vols. Shanghai: Liangyou tushu gongsi, 1935–36.

Zheng Zhenduo 鄭振鐸. *Zheng Zhenduo xuanji* 鄭振鐸選集 (Selected works by Zheng Zhenduo). Fuzhou: Fujian renmin chubanshe, 1984.

Zheng Zhenduo with Fu Donghua 傅東華, eds. *Wenxue baiti* 文學百題 (One hundred questions about literature). Shanghai: Shenghuo shudian, 1936.

Zhongguo jindai wenlun xuan 中國近代文論選 (Selected modern Chinese literary essays). 2 vols. Beijing: Renmin wenxue chubanshe, 1981.

Zhongguo xiandai duanpian xiaoshuo xuan 中國現代短篇小說選 (Selected modern Chinese short stories). Edited by Modern Literature Research

Room, Chinese Academy of Social Sciences. 7 vols. Beijing: Zhongguo shehui kexueyuan, 1980.

Zhongguo xiandai wenxue qikan mulu (chugao) 中國現代文學期刊目錄（初稿）(Draft catalogue of modern Chinese literary periodicals). Shanghai: Shanghai wenyi chubanshe, 1961.

Zhou Zuoren 周作人 [Zhou Xiashou 遐壽]. *Lu Xun xiaoshuo li de renwu* 魯迅小說裏的人物 (The characters in Lu Xun's fiction). Beijing: Renmin wenxue chubanshe, 1981.

Zhuang Zhongqing 莊鍾慶, ed. *Mao Dun yanjiu lunji* 茅盾研究論集 (Research articles on Mao Dun). Tianjin: Tianjin renmin chubanshe, 1974.

Zuolian huiyi lu 左聯回憶錄 (Reminiscences of the League of Left-Wing Writers). 2 vols. Beijing: Zhongguo shehui kexue chubanshe.

JOURNALS

Asian and African Studies. Bratislava: Department of Oriental Studies, Slovak Academy of Sciences, 1965–.

Beidou 北斗 (Big dipper). Shanghai: Hufeng shuju, 1931–32.

Beixin 北新 (The north renewed). Shanghai: Beixin shuju, 1926–30.

Benliu 奔流 (Currents). Shanghai: Beixin shudian, 1928–29.

Chinese Literature. Beijing: Guozi shudian, 1951–.

Chinese Literature: Essays, Articles, and Reviews. Madison: University of Wisconsin, 1979–.

Chuangzao yuekan 創造月刊 (Creation monthly). Shanghai, 1926–29.

Chuangzao zhoubao 創造周報 (Creation weekly). Shanghai: Taidong tushuju, 1923–24.

Dazhong wenyi 大衆文藝 (Mass literature). Shanghai: Xiandai shuju, 1928–30.

Dongfang zazhi 東方雜誌 (Eastern miscellany). Shanghai: Shangwu yinshuguan, 1904–48.

Gudai wenxue lilun yanjiu 古代文學理論研究 (Compendium of research on ancient literary theory). Shanghai: Shanghai guji chubanshe, 1979–.

Kangzhan wenyi 抗戰文藝 (Resistance literature). Hankou and Chongqing, 1938–46.

Libailiu 禮拜六 (Saturday). Shanghai: Zhonghua tushuguan, 1914–23.

Lunyu 論語 (Analects). Shanghai: Shanghai shuju, 1932–49.

Mengya yuekan 萌芽月刊 (Sprouts monthly). Shanghai: Guanghua shuju, 1929–30.

Modern China. Beverly Hills, Calif.: Sage Publications, 1975–.

Modern Chinese Literature, San Francisco: San Francisco State University Center for the Study of Modern Chinese Literature, 1984–.

Renditions: A Chinese-English Translation Magazine. Hong Kong: Chinese University of Hong Kong, 1973–.

Shizi jietou 十字街頭 (Crossroads). Shanghai, 1931–32.

Taidong yuekan 泰東月刊 (Taidong monthly). Shanghai: Taidong tushuju, 1927–29.

Taiyang yuekan 太陽月刊 (The sun monthly). Shanghai: Chunye shudian, January–July 1928.

Tamkang Review. Taipei, Taiwan: Tamkang College of Arts and Sciences, 1970–.

Tuohuangzhe 拓荒者 (Pioneers). Shanghai: Xiandai shuju, January–May 1930.

Wenhua pinglun 文化評論 (Cultural review). Shanghai, 1931–32.

Wenhua pipan 文化批判 (Cultural criticism). Shanghai: Chuangzao she, January–May 1928.

Wenxue 文學 (Literature). Shanghai: Shanghai wenxue chubanshe, 25 April 1932 (one issue only).

Wenxue 文學 (Literature). Shanghai: Shenghuo shudian, 1933–37.

Wenxue jie 文學界 (The literary world). Shanghai: Wenxue jie yuekan she, June–September 1936.

Wenxue jikan 文學季刊 (Literature quarterly). Beijing: Lida shuju, 1934–35.

Wenxue pinglun 文學評論 (Literary review). Beijing: Zhongguo shehui kexue chubanshe, 1957–.

Wenxue yuebao 文學月報 (Literature monthly). Shanghai: Guanghua shuju, June–December 1932.

Wenxue yuebao 文學月報 (Literature monthly). Chongqing: Dushu shenghuo chubanshe, 1940–41.

Wenxue zazhi 文學雜誌 (Literature magazine). Shanghai: Shangwu shuguan, 1937–48.

Wenxue zhoubao 文學周報 (Literature weekly). Shanghai: Kaiming shudian, 1925–29.

Wenyi bao 文藝報 (Literary gazette). Beijing: Zuojia chubanshe, 1949–.

Wenyi xinwen 文藝新聞 (Literature and art news). Shanghai, 1931–32.

Wenyi yuekan 文藝月刊 (Literature and art monthly). Nanjing: Zhongguo wenyishe, 1930–37.

Wenyi zhendi 文藝陣地 (Literary front). Hankou and Chongqing, 1938–40, 1942–43.

Women yuekan 我們月刊 (Us monthly). Shanghai: Xiaoshan shudian, May–July 1928.

Xiandai 現代 (Les contemporaines). Shanghai: Xiandai shuju, 1932–35.

Xiandai pinglun 現代評論 (Contemporary review). Beijing and Shanghai, 1924–28.

Xiandai wenyi 現代文藝 (Contemporary literature and art). Shanghai, April–May 1931.

Xiandai wenyi 現代文藝 (Contemporary literature and art). Fujian: Gaijin chubanshe, 1940–42.

Xianshi wenxue 現實文學 (Realist literature). Shanghai: Wenyi banyue kanshe, July–August 1936.

Xiaoshuo yuebao 小說月報 (Short story magazine), Shanghai: Shangwu yinshuguan, 1910–31.

Xin qingnian 新青年 (New youth). Beijing, 1915–22.

Xin wenxue shiliao 新文學史料 (Historical materials on the new literature). Beijing: Renmin wenxue chubanshe, 1979–.

Xinchao 新潮 (New tide). Beijing: Beijing daxue chubanbu, 1919–22.

Xinliu yuebao 新流月報 (New current monthly). Shanghai: Xiandai shuju, May–December 1929.

Xuedeng 學燈 (Lantern of learning). Supplement to the newspaper *Shishi xinbao* 時事新報, Shanghai: 1918–26.

Yu si 語絲 (Spinners of words). Shanghai: Beixin shuju, 1924–30.

Zhongguo wenhua 中國文化 (Chinese culture). Beijing, 1939–41.

Zhongguo xiandai wenxue yanjiu congkan 中國現代文學研究叢刊 (Compendium of research on modern Chinese literature). Beijing: Beijing chubanshe, 1979–.

Zhongliu 中流 (Midstream). Shanghai, 1936–37.

Zuojia 作家 (Author). Shanghai, April–November, 1936.

Zuojia 作家 (Author). Nanjing: Zuojia chubanshe, 1941–44.

Zuopin 作品 (Composition). Shanghai, June–July 1937.

Index

Compositor: Asco Trade Typesetting, Ltd.
Text: 10/13 Sabon
Display: Sabon
Printer: Edwards Brothers, Inc.
Binder: Edwards Brothers, Inc.